W9-ADM-255

AUTOCRACY, MODERNIZATION, AND REVOLUTION IN RUSSIA AND IRAN

AUTOCRACY, MODERNIZATION, AND REVOLUTION IN RUSSIA AND IRAN

Tim McDaniel

PRINCETON UNIVERSITY PRESS PRINCETON, NEW JERSEY

Published by Princeton University Press, 41 William Street,
Princeton, New Jersey 08540
In the United Kingdom: Princeton University Press,
Chichester, West Sussex

Library of Congress Cataloging-in-Publication Data

McDaniel, Tim.
Autocracy, modernization, and revolution in Russia and Iran/
Tim McDaniel.
p. cm.
Includes bibliographical references and index.
ISBN 0-691-03147-9
ISBN 0-691-02482-0 (pbk.)
1. Soviet Union—History—Revolution, 1917–1921—Causes.
2. Iran—History—Revolution, 1979—Causes. 2. Soviet Union—
Social conditions—1801–1917. 4. Iran—Social conditions.
I. Title
DK265.M3743 1991
303.4′3′0947—dc20 90-20191 CIP

First Princeton Paperback printing, 1993

This book has been composed in Linotron Galliard

Princeton University Press books are printed on acid-free paper,
and meet the guidelines for permanence and durability of the
Committee on Production Guidelines for Book Longevity of the
Council on Library Resources

Printed in the United States of America

10 9 8 7 6 5 4 3 2

TO DEAR CHILDREN

OF FRIENDS AND RELATIVES,

IN ORDER OF AGE:

Misha, Jacob, Tim, and Ryan

Contents

Acknowledgments

I AM GRATEFUL for the help of many friends and colleagues who read this book in manuscript form and made valuable suggestions for improvements. Above all, I want to acknowledge the encouragement of Andy Scull, who at many points had more confidence in the outcome of this project than I did, and whose comments were invaluable. A number of other people read the manuscript carefully and offered much advice, saving me from errors of fact and interpretation. In this regard I particularly want to thank Ervand Abrahamian, Said Amir Arjomand, Victoria Bonnell, Daniel Chirot, Ali Gheissari, Jack Goldstone, Michael Mann, and Jeff Weintraub. I have discussed my ideas on these issues with Gershon Shafir and Carlos Waisman, from whose knowledge and friendship I have benefited in innumerable ways. Nikki Keddie was kind enough to invite me to a conference she organized at UCLA, at which I was able to discuss my work with a number of Iranian specialists. I am grateful to her for the invitation and encouragement. Pat Stewart and Barbara Stewart gave advice on the preparation of the manuscript and facilitated its completion. My editors at Princeton, Margaret Case and Gail Ullman, have done a wonderful job with a manuscript that does not fit any easy classifications. I am also grateful to Brian MacDonald, my copy editor, for a first-rate job with the text. Finally, I would like to acknowledge the importance of something less tangible, the atmosphere created by my colleagues at the Department of Sociology at the University of California, San Diego, who have provided an unusually supportive environment for this kind of endeavor.

A Note on the Transliteration

Readers will notice some inconsistencies in spelling of a number of Middle Eastern words and names. The reason is the following: I adopted a single transliteration for my own use, but when the name appeared in another form in a text that I cited, I followed the latter. This explains, for example, the usage of both Al-e Ahmad and Al-i Ahmad for the same man.

AUTOCRACY, MODERNIZATION, AND REVOLUTION IN RUSSIA AND IRAN

Introduction

A Contradictory Route to Industrial Society

THE RUSSIAN Revolution of 1917 and the Iranian Revolution of 1978–1979 were stunning events that altered the temper of their times. Although both events were preceded in their respective countries by decades of revolutionary agitation against the regimes and episodes of dramatic mass mobilization, the events that culminated in the downfall of the governments came as a shock to world opinion. In the case of Russia, seasoned observers and the general public alike found it hard to believe that a system of government that, in one form or another, had lasted roughly six centuries, could collapse with such rapidity. No matter how shaky the foundations of tsarism might have seemed in the abstract, it was subliminally accepted as part of the very nature of Russia. In its own way the Iranian Revolution was just as dramatic. Never before had a revolution of such depth occurred in the Moslem world. The movement led by clerics was victorious over a regime with its formidable repressive apparatus, its secret police and army, largely intact. Few would have dared predict that hundreds of thousands of people would have been willing to sacrifice themselves in the streets to bring an end to the shah's rule.

Astonishing as the two revolutions were for the ways they brought down the old regimes, they are just as remarkable for setting their countries on paths new both to them and to the world at large. The Russian Revolution ushered in the world's first socialist regime basing itself on Marxist principles. The Iranian Revolution was equally unprecedented: no modern revolution has been led and supported in the name of ancient religious values claimed to provide a truer and more just foundation for modern society than do Western ideas of progress.

Equally startling for their drama and lack of precedent, the two revolutions seem at first glance to share little else in common. How could a revolution led by Lenin be compared with one inspired by Khomeini? What is the similarity between a revolution based primarily on the urban working class and one founded to a significant degree on traditional groups like the *bazaaris* (traditional merchants), small craftsmen, and religious students and preachers? One is tempted to agree with the Ayatollah Motahhari, one of the most respected and influential of the clerical leaders in Iran, that "the nature of the Islamic movement is in no case similar to the French revolution or to the great October revolution of Russia."[1]

Much depends, of course, on which aspects and dimensions of the two revolutions are to be compared. Revolutions are complex phenomena, generally having deep roots in the societies that give birth to them, unexpected twists and turns in the revolutionary process itself, and long-term consequences that take years and perhaps even generations to discern. Theories of revolution have not been able, and may not have the capacity, to integrate an understanding of the causes, process, and outcome of revolution in the same model. Not even the two classic theoretical perspectives on revolutions, those of Tocqueville and Marx, managed to incorporate all these factors within a single framework. Tocqueville's *The Old Regime and the French Revolution* focuses on the long-term causes of the revolution that also conditioned its impact on French society, but devotes little attention to the actual political phenomenon. (Whether Tocqueville's subsequent book on revolutionary politics, which was left uncompleted at the time of his death, could have been integrated with his earlier ideas is an open question.) The major strength of Marxist studies of revolution, in my view, lies in their frequently illuminating discussion of the class conflict at the heart of at least some revolutionary processes; they tend to be much weaker on long-term outcomes.

The failure of any given theoretical perspective to do justice to all three dimensions of revolution can be traced to the complexity of the phenomenon itself. Structural causes, revolutionary processes, and long-term outcomes are partly independent of each other, affected not just by the logical unfolding of a revolutionary trajectory but by new issues and dilemmas that make their appearance at every step—the imperatives of state building, revolutionary survival, the transition to normalcy, and the like. Tocqueville, in arguing that the main outcome of the French Revolution—the concentration of political power in the central government—was rooted in trends that long antedated the revolution, recognized this independence far more than Marx, whose theoretical model linked causes, revolutionary processes, and outcomes much more tightly.

The complexity of revolutions thus allows, even forces, one to highlight certain dimensions of the phenomenon for analytical purposes. And revolutions that seem incomparable in some respects can usefully be juxtaposed for other purposes. The present study is founded on a striking shared characteristic of the Russian and Iranian revolutions that, in my view, was decisive for the genesis of the revolutionary crisis and also affected the play

[1] Ayatollah Murtada Mutahhari, excerpts, in *Expectation of the Millennium*, ed. Seyyed Hossein Nasr, Hamid Dabashi, and Seyyed Vali Reza Nasr (Albany: State University of New York Press, 1989), 404.

of forces during the course of the upheaval and the immediate outcome of the revolutionary process: both revolutions occurred after two or three decades' experience of what I call autocratic modernization.

A great many theories of revolution have attempted to link patterns of modernization and industrialization with the outbreak and results of revolutions. Marx himself pioneered this approach, predicting the outbreak of socialist revolutions on the basis of the dilemmas of capitalist development. Barrington Moore, among many others, has worked out more differentiated models of the different paths to modernization, examining how they affect the possibilities for different political outcomes.[2] Basing his conclusion on six case studies, Moore identified three alternative routes to the modern world: bourgeois revolution leading to liberal democracy; conservative revolution from above culminating in fascism; and peasant revolution leading to communism. It should be noted that Moore's understanding of the term *revolution* differs from another more commonly accepted usage, which restricts the concept to rapid and violent political change accompanied by profound social change. In this second sense the wide-ranging social changes of the Meiji era in Japan or late imperial Germany would not qualify as revolutions.

My central argument is that autocratic modernization is another distinctive route to modernity not identified in Moore's work. Related to his "conservative modernization" (though quite different in emphasizing specifically political dimensions of social change, and also connected to more general models of modernizing dictatorship), it nonetheless has traits and political consequences specific enough to constitute an independent type. Together with my claim that this route is sociologically distinctive enough to require separate analysis, I argue that the two major examples of autocratic modernization, Russia and Iran, culminated in the only clear-cut examples of what Huntington calls "western revolutions" in the twentieth century—that is, revolutions that take the form of a rapid crisis and breakdown of the state rather than a prolonged civil war in which the revolutionary contender has the opportunity to control territory and mobilize its entire population.[3]

The substantiation of these dual claims—that autocratic modernization constitutes a discrete developmental path especially vulnerable to "western" revolution and that Russia and Iran exemplify this path uniquely well—requires further specification of both parts of the compound concept. By autocracy I do not mean just any form of personal dictatorship but one that remains highly traditional in the political sense, and thus is

[2] Barrington Moore, *Social Origins of Dictatorship and Democracy* (Boston: Beacon Press, 1966).

[3] Samuel Huntington, *Political Order in Changing Societies* (New Haven: Yale University Press, 1968), 266–68, 271–74.

inconsistent with the creation of significant modern political parties or the formulation of compelling official modern ideologies. Similarly, my interest in modernization does not extend to all stages and dimensions of this very broad set of processes.[4] Rather, I am concerned only with the period of attempted transition to a mature industrial society, with its new social groups and classes. This particular transition entails economic, social, and political questions and challenges not encountered in less far-reaching processes of change. It is also true that many of the contradictions encountered in autocratic modernization find their parallels in other forms of dictatorship and other stages of modernization. Although some hypotheses will be offered, systematic comparison between autocratic modernization and other types is not the purpose of the present study.

As just noted, the concept of autocracy employed here is not simply synonymous with dictatorship. If it were, Nicholas II's and the shah's regimes would be part of a very large company. Rather, my understanding of autocracy is the classic one that can be found in the work of, among many others, Montesquieu. In this tradition, autocracy means personal power, in theory unlimited and often, though not necessarily, based on a claim to divine selection and guidance. Autocratic power is not necessarily very effective; indeed, the paradoxical weaknesses of autocratic rulers in their efforts to force modernization will be one of the major themes of the study. Yet it is always in principle uncontrolled by competing powers and unconstrained by fixed law. In this sense, it is always arbitrary in its exercise, dependent on the will of the monarch more than the workings of institutions. For this reason, autocratic rulers put their trust in individual men, not in formalized procedures or organizations. In perhaps the most extreme case of autocratic rule in modern times, Haile Selassie's in Ethiopia, the emperor was not willing to trust the written word in any form, so limiting would it be to the autonomous expression of his ever-changing will.[5] Apart from this idiosyncratic case, it is true that autocrats distrust official ideologies and resist the formation of proregime social movements or political parties.

To say that the Russian and Iranian regimes were autocratic is not to say

[4] For a very comprehensive list of different political, social, economic, and intellectual aspects of modernization—which implies no judgment as to their superior value—see John Whitney Hall, "Changing Conceptions of the Modernization of Japan," in *Changing Japanese Attitudes toward Modernization*, ed. Marius Jansen (Princeton: Princeton University Press, 1965), 20–23. Although I am well aware of the controversies surrounding the "theory of modernization" in recent years, to me the concept itself still seems valid, indeed indispensable. So would it seem, I think, to intellectuals in Third World countries undergoing some aspects of these changes, even if they dispute the benefits of the change. Renewed theoretical discussion of the concept of modernization and the theories associated with it is, in my judgment, long overdue.

[5] Ryszard Kapuscinski, *The Emperor* (San Diego: Harcourt Brace Jovanovich, 1983), 7–8.

that they were pure embodiments of the principles of autocracy. Nor is it to affirm that there is some unchangeable essence of autocracy that can exist apart from historical and institutional circumstances. Indeed, we will need to inquire into the challenges and limitations of autocratic rule in the two countries as well as the very different contexts in which it was exercised (see chapter two). No concept can ever find unalloyed expression in real life. Nonetheless, the traits of monarchy in the two countries provide a close enough approximation to the concept to make its employment illuminating.

One point deserves further emphasis to avoid possible misunderstanding. Autocracy does not imply absolute control of society or the ability to transform it at will. More germane for our purposes are some traits inherent in the phenomenon, particularly the arbitrary nature of power and the inability to generate modern ideologies or organizations for political mobilization of the masses. Arbitrariness has political consequences no matter how large the degree of power. It inhibits the emergence of rational bureaucratic organizations. It constrains the development of social organizations able to represent the will and embody the collective efforts of social groups. It also shapes the exercise of power in other spheres of society, conditioning, for example, the relationships between industrialists and workers, landlords and peasants. Thus, the amount of power should be clearly distinguished from its attributes.[6] Many of these limits to autocratic power can only be transcended through the transformation of the regime into a new type—that of one-party mobilizational systems that, while maintaining many traits of traditional autocracy, also establish a new and very different relationship between state and society.

Some few autocracies in this sense have survived into modern times—one thinks, for example, of Ethiopia's Selassie, Haiti's Duvalier, or even of Vietnam's Diem and Cambodia's Sihanouk. Nor were the last tsar and final shah alone in seeking to modernize their societies. Of Selassie it has been reported that every day, between four and five o'clock in the afternoon, "he received processions of planners, economists, and financial specialists." Similarly, "a map of the Empire's development hung in the Palace, on which little arrows, stars, and dots lit up."[7] What distinguished the regimes of Nicholas II and Muhammad Reza Shah from these similar cases was the effort to create an urban industrial society as a prerequisite for present or future claims to great-power status.

Even though the rulers were aware that the rapid transition to an urban

[6] Tocqueville, too, was less concerned with the government's real power than the effect of its arbitrary actions on the political life of society, particularly its ability to prevent the emergence of intermediary social institutions. For comments along these lines, see François Furet, *Interpreting the French Revolution* (Cambridge: Cambridge University Press, 1981), 143.

[7] Kapuscinski, *The Emperor*, 86–87.

industrial society might pose challenges to their own position, they felt compelled to pursue the achievements of modern society. Nicholas II was particularly ambivalent about the benefits of urbanization and industrialization, but also knew that a modern economy was indispensable for Russia's position in the world. Despite concern over the relative decline of agriculture and the landed nobility, which at certain times led to reversals of government sponsorship of industry, the state could not alter this fundamental commitment. The shah was probably also sincere in his belief that economic development was absolutely essential for the long-term welfare of the country and that his regime had no choice but to pursue it, creating what he called a "permanent state of urgency."[8]

The main features and accomplishments of the two regimes' modernization programs, as well as the very significant differences between them, will be discussed at some length in chapter three. However, the central dilemmas entailed in these efforts to combine political autocracy and advanced modernization should be indicated at the outset.

In general terms, effective economic and social modernization at this relatively advanced stage of development requires both stable political institutions and the involvement and initiative of society. Although autocratic rulers like Peter the Great of Russia, Reza Shah of Iran, or Mahmud II and Abdulhamid of Ottoman Turkey may be able, through the exercise of state power, to lay many of the foundations of a modern society and economy, further change in this direction will at some point require more modern forms of social and political organization. Societies without reasonably strong corporate organizations, such as trade unions and professional associations, as well as relatively legitimate social elites, will lack both stability and dynamism. Similarly, governments without a fixed administrative structure and a public organized into one or more political parties will be incoherent and unable to shape and mobilize social groups for their own purposes.

The general principle that political life and institutions need to adapt to transformations in the society if they are not to lose their efficacy and legitimacy is frequently encountered. It is in this light that Ervand Abrahamian, drawing on Marx's writings on the French revolutionary episodes, interprets the revolutionary crisis in Iran:

> The revolution came because the shah modernized on the socioeconomic level and thus expanded the ranks of the modern middle class and the industrial working class, but failed to modernize on another level—the political level; and that this failure inevitably strained the links between the government and the social structure, blocked the channels of communications between the political system and the general population, widened the gap between the ruling circles and the

[8] Mohammed Reza Pahlavi, *The Shah's Story* (London: Michael Joseph, 1980), 153.

> mass social forces, and, most serious of all, cut down the few bridges that had in the past connected the political establishment with the traditional social forces, especially with the bazaars and the religious authorities.[9]

My approach in the following chapters in no way contradicts this perspective, which centers on the emergent political requirements of a society at a relatively advanced stage of development. Indeed, it builds upon and elaborates this idea by demonstrating the consequences for state, society, and their interrelations if political reforms are not accomplished within an autocratic system. As will be seen, rapid socioeconomic modernization disarticulates the autocratic state, undermines its effectiveness and legitimacy, and widens the barriers between state and society, depriving the regimes of a significant social base. Conversely, the autocratic state weakens and atomizes social groups, thereby hindering the accomplishment of its own goals, including the creation of social stability and the emergence of a significant degree of social consensus.

Because of these persistent contradictions, autocratic modernization is likely to generate social and political impasses that call into question the country's institutions and leadership. In comparative terms, this pattern of development exhibits less dynamism and ultimately proves less viable than Moore's alternative routes to modern industrial society. In their different ways, these other three patterns of social change all involve establishing links between increasingly powerful states and rapidly changing societies.

The contrast between Moore's first pattern, the liberal democratic route, and autocratic modernization are too obvious to require further comment, but brief comparisons with the other two patterns help illuminate the distinctiveness of autocratic modernization. The second main route, best exemplified by Germany and Japan, is capitalist and reactionary. It is capitalist in the sense that relatively powerful social elites control the economy and are responsible for economic development. Yet class relations are infused with premodern patterns of authority and the state allies itself with the elites to limit the spread of democracy. The significant point of contrast between reactionary capitalist development and autocratic modernization lies precisely in the discrepant positions of social elites. In autocratic modernization, the state undermines the formation of strong and legitimate social elites and inhibits the maturation of hierarchical relations among classes. Thus, in contrast to Russia and Iran, Japanese and German elites played a much more vital role in economic growth, provided the regimes with a social base, and, through their hierarchical links with subordinate classes, enhanced social stability.

Moore's third route to modernity, peasant revolution culminating in

[9] Ervand Abrahamian, *Iran between Two Revolutions* (Princeton: Princeton University Press, 1982), 427.

communism, combines two phenomena that should, in my view, be split. The Russian Revolution cannot really be classified as a peasant revolution, and so the social roots of communism cannot be identified so simply.[10] But for present purposes, what is significant is not the social prelude to communist modernization, but the phenomenon itself—with its prototype in the Stalinist period. Here communist regimes can be loosely grouped with some noncommunist states such as Ataturk's Turkey as modernizing one-party dictatorships. Although it is not inappropriate to label rulers such as Stalin or Ataturk autocrats, it is autocracy with a difference: no longer claiming personal rule based on traditional legitimation, these rulers break with the past by propagating modernizing ideologies and sponsoring mass participation through the development of mass political organizations. Even though much of this participation is sham and the ideologies can be malleable to the point of emptiness, dynamic links between the regime and select social groups are forged, partly by identifying common enemies; such autocratic mobilizational systems have clearly proved able to create the foundations of modern industrial society. In the case of the most extreme example, the Stalinist system, they did so at the cost of virtually abolishing the separate existence of a civil society—a fact that indicates the immense price these regimes were willing to pay for their version of progress. Neither Nicholas II nor the shah were willing or able to embark very far on this deadly new strategy. (Nor, indeed, was Ataturk.) Rather, they remained trapped in a more contradictory system whose very limits made it more politically volatile. Whether such autocratic mobilizational systems can prove adequate to the task of guiding their societies along a path of continuing growth and innovation—this is the great issue being played out in much of the communist world at the present time.

My aim, then, is to explore the various tensions and contradictions in this path to modern society that make the regimes and societies especially vulnerable to revolutionary crises. I do not claim that the model predicts revolution as an inevitable outcome of autocratic modernization. I agree with Arthur Stinchcombe that "rather than explaining the occurrence of revolution, a sociological theory [I would say model] ought to try to explain the occurrence of a revolutionary situation."[11] Concrete events and situations—World War I, the shah's cancer, Jimmy Carter's human rights policy—play too great a role in the genesis of revolutions to allow for prediction. Sociologists should, however, be able to analyze the differential vulnerability of different kinds of societies to revolutionary threats. This may also be the time to make clear that I am not arguing a general causal

[10] See Tim McDaniel, *Autocracy, Capitalism, and Revolution in Russia* (Berkeley: University of California Press, 1988), 1–9, for a summary of the role of industrial labor in the revolution.

[11] Arthur Stinchcombe, "Social Structure and Organizations," in *Handbook of Organizations*, ed. James March (Chicago: Rand McNally, 1965), 169.

proposition—autocratic modernization causes revolution—partly because of the contingencies already referred to and partly because I am well aware that other kinds of political configurations can also give rise to revolutions.

Beyond the manifold and, I hope, surprising similarities observable in the patterns of social change in these two very different societies, what of general significance can emerge from the study of a type of development that, in relatively pure form, only embraces two cases? The insights to be gained are, in my view, both substantive and methodological. Substantively, the analysis of this type potentially contributes to the study of comparative development through supplementing and even calling into question other typologies. For example, if autocratic modernization has a distinctive logic especially prone to generate revolutionary situations, then Russia and China should not be grouped together, as Barrington Moore does. Further, the comparison makes plain why Russia and Germany should belong to different categories—a matter by no means clear from Moore's analysis of conservative modernization from above, which Russia appears to fit in many ways. These modifications arise from the incorporation of fundamentally political distinctions into the typology in place of Moore's more sociological analysis centered on elite coalitions. From the present perspective, which, going back at least to Montesquieu, seems in many ways old-fashioned, personal autocracy has very different consequences for development than other forms of dictatorship.

The second set of substantive implications is located precisely in the area of a comparative analysis of dictatorship and social change. The systematic exploration of these issues lies beyond the scope of this study, but the analysis does suggest that the different forms of dictatorship can be analyzed in conjunction with different stages of modernization in order to generate insights about social change. For example, personal autocracy seems to be both effective and viable in early stages of development, as the experiences of Russia under Peter the Great and Iran under Reza Shah suggest. The dilemmas emerge at a later stage, at the point of attempted transition to a mature industrial society, with its new array of social groups and classes. By contrast, it appears that this transition can be successfully accomplished by dictatorships less corrosive of social elites and traditional authority patterns, as the experience of late imperial Japan suggests. A final example: one-party mobilizational regimes are able to accomplish the transition to a modern urban and industrial society, but they may be incapable of ruling over the societies they have called into existence for a long period of time, or of ensuring their further progress.[12]

Apart from such hypotheses about comparative development or the

[12] Moshe Lewin, *The Gorbachev Phenomenon* (Berkeley: University of California Press, 1988).

study of dictatorship and social change, the relatively intensive focus on two cases within a single type has methodological advantages that compensate for a certain lack of generalizability. First, the similarities and differences can be more carefully compared in order to disclose aspects of processes and institutions that might otherwise be less evident. For example, the comparison between prerevolutionary Russia and Iran will allow us to trace the stronger class dimensions of the Russian Revolution to differences in the relationship between the state and social elites in the two countries. Similarly, the comparison generates insights about the different contributions of the countryside to revolution in the two societies. Comparison can in this sense have a heuristic value, as the two cases are used to illuminate each other. The insights that emerge will be rooted in the specific comparison. For example, comparison of Russian and Iranian modernization reveals significant ways in which Russian social relations were Western; a comparison between Russia and, say, Germany would indicate the limits of Russia's Westernism.

In addition, the specificity of analysis that the small number of cases makes possible facilitates the incorporation of historical context into the argument. I can discuss not only the general traits and implications of autocracy, but also the specific historical and cultural features in each society that help explain differences outside the bounds of the more general model. The limits of the comparison can therefore be plumbed without calling into question its validity, which depends upon the central analytical parallel.

Finally, and perhaps most important, the closer focus permits a more inclusive approach to the question of modernization and social change than is generally found in the recent literature on revolutions, with its emphasis on particular contending actors or specific variables. I believe that the comprehension of revolutions must involve the elaboration of more global models of how societies, or particular types of society, function; of how their institutions are related to each other; of how changes in one institution affect others; of how culture, economics, and politics are interconnected. Concepts like contradiction or institutional imperative are necessary to analyze these patterns of interrelations. They do not imply moral judgments or a preference for the status quo.

Only through such global approaches are we in a position to understand one of the fundamental traits of many, though not all, revolutions—the fact that they are the culmination of many years of protest and the accumulation of a great amount of historical experience rooted in a common set of fundamental contradictions. Frameworks such as Charles Tilly's that focus on the breakdown of the state and the resources of contending actors miss these continuities rooted in enduring crises endemic to the societies in a particular historical period. Thus, the Russian Revolution of 1917 cannot be interpreted simply as a result of war and political breakdown, but must also be seen against the background of the previous decades of modernization. Iran also had a remarkable history of protest in the decades preceding the revolution, all of it connected to the fundamental traits of the overall pattern of development. It is simply insufficient to focus all attention on new opportunities for action brought about by discrete events.

All of this, I know, sounds rather old-fashioned. But I believe that in the critique of societal or functional models of revolution, some of it deserved, much of great value was discarded. The two greatest contributions to the study of revolutions, the works of Tocqueville and Marx, both embarked from a global understanding of particular social formations. Their works were *not* attempts to develop models for revolutions at all times and for all places, but to understand the functioning of particular kinds of societies. More concentrated scrutiny of two societies permits closer attention to the logic and patterning of institutions and intergroup relations, thus facilitating the more global analysis required, in my view, by the subject matter. More than for any other social phenomenon, the secrets of revolutions are not disclosed through the fragmented approaches typical of modern social science.

One

Historical Legacies

THE COMPARISON of complicated periods of social change in different countries is not without its conceptual challenges and pitfalls. Russia under Nicholas II and Iran under Muhammad Reza Shah both witnessed experiments in autocratic modernization, and for this reason the patterns of social change in the two periods may fruitfully be contrasted with each other. It is not a weakness of comparative sociology, but fundamental to its very nature, that such comparison cannot approximate a controlled experiment with clear-cut causal inferences. The periods under consideration, despite considerable distinctness and coherence, cannot be cleanly separated from previous historical patterns, and so sociological regularities rooted in a shared structure are intertwined with historical particularities. One example can illustrate how historical and sociological analysis must supplement each other. The actions of the clergy in late 1970s Iran were partly a response to the shah's modernization program, but also the expression of their role in Iranian society as this had developed over the previous centuries. Thus, a purely synchronic analysis of autocratic modernization cannot account for many of the fundamental traits of their political stance.

Similarly, both the particular experiences of autocratic modernization and the historical backgrounds to these in the two countries diverged from each other in significant respects. Although both Tsar Nicholas II and Muhammad Reza Shah were autocratic rulers, the historical contexts of autocracy, with all the rich variations and associations in each country, and the nature of the ruler's own autocratic rule were in many ways very different. The same variations characterize the gamut of concepts that comparison must employ—for example, merchantry, industrialization, clergy, political party, social class. Although perfectly appropriate for purposes of comparison, such concepts must also be fleshed out for the two cases with a degree of historical concreteness.

These glancing references to some of the methodological complexities of comparative sociology will not be further developed here. Their purpose, rather, is to provide a context and rationale for the present chapter, and to suggest how it fits into the overall logic of this study. It is difficult to imagine a marriage of history and sociology satisfactory to scholars in both disciplines. The concepts, generalizations, and propositions of analytic sociology will offend the historian concerned with evidence, nuance, and particularity. The rich detail, complexity and tentativeness of the historian will often leave the sociologist with an unsated appetite for generality and causal structure.

The comparison of two cases strikes a partial compromise between the historian's accustomed attention to a single case and the sociologist's preference for maximizing the number of cases in search of the most broadly based conclusions. More specifically, insistence on the similarity of the core process of autocratic modernization can be combined with an appreciation of historical contrasts in order to interpret both similarities and differences in the revolutions. Such a compromise will not satisfy all tastes. I will not be able to avoid abstraction and generalization—indeed, this is precisely one purpose of the study. Yet these abstractions will be too historically grounded to admit of easy extension to other developing countries or other revolutions, except insofar as they can provide a foundation for contrasts between types. Although I will at points allude to cross-type comparisons, the purpose here is to lay bare the fundamental traits and tensions of one pattern of modernization and its implications for social change.

Let me, then, summarize the overarching logic of the comparison. I have chosen a general problem, the nature and consequences of autocratic modernization as a pattern of development. However little else they shared, both Nicholas II's Russia and Muhammad Reza Shah's Iran encountered the dilemmas of this contradictory path to the modern world. But the historically shaped social physiognomies of the two countries led to very different patterns of change. Through contrast and counterpart the historical traits and experiences of the two countries can be shown to illuminate each other, both in terms of commonalities and particularities. The goal of the comparison is not simply generalization, but also insight into each concrete case through contrast, a kind of dialogue of theme and variations.

From these methodological bearings follows the necessity of beginning with an account of the fundamental long-term historical traits of the two societies. A consideration of the historical backgrounds of the regimes, their social and cultural foundations, the relation of the states to other institutions, the nature of the dominant social elites, and the societies' historical experiences with modernization will help interpret the characteristics and interrelations of the key contending actors during the periods of rapid development.

Background of the Modern State

Both Russia and Iran were geographically exposed, vulnerable to invasions and cultural influences from east and west. Russia is situated on an immense plain, with no physical barriers to foreign depredations, by which it has been victimized for centuries. Norsemen, Mongols, Poles, French, and Germans have taken advantage of its flat expanses of land and advantageous river routes to conquer or despoil the Russian territories. Iran's geography is more rugged, its mountains, deserts, and lack of navigable rivers posing barriers to conquerors and centralized rule. But its placement between the Mediterranean and Asia made it an obvious target of foreign aggressors, of whom there was no lack from Alexander the Great and later the Arabs to the English and Russians of modern times.

Perhaps it was partly this vulnerability to foreign threat that explains the relatively early formation of distinct territorial states in Russia and Iran. The struggle of the Russians against Tartar domination in the thirteenth and fourteenth centuries culminated in the consolidation of power by the Moscow princes (partly through their astute cooperation with the Mongol authorities) over the other branches of the House of Riurik. They had to impose themselves not only against the Mongols, but also against the status quo of fragmented rule embodied in the appanage system of princes. The so-called appanage period of Russian history, from the mid-twelfth to the mid-fifteenth centuries, was characterized by a multitude of petty princes with limited authority even in their own territories, and by a tendency toward further fragmentation through the division of the prince's patrimony among all his sons. The struggle of the Moscow princes for supremacy in the face of foreign threat and internal centrifugal forces exemplifies one of the main themes of Russian history: the interplay between centralized power, incarnating order, and later, in its own view, rationality, against the manifold forces of chaos and dissolution. Chaos, spontaneity, disorder, the threat of anarchy, and the collapse of the state: all of these would form a powerful set of images justifying further concentration of power and the development of statist mythology with great appeal to a people well aware of the dangers of spontaneous social forces.

By the late fifteenth century the power of the Mongols had collapsed. With the fall of Constantinople to the Turks, the Russian church was able to establish its independence from the Greeks. The previous subordination, political and cultural, of the Russians to the Mongols and to Byzantium was now at an end, and the Moscow princes, beginning with Ivan III (1462–1505), proclaimed themselves tsars, and Moscow could now envision itself as the Third Rome. Territorial unity, national identity (primarily as the union of the true Orthodox believers), and autocratic power created the preconditions for a dramatic expansion of the Russian state in the following centuries.

Roughly contemporary developments in Iran offer interesting points of similarity and contrast. Iran, as a general term referring to the Iranian plateau east of Mesopotamia and west of Central Asia, was heir to ancient imperial traditions, but after the Arab conquests these had been eclipsed.

In the Islamic middle ages, Iran, like Mesopotamia, witnessed a system of decentralized rule combining the power of petty rulers, the emirs,[1] and the influence of local notables in the cities. The power of the emirs was arbitrary but limited and often ineffective, and there was constant warfare among them. This pattern was interrupted and partly transformed by the Mongol invasions of the mid-thirteenth century, which led to the imposition of Mongol rule until the conquests of Timur (late fourteenth century), who himself built upon the Mongol political inheritance. Although the Mongols frequently delegated power to local emirs, they also imposed elements of an imperial structure, including an emphasis on the absolute power of the ruling family. In addition, they reintroduced Turkic-Mongolian tribal and military chieftainships (first brought in by the Seljuks in the eleventh century), with their unstable alliances and competitions for power, which proved capable of posing continual threats to centralized monarchy well into the twentieth century. Finally, they encouraged a pastoralist mode of life that would later pose obstacles to the consolidation of a modern nation-state.

There were thus traditions and resources available for the creation of an absolutist state in Iran, as there were also numerous serious impediments. It was the achievement of the Safavid shahs to promote this process of state building in the sixteenth and seventeenth centuries with remarkable energy. Originating as a Sufi order in northwestern Iran in the late thirteenth century, the Safavid movement gained widespread support, especially among the nondominant Turkic tribes in the region, for its opposition to the ruling Aqquyunlu and for its elaboration of a militant religious doctrine. In 1501 Ismail, leader of the movement, declared himself shah of Iran, founding the dynasty that endured until 1722. At its high point, during the reign of Shah Abbas I (1588–1629), the shah ruled in absolutist fashion over a vastly expanded empire administered by a strong professional bureaucracy. Together with the Ottoman and Mogul empires, the Safavid state constituted one of the three great Islamic territorial formations of the early modern period. To buttress their temporal authority, the Safavids developed a distinctive caesaropapist conception of kingship, under which the king was regarded as the Shadow of God. Shiʿism was declared the state orthodoxy and forcibly imposed upon the people, who until that time adhered to a variety of Sunni, Shiʿite, and Sufi beliefs.

It is not easy to summarize in brief compass the nature of Shiʿism and its key differences from the majority Sunni belief. The historical foundation of the split was the conflict over the succession to Muhammad at the Saqifah assembly: whether the choice of leader should be restricted to the

[1] Emir (or amir): a general or other military commander; in medieval Islam, the term also referred to many independent rulers and occasionally to members of their families.

Prophet's household (Banu Hashim) or whether the head of the community should be selected through consensus. The partisans of Ali favored him as the cousin and son-in-law of Muhammad, whom they claimed the Prophet had chosen to succeed him before his death. Their opponents argued that Muhammad had deliberately not chosen a successor, leaving this responsibility to the community, which he deemed fully capable of choosing the most competent person.

To this historical dispute were added, over the centuries, various other cultural and ideological differences that, when combined with the opposing historical experiences of the two communities, transformed these two positions into conflicting and often incompatible religious traditions. To oversimplify: Sunnis stood for the tradition of the community, consensus, law (the shariʿa), and the integration of political and religious elites. Shiʿism came to represent a hostile, or at least skeptical, stance toward the status quo, with an underlying millenarianism; emphasis on the authority of the religious elite, who were given the right to interpret the tradition on the basis of their religious knowledge; and the elevation of esoteric knowledge and inner experience over external law. This is not to say that Sunnism was conservative, Shiʿism revolutionary. In fact, the Sunni model of the community guided by law always posed an implicit challenge to imperfect secular authorities; and the Shiʿa often retreated into an apolitical, otherworldly perspective based on a deep sense of the corruption of all worldly affairs. Yet it is also true that Shiʿism more than Sunnism was the repository of a dissident tradition within Islam, which frequently expressed itself historically in a greater degree of distance from the political authorities.

Building on earlier foundations, by the late sixteenth century autocratic monarchy attained unprecedented scope and power in both countries. Ivan the Terrible and Abbas I ruled vast territories over which they claimed absolute dominion. In their persons spiritual and temporal powers were united, and the legitimating concepts of the Shiʿite state and Moscow as the Third Rome buttressed their authority. State control over religious institutions was extended while the power of local elites was significantly reduced. Russia and Iran emerged as relatively well-formed states with defined (if changing) boundaries and peoples set off against their neighbors by a widely shared religious identity.

The differences were equally significant and provide keys to the very different historical developments of the two countries over the following centuries. The Iranian monarchy never lost its tribal foundations,[2] nor was it able to control the power of rival tribal groupings. Iranian political life did

[2] The Safavid movement was not strictly tribal in its inception, though, as pointed out, it gained its major support from the Turkic tribal groups in northwestern Iran and took on a tribal identity.

not lose its segmentary character until at least the reign of Reza Shah in the early decades of the twentieth century. Such an apparently modern movement as the Constitutional Revolution of 1906 could thus partly be interpreted in terms of the model of urban-tribal relations worked out by Ibn Khaldun for medieval Islam. All Iranian regimes until Reza Shah had a tribal basis, and all of them confronted tribal challenges to their power. The shahs were autocratic rulers because their power was arbitrary and in theory unlimited and because legitimate countervailing institutions were weak, but their governments were seldom able to control tribal forces effectively or deeply to penetrate society.

Russia had its own centrifugal forces, especially the various national groups that multiplied as the empire expanded. Yet the Muscovite state benefited from certain advantages and developed effective ways to handle the potential challenges. First, the national groups occupied distant and outlying areas. Their distance, diversity, and distinctness from Russian culture impeded the formation of alliances with rival sectors of the Russian political elite. In addition, the tsars adopted a policy of conversion, baptism, and often incorporation of the foreign elites into the state apparatus,[3] thus limiting their potential role as local communal leaders. These efforts were not and could not be wholly successful, as the experience of the Ukraine testifies, but by Iranian standards the universality implicit in the nontribal nature of the Russian autocracy gave immense advantages.

A second crucial contrast lay in the manner in which the Russian and Iranian rulers responded to the classic dilemma of patrimonial regimes: how to establish control over the social elites upon which the ruler depends for the extension of his power over the population. Nobles can too easily usurp what are in theory contingent grants of land, withhold tax revenues due the ruler for their own purposes, or form military contingents loyal to themselves rather than to the central government. In response to these familiar problems the Russian rulers initiated policies to weaken the independent nobility and to form a service elite defined and controlled by the ruler. In the *mestnichestvo* system of seventeenth-century Russia, noble lineage was recognized as one ingredient in the official social hierarchy, but the overall rank also depended on the quality of state service. The emphasis on state service was further strengthened by the administrative reforms of Peter the Great (1682–1725), which established a formal ranking system based almost wholly on this criterion. In Iran the tribal basis of the ruling elite and the social cohesion produced by regional tribal solidarities hindered such a solution. Tribal elites and noble landowners maintained a degree of independence inconceivable in Russia after Ivan the Terrible's

[3] Marc Raeff, *Understanding Imperial Russia* (New York: Columbia University Press, 1984), 15.

attacks on the boyars. Thus, early eighteenth-century Iran produced no Peter the Great but degenerated into political anarchy marked by provincial revolts and Afghan, Afshar, Zand, and Qajar tribal movements.

Special note must also be taken of the international influence operating on the two monarchies before the eighteenth century. The exposure of the Russian court to European ideas, particularly through its contact with the Polish nobility and because of influences coming from the newly incorporated Ukraine, stimulated new ways of thinking about state, society, and religion. Novel activist conceptions of the responsibility of the state for the welfare of society, of the need for corporate organization of the elite, and the necessity of religious reform gained wide currency in ruling circles. These conceptions did not penetrate the popular classes, however, and the diffusion of Western ideas already at this early date created a gap between the political elites and the people. The church reforms of the late seventeenth century were an expression of this divergence, and the schism they precipitated solidified the separation between the state and a significant part of its population. Both this separation and the activist conception of the state would find fuller expression in the dramatic but historically rooted reforms of Peter the Great. The Iranian monarchy, by contrast, was subject to no such influences. The politics of the Qajar rulers in the late nineteenth century could largely be interpreted in the political categories of previous centuries.

These crucial differences provide clues to the development of the Russian and Iranian states over the next two centuries. For despite the remarkable similarities already noted, the Russian autocracy, governing apparatus, and society underwent noteworthy transformations in the eighteenth and nineteenth centuries, allowing Russia to maintain itself as a great European power, while Iran remained politically fragmented and economically sluggish, prey to British and Russian territorial and economic incursions.

Nineteenth-century Russian intellectuals endlessly debated the question of whether Russia belonged to the East or the West. By East, they had in mind a complex of traits including arbitrary and personal government, the formlessness and sluggishness of social groups, the insignificance of urban life, and the enserfed peasantry. The Western elements, of course, were those introduced into Russian life as a response to the influence and challenge of the West. Peter the Great, coming to power at a time when the old Muscovite system was in considerable disarray, was the first great Westernizing monarch, responsible for traumatic changes irrevocably breaking with the Russian past. Russia did not become a fully Western nation—if nothing else, Peter's brutal and autocratic methods of rule demonstrated the great gaps that remained. But Russia had been set, against the will of much of the population, on the path of progress, with results even more ambiguous than for western Europe.

Peter's rule and the social changes to which it gave birth commingled Muscovite and Western traits. The autocracy expanded its power, further transforming the nobility into a service elite and harnessing the church to its purposes. It committed itself to an activist conception of government, whereby the state had the responsibility to regulate and transform society. The conceptions of the autocratic ruler and the modernizing monarch were wedded to each other, diverging from the new partnership between state and society observable in the "well-ordered police states" of Europe.[4] Thus, in breaking with tradition, Peter also broke with a large part of his own society, calling into question the traditional bases of legitimacy. For many Russians Peter was the anti-Christ, his changes a perversion of Russian ways. Nor could they be fully acceptable to those with more Western perspectives: as noted, they expanded the powers of the state not through but at the expense of society, thus subverting the most fundamental of all Western innovations, the growing autonomy and dynamism of independent social groups.

Progress in Peter's Russia was undeniable. New directions were taken in industry, administration, science and technology, education, military science, and a host of other fields. But many of his changes, initiated by the state, could not permeate society, and they often aroused opposition, sometimes active, more often passive. In the end, they mainly affected the elites of Russian society, and they delayed or even hindered the more fundamental task of the creation of a society founded on individual and group initiative.

The reign of Catherine the Great (1762–1796), like that of Peter, marked a new stage in the development of the Russian autocracy, as she wrestled with the dilemmas of the Petrine system. Also like Peter's, her legacy is controversial: for some she was insincere, launching reforms that she had no intention of realizing; for others she was deeply committed to progressive ideals out of place in the Russia of her time.[5]

One of the key weaknesses of Peter's reforms had been their lack of social rootedness. He did little to improve local administration, and Russian society was not sufficiently organized to absorb and promote his policies through a network of associations. Coming to power at a time when the gap between Europe and Russia had widened significantly, Catherine sought to introduce into her country elements of the estate system, which was already becoming an anachronism in Europe. Reversing Peter's tactics,

[4] See Marc Raeff, *The Well-Ordered Police State* (New Haven: Yale University Press, 1983).

[5] For an authoritative defense of Catherine, see Isabel de Madariaga, *Russia in the Age of Catherine the Great* (New Haven: Yale University Press, 1981).

she wished to organize and enlist the support of social groups in the name of progress.[6] The famous Charters to the Nobility and to the Towns (1783) were the most significant measures in this direction, granting corporate status and rights to the provincial nobility and to urban elites. Yet the self-organization of Russian society was not allowed to proceed very far, testifying to the ironies and limitations of state initiative in the modernization of society.

The political history of nineteenth-century Russia is dominated by this dilemma: how to combine the autocratic state, the historically dynamic factor in social change, and a civil society, necessary for the further modernization of the country and thus indispensable to the state's own purposes. The autocratic state's efforts to change society in the previous century had led to more rationalized administration. Under Nicholas I, the regime continued this process and searched for an ideological justification for itself in the context of a newly developing civil society. Thus, in its efforts to develop society and through its encounter with the society it had helped spawn, the autocratic regime itself underwent transformation over a prolonged period.

Nicholas I (1825–1855) attempted to continue autocratic rule over a society far more complex and independent than Peter's Russia. The influence of European ideas on the nobility had found expression in the Decembrist movement of young officers that had challenged Nicholas at his accession. This was only one indication of the profound changes in Russian culture brought about by the continuing development of civil society, which included the emergence of an educated public and the birth of an intelligentsia. Nicholas's response was the imposition of new controls over public expression and education, a policy that led to widespread condemnation of him as a reactionary. But he also shared his predecessors' belief in some aspects of progress and furthered administrative rationalization, technical education, and economic growth. He also seems to have favored the abolition of serfdom, although he was not ready to tackle the issue himself. In order to strengthen his links with his people, he promoted a rudimentary theory of government based on the ideas of Orthodoxy, autocracy, and nationality, which incorporated many rationalist enlightenment ideas, and he formed his political police as a way of extending his patriarchal benevolence to his people. Yet ultimately his conservative strategy to rejoin state and society failed, for reasons well expressed by his own state ideologist, Michael Pogodin:

[6] See Raeff, *Police State*, 237–38. "Catherine's recognition of the beneficial role of a comprehensively structured society, rather than reliance on an atomized population ruled by state servants, constitutes her most important contribution to the political history of Russia."

> Carried away by the brilliant example of his ancestor, he failed to realize that things have changed since the time of Peter I, that Peter's activity, transferred into our own age, becomes an optical illusion; that most affairs, in spite of an apparent direct dependence on the sovereign, become in this manner a prey of the arbitrariness of subordinates, protected by the sacred name of the Tsar and thus unpunishable; or these affairs follow, so to speak, their own course, according to the established pattern, often against His wishes, to the detriment of general welfare, emphasizing the contrast between Russia on paper and Russia in reality.[7]

One need only add one qualification: Pogodin exaggerates the power of Peter, who in fact faced the same dilemmas of translating his will into reality in the absence of an organized society.

If Nicholas I tended toward the "Petrine" solution to the dilemma, Alexander II (1855–1881) tended to favor the "Catherine" pole. The distinction between the two rulers has its limitations: much of Alexander II's reform program was actually conceived during his father's reign. Yet it is true that Alexander II, the Tsar Liberator, saw much more urgency in the need to liberate civil society, starting with the emancipation of the serfs and including reforms in the military, the justice system, urban and rural administration, and education. He met opposition from conservatives and radicals alike, and his reforms proved to be only partly successful. In addition, in looking at his "great reforms" we encounter the same contradiction noted for Catherine's reform: civil society cannot be liberated by fiat by an enlightened autocracy seeking to define and control the process from above.

The concept "autocracy" in Russia thus embraces a rich historical experience, as the autocrats, in seeking to extend their overall social power administratively, militarily, and economically, encouraged the development of a civil society. Civil society and its needs, in turn, compelled the autocracy to introduce further changes and eventually challenged autocratic claims. Thus, in the final period of rapid change, in Nicholas II's industrializing Russia, the tsar had a wealth of possible historical models of autocracy upon which to rely. Unfortunately, his image of autocracy harkened back to the Muscovite period, shutting him off from the realities of the society he sought to rule.[8]

If the autocracy was the most dynamic force in Russian society, the Ira-

[7] Quoted in Nicholas Riasanovsky, *Nicholas I and Official Nationality in Russia, 1825–1855* (Berkeley: University of California Press, 1955), 206.

[8] Richard Wortman, "Moscow and Petersburg: The Problem of Political Center in Tsarist Russia, 1881–1914," in *Rites of Power*, ed. Sean Wilentz (Philadelphia: University of Pennsylvania Press, 1985).

nian monarchy embodied many of the obstacles to social change in seventeenth- through nineteenth-century Iran. The institution's history is not so dramatic; no figure parallel to Catherine or Alexander II emerged to modernize the system of rule. The entire period is one of political decadence and decay. Correlatively, it was not until the end of the nineteenth century that Iranian society forced the regime seriously to confront the question of social and political change.

After the death of Abbas I (1629), the Safavid state experienced a period of decline.[9] The rulers were mediocre, the army and administration deteriorated, taxation was irregular, and early in the eighteenth century tribal revolts proliferated, leading to a period of weakness and anarchy. In 1722 an Afghan tribe occupied Isfahan, the Safavid capital, and the Russians and Ottomans divided large parts of Transcaucasia between themselves. Afshar and Zand tribal groups occupied the throne until the victory of the Qajars, a Turkoman tribe whose khans had previously served the Safavids.

The Qajars ruled Iran from 1779 to 1925, but they were never able to establish effective control of the country.[10] The army was little more than an assembly of tribal military forces, of doubtful reliability and without a professional officer corps. The government administration even by the end of the nineteenth century was rudimentary, undermined by favoritism and corruption. The state was threatened by tribal movements, and in the early part of the nineteenth century by Russian and British territorial encroachments. In the latter half of the century the regime granted extraordinary economic concessions to British and Russian interests, a policy that may have relieved the problem of state revenues but also stimulated broad coalitions of opposition.

Though limited in its ability to control society, Qajar power was arbitrary and unconstrained, a threat to the property and security of its subjects. Seeing themselves almost as an occupying power, they seem to have regarded Iran as a property to be exploited, not a country to be improved. Writing of Fath Ali Shah (1797–1834), Fraser observes that "the throne having come into the hands of his family by conquest, he treats the whole country (except, perhaps, the seat of his own tribe in Mazunderan) like a conquered nation; and his only concern is how to extort from them the greatest possible amount of money."[11]

Precarious in their hold on power, the Qajars revived the Safavid idea of the shah as the Shadow of God on earth and surrounded their court with

[9] Ira Lapidus, *A History of Islamic Societies* (Cambridge: Cambridge University Press, 1988), 299–300.

[10] For a good outline of Qajar politics and society, see Ann Lambton, *Qajar Persia* (London: I. B. Tauris, 1987), 87–107.

[11] Cited in Ann Lambton, *Landlord and Peasant in Persia* (London: Oxford University Press, 1953), 135.

extraordinary pomp. As Malcolm wrote, "nothing can exceed the splendour of the Persian court on extraordinary occasions. It presents a scene of the greatest magnificence, regulated by the exactest order. To no part of the government is so much attention paid as to the strict maintenance of those forms and ceremonies, which are deemed essential to the power and glory of the monarch."[12]

In another sense, the parallel with the Safavids is misleading, for the Qajars lacked the religious basis of authority accorded to the earlier dynasty. As is well known, Islam makes no strict separation between secular and religious authority, in principle if not always in practice. The Safavids exemplified caesaropapist tendencies implicit in Islam. By contrast, early nineteenth-century Iran represents, within Islam, an extreme working out of the principle of the separation of the realms of God and Caesar. The Shiʿite hierocracy had achieved a strong degree of institutional independence and authority over religious life; the temporal authorities were granted the sanction to rule over the secular realm in general accord with the norms of Islam. Religious thinkers worked out a theory of the two differentiated powers, the ulama and the rulers, based on complementary functions until the return of the imam, at which time unity of authority would be reestablished.[13] Although this thesis, and the cooperation between the state and the ulama that it implied, could be seen to support the position of the shahs, it also expressed a contingency in the religious legitimation of authority very different from the Safavid conception. Islamic norms were all-embracing and defined by the Shiʿite hierocracy; the shah's authority was legitimate only insofar as he respected them. The theory of the differentiation of the complementary powers thus included the potential for a religious attack on state policy.

If Qajar rule in the early nineteenth century was far from dynamic, by the middle and late nineteenth century the shahs increasingly perceived the need for political modernization. There had been some initiatives earlier in the century, such as the 1826 proposal for a new military corps, but this had been withdrawn due to the opposition of the ulama. Nasir al-Din Shah (1848–1896) embarked on a fitful course of military and administrative reforms, including a new system of military recruitment and the creation of a Russian-inspired local government administration. Some of his advisors, inspired by the Ottoman example, wanted to go much further. Mirza Malkum Khan, the leading Westernizing reformer of the late nineteenth century, urged Iran to "profit from the example of the Ottoman Empire. . . . Henceforth all governments in the world will have to be ordered [*mun-*

[12] Lambton, *Qajar Persia*, 94.

[13] Said Amir Arjomand, *The Shadow of God and the Hidden Imam* (Chicago: University of Chicago Press, 1984), 225–29.

azzam] like those of Europe, or to be subjugated and conquered by European power."[14] He favored the development of a new body of secular law and the formation of a legislative council and an executive cabinet to enact reforms.

But Malkum Khan was wrong in his estimate that Iran was "not in the least different from the Ottoman Empire."[15] The Ottoman state furnished a stratum of reformist bureaucrats in the early nineteenth century that had no counterpart in Iran, whose reformers were isolated individuals, associated at best in secret societies. The Ottoman ulama had nothing like the independence of their Iranian counterparts, and were in no position to oppose the Ottoman reformers. Equally significant, in the Ottoman Empire the Western threat encouraged independent state initiatives to counter the challenge, whereas in Iran the financial hardships of the monarchy led it to promote foreign concessions as a source of funds, thus arousing nationalist and religious opposition. Ironically, those who wanted to modernize the state came to be seen in many quarters as the betrayers of the nation's independence. Diverse combinations of secular nationalist, merchant, and ulama opposition led to the withdrawal of the economic concessions granted to the Europeans and the failure of the proposals for governmental reform.

By the late nineteenth century a weak state with challenged legitimacy confronted a potentially very broad opposition of Western-style constitutionalists, disaffected ulama, and nationalists of various stripes (including Islamic reformers inspired by Afghani). As a result of economic crises and various provocations from the government, these groups were able to ally with each other to wrest a constitution from Muzaffar al-Din Shah as a result of the Constitutional Revolution. Instead of introducing in practice the constitutional monarchy established on paper, the revolution ushered in a period of instability and chaos, which lasted until the rise of Reza Khan. Russian and British troops occupied Iran during World War I, and with the fall of the tsarist regime the country came under greatly increased British influence.

The nature and origins of the Constitutional Revolution of 1905–1911 help us understand the very different historical relationship between state and society in the modern period in the two countries. Precipitated by the brutal punishment of several sugar merchants by the governor of Teheran, and against a background of food shortages, governmental waste, and concern over foreign influence, the revolution quickly involved a broad coalition of traditional and modern groups, including merchants, significant

[14] Quoted in Hamid Algar, *Mirza Malkum Khan* (Berkeley: University of California Press, 1973), 70.

[15] Ibid., 70.

sectors of the clergy, and a small group of secular intellectuals. Outraged by the government's unlawfulness and preoccupied with the state's inability to protect the society against foreign encroachments, the revolutionaries demanded above all the rule of law and the granting of a constitution. Under great pressure a constitution was granted and a representative assembly set up. This victory was precarious, however, and many of the reforms were later reversed, in fact if not always in law. Nonetheless, the revolutionary period left a strong imprint on Iranian political culture, establishing a widespread commitment to individual rights, the rule of law, and constitutionalism, particularly among the modern sectors.

Many, though not all, of these same reforms had been announced by the Russian government already in the 1860s, the era of the great reforms. Much more influenced by the European experience, the tsars themselves initiated many of the measures that in Iran could only come from society against the state. Although the constitutionalist reforms did enjoy the sympathy of some reformist government officials, they evoked only hostility from the new shah, Muhammad Ali Shah. Although the reforms conceded by the Russian tsars were also precarious, they left a much more substantial institutional residue than in Iran. It was in part for this reason that liberalism, based on the belief in nonrevolutionary political reform, weak as it was in Russia compared with that in Europe, was still far stronger than in Iran.

The break with tradition, and the first great steps toward political and economic modernization, occurred during the reign of Reza Shah, brought to power with the help of the British in the early 1920s. Under the Qajars, modernization had been connected with Western political ideas and foreign economic control, traits that had further weakened the tenuous power of the dynasty. The tribal Qajars were also in no position to reduce the role of the tribes in Iranian politics. The Pahlavi dynasty was novel in its nontribal social foundation, and Reza Shah had no truck with Western ideas of the separation of powers, ministerial governments, or constitutions. He also acted to reduce the role of foreign economic interests and advisors.

Reza Shah was able to accomplish what had proved impossible for the Qajars, the creation of a relatively powerful state possessing an effective bureaucracy and a modern army. (The military budgets increased dramatically, and a new draft law ensured a reliable supply of recruits.) The shah's power was also founded on the increasing wealth of the royal house, much of it accumulated by the ruler through force and fraud. As a result of these measures, the strengthening of the state could be tied to nationalism, as had been impossible under the Qajars, with their perpetual turning to foreign financing.

In much of his policy, including his brutality against his enemies, Reza

Shah was reminiscent of Peter the Great. Especially striking is the parallel policy of an enforced change of dress, the traditional attire being seen as symptomatic of backwardness. In some respects his actions went considerably beyond Peter's, for he strove to create a modern nation-state out of a culturally and politically fragmented society. Toward this goal he discouraged the use of non-Persian languages, especially Azeri, Arabic, and Armenian, through the closing of schools and publishing houses.[16] Also, he had the resources of modern propaganda to celebrate the New Order and the great pre-Islamic heritage of Iran. In his forced Westernization and secularization, he resembled Ataturk, but unlike his Turkish counterpart he did not head a movement or a party. The first giant stride in the modernization of Iran was taken by an individual autocrat, son of a soldier of modest rank.[17]

The political system bequeathed by Reza Shah to his son Muhammad was, by the standards of early twentieth-century Russia, still quite primitive. The Russian autocracy had accumulated two centuries of experience of social change from above, and so had formed a complex administrative apparatus and had participated in the creation of more than the mere rudiments of a civil society. This developing civil society had in turn made the state more complex, furnishing it with educated professionals, challenging it to reform itself, establishing links with government bodies. Thus, the Russian autocracy had complex and manifold links with society, and embraced within itself both reformist and reactionary traditions and perspectives. This greater complexity benefited the tsars in their ability to shape society—they no longer sought to impose modernization on a largely unprepared society. But the subtle interconnections of the autocratic regime with a partly modernized society also had its drawbacks, as the remaining autocratic controls jarred even more strongly with the demand for political participation, and as the profound contradictions of the process of autocratic modernization were reflected in the state apparatus itself.

In Iran this process of partial mutual adaptation between the autocratic state and civil society had hardly begun under the last shah. The Iranian autocracy had much more the appearance of a premodern despotism, more capricious and unpredictable than the Russian autocracy. In many respects the contradictions of autocratic modernization were quite similar under Nicholas II and Muhammad Reza Shah, yet the historical context of the autocracies also determined significant differences in the nature of the state and its relationship to society. In Muhammad Reza Shah's Iran, a less well

[16] Abrahamian, *Iran between Two Revolutions*, 142.

[17] For Reza Shah's background, see Donald Wilber, *Riza Shah Pahlavi: The Resurrection and Reconstruction of Iran, 1878–1944* (Hicksville, N.Y.: Exposition Press, 1975), 3–15.

established, yet more voluntaristic, autocracy would dominate and disorganize a nascent civil society with strong traditional social groups. In Russia a traditional autocracy would attempt to control and submerge the social groups to which it had given rise and upon which it depended for economic progress and social support.

Social Elites

Russia until the turn of the nineteenth century and Iran until the rule of Muhammad Reza Shah were both overwhelmingly agrarian countries. In Russia roughly 96 percent of the population was rural as late as 1796;[18] in Iran the urban population in the nineteenth century was estimated at 20 percent, although the reliability and comparability of this figure is dubious.[19] Even though Russia had become an industrial power by 1900, at least three-quarters of its population still consisted of peasants. In accord with the nature of the economies, the dominant social elites in both countries were the landed nobility. Parallel to, and partly because of, the very different historical evolutions of the state, the nobilities in the two countries also played very different historical roles in politics and society. Neither showed the dynamism of some Western nobilities, and both agricultural economies remained technologically backward and relatively unproductive. Yet, for reasons to be explored, the Russian nobility was partially able to impede far-reaching social and political reforms despite its economic decline, whereas the Iranian nobility proved quite unable to protect itself from the modernizing state.

Historically, the experience of the Russian nobility is highly uneven, with dramatic changes in its social and political fortunes. These reversals stemmed from the fact that its evolution was not primarily rooted in processes of economic or social accretion, but in the actions of the Russian state, which imposed changes that would not have occurred spontaneously. In the period before the rise of the Muscovite autocracy, the landed elite in Russia was composed of a multiplicity of princes and boyars. Ties of vassalage and fealty were weaker than in feudal Europe and landlords had the right to choose whom they served, casting in doubt the applicability of the term *feudalism* to the Russian context. From this condition of relative autonomy, the Russian nobility moved to a position of greater dependence in the Muscovite period. The *pomestie* system, involving grants of land based on service to the state, began to replace the *votchiny*, the

[18] Nicholas Riasanovsky, *A History of Russia*, 4th ed. (New York: Oxford University Press, 1984), 287.

[19] Abrahamian, *Iran between Two Revolutions*, 11.

hereditary landholdings typical of the pre-Muscovite period. The state rewarded and promoted the interests of the service gentry by granting land and extending serfdom; the imposition of state service and the development of the *mestnichestvo* ranking system led to incessant struggles within a uniform and imposed status system as well as a certain coalescence of the nobility as a social group.

Peter the Great perfected the concept of a service nobility, further reducing their independence and yoking their position to the state through the famous Table of Ranks. Yet there was also a tension in his program evident in his policies of increasing landowner control over the serfs, converting their landholdings into private property, and encouraging new ideas through education and foreign experience. In the course of the eighteenth century this inconsistency in the position of the gentry due to the tensions of modernization from above was resolved in favor of greater autonomy for the nobles. Indeed, under Catherine the nobility entered its "golden age," as the state granted it considerable independence and supported it socially and economically. Examples of the latter policy include government initiatives to organize the gentry as an estate on European lines and the creation of a state lending bank in 1786.

With their service obligations removed and with government loans available, some members of the gentry invested in and managed their estates, turning them into productive enterprises. Others pioneered in some branches of industry, especially those, like sugar production, connected with agricultural production. But on the whole the landowners were unable to adapt to the more competitive market conditions of early nineteenth-century Russia, and the percentage of nonnoble landowners and the weight of noble indebtedness increased. The great blow for the nobility was the emancipation of the serfs in 1861, an act that illustrated once again that their fortunes depended on the state. The governments of Alexander III and Nicholas II did what they could to enhance the declining economic position of the landowners, and the nobles maintained their great influence in the court as well as their ties to the bureaucracy, despite the fact that their dominance in the latter decreased with its professionalization. Although the economic decline was irreversible, the historical interweaving of gentry elite and the autocratic state provided the foundation for continuing political power. It was, indeed, they whom the challenged monarch sought out when the autocracy seemed on the verge of collapse.

By the time of the Safavids, settled agriculture already had had a long and complex history in Iran. The various conquests and changes in dynasty had bequeathed a complicated mix of pre-Islamic Persian, Islamic, Seljuk, and Mongol principles and practices of land tenure. For example, the pre-Islamic conception of the absolute authority of the ruler survived the Islamic egalitarian emphasis,[20] to be assimilated later with the Turkish notion of the khan as sole landowner.[21] Upon the Safavid rise to power, this complex heritage was again modified to meet the needs of a centralizing state. The resulting subtleties need not be discussed here.[22] In general terms, the rulers followed the customary patrimonial policy of attempting to transform inalienable and hereditary rights into grants of land in exchange for service to the state, a practice that was often successfully resisted by the grantees, whose goal was full proprietary rights.

Several factors prevented land ownership in Iran from developing feudal traits. The small, dispersed villages of rural Iran and the frequency of absentee landlordism inhibited the growth of a manorial system.[23] The economic significance of trade and the regard in which it is held in Islam facilitated the cities' cultural domination of rural areas and weakened the stability of the agrarian order. Even leading tribal khans in the premodern era were oriented to the cities, hardly the rough-hewn warriors of popular imagery.[24] Pastoralism was a constant threat to settled agriculture and tribal power a source of social and economic disruption. Finally, the political institutions of Iran were inconsistent with the social underpinnings of feudalism in the strict sense; vassalage, institutionalized personal loyalties, fixed rights, and contractualism could find no place amid the arbitrariness of power in Iran.[25]

One final source of weakness of the agrarian elite deserves mention: its great heterogeneity. Among the most substantial landowners were prominent members of the clergy and tribal khans. Clearly their social backgrounds and cultural orientations separated them out from other members of the landed elite. Crosscutting communal loyalties inhibited the formation of collective identities, and in fact there was nothing resembling a noble estate in Iran: no charters of rights, no estate organizations, probably little sense of shared status.

All of this is not to deny the immense weight of the landed nobility in

[20] For example, water and pasture were held to be the common property of all Muslims in theory. See Lambton, *Landlord and Peasant*, 16. This work describes land tenure in Iran from the Arab conquest to approximately 1950 and gives a good idea of the complexity of the issues involved.

[21] Lambton, *Landlord and Peasant*, 76.

[22] See Bert Fragner, "Social and Internal Economic Affairs," in *The Cambridge History of Iran*, vol. 6, *The Timurid and Safavid Periods*, ed. Peter Jackson and Laurence Lockhart (Cambridge: Cambridge University Press, 1986), 499–524.

[23] See Marshall Hodgson, *The Venture of Islam* (Chicago: University of Chicago Press, 1974), 2:79–81, for a general discussion of the "precariousness of the agrarian power" in Middle Eastern history.

[24] Lois Beck, *The Qashqa'i of Iran* (New Haven: Yale University Press, 1986), 86–87. Sometimes urban residence was enforced on the khans or their family members as a form of control.

[25] Lambton, *Qajar Persia*, x–xi.

Iranian social and political life. Under the Qajars, land assignments tended to become private property, no matter what they might have been in principle. The landlords' control over the peasants mirrored the arbitrary power of the shahs, and there was a tendency to concentrate juridical authority over the peasantry in their hands.[26] In addition to their local prerogatives, the landowners had great social prestige, were often appointed to government office, and in general throughout the Qajar period constituted the most powerful social group in the kingdom.

In its departure from the "feudal model" of an established and independent agrarian power, the Iranian landed elite appears to resemble the Russian nobility. Yet in crucial respects it is equally far from its Russian counterpart, which for centuries had been disciplined and mobilized by the state. Much of the Iranian landed gentry, and particularly the tribal khans, enjoyed great political independence, often constituting petty rulers in their own lands with their own military contingents. The Qajars, unable to break the power of their potential rivals, engaged in a strategy of co-optation and the manipulation of communal rivalries for their own benefit.[27] Key nobles and khans were appointed to court positions or as local government officials; and a series of obligations, including the levying of taxes and the delivery of military contingents, was imposed upon the landed elite. These controls had some effect, at least enough to keep the Qajars precariously in power until the beginning of the twentieth century, but the elites' unusual autonomy was clearly inconsistent with the further development of the modern state.

Over the centuries the Russian state had brought into being a nobility indispensable for its own power. The nobility's independence was compromised, but the autocracy also trained, educated, and mobilized the nobles for new tasks. It even sought, with only modest success, to organize them into an estate and strengthen their economic position. In Iran, few such measures were taken; taken together with their threat to the autocracy, their archaic nature as a class made them dispensable to the regime. First Reza Shah, then his son, were thus able to attack them, radically transforming their position in society.[28]

The struggle between kings and burghers so characteristic of much of western European history had few parallels in Russia. The strength and

[26] Lambton, *Landlord and Peasant*, 176.

[27] Gene Garthwaite, *Khans and Shahs: A Documentary Analysis of the Bakhtiyari in Iran* (Cambridge: Cambridge University Press, 1983), 96; Lambton, *Qajar Persia*, 95–96.

[28] Reza Shah's policy toward the landed elite was complicated. He dispossessed many of them and attacked the independence of the khans; but he also strengthened private property and made them more of a modern social class. See Lambton, *Landlord and Peasant*, 259–60, and Said Amir Arjomand, *The Turban for the Crown* (New York: Oxford University Press, 1988), 70–71.

independence of Novgorod, the leading city-state, with a flourishing commercial economic base, was destroyed during Moscow's consolidation of power. It was not until the last two decades of the imperial regime that the Russian state had to take into account the demands of increasingly assertive urban elites, particularly an emerging class of industrialists. Although commerce and industry already had a long genealogy in Russia, cities were not autonomous and the merchant estate was heterogeneous and of only slight political significance. In Iran before Muhammad Reza Shah, the weight of industrialists in politics and social life was even less noticeable, but the traditional merchant class had great social prestige and was one of the most significant forces in national politics.

Although Peter had given an impetus to industrial development, before the nineteenth century industry was often located near raw materials, distant from the major urban areas. Often, too, factories were established by state order to fulfill military needs and were state-run or administered by merchants granted control over a serf labor force ("possessional factories"). Toward the end of the eighteenth century some gentry industrialists had emerged, and there had even begun to arise a stratum of serf entrepreneurs paying quitrents to their masters. In the early nineteenth century, the Russian textile industry experienced impressive growth, particularly in the Moscow region. Although heavy industry remained backward until the second half of the century, by midcentury modern industry comprised roughly 10 percent of the Russian economy.[29]

The entrepreneurs were of diverse social origin, often craftsmen or merchants. Old Believers, persecuted under Nicholas I, were especially prominent among the new entrepreneurs. This emerging economic elite had few of the hallmarks of a social or political elite. Its members tended to display deference toward their social betters, the nobility, and the most successful of them eagerly accepted ennoblement or went into the more prestigious professions.[30] They tended to be socially conformist, politically quiescent, and regarded with suspicion or condescension by the rest of society. Their position was in many ways the converse of that of the nobility: whereas the industrialists were in economic ascendancy but politically marginal, the nobility was economically feeble but well integrated into the tsarist political system.

The merchants occupied a more recognized place in Russian society. By the statutes of Peter the Great they were part of the urban estate and belonged to guilds defined according to wealth. This structure, like the arti-

[29] William Blackwell, *The Beginnings of Russian Industrialization* (Princeton: Princeton University Press, 1968), 40, 42, 65.

[30] See Roger Portal, "Muscovite Industrialists: The Cotton Sector (1861–1914)," in *Russian Economic Development from Peter the Great to Stalin*, ed. William Blackwell (New York: New Viewpoints, 1974), 165–69.

san craft unions, was not a natural outgrowth of social processes, but a definition imposed by the state for purposes of organization and taxation. Thus, the mobility of town dwellers (the category was hereditary) was restricted by a system of collective guarantees for taxes and other obligations.[31] In her Charter to the Towns (1785) Catherine introduced legal changes in the status of the urban estate in line with her general policy of encouraging a greater degree of group self-regulation in Russian society. It is unclear from the evidence how these new regulations operated in practice, but nothing remotely like a "third estate" came into being in Russia.

The industrialization of Iran did not begin in earnest until the 1930s. As had been true in Russia more than two centuries earlier, the impetus for the growth of modern industry came from the state, and as late as 1946 over 60 percent of Iranian factories were state-owned.[32] It was not until the 1960s that a stratum of modern industrialists became a conspicuous part of the Iranian social elite. On the other hand, modern Iranian history has witnessed the survival and repeated political activism of a traditional merchant group, a phenomenon perhaps unmatched elsewhere in modern history.

The Iranian merchantry suffered from many of the debilities of its Russian counterparts. It was perhaps even more heterogeneous, as Koranic injunctions against usury facilitated the entrance of Armenians, Jews, and Zoroastrians into moneylending and commerce. Further, a merchant elite well connected with the landowners and high government officials was clearly distinguishable from the mass of middling or small traders. Finally, the expansion of foreign trade and the growing importance of foreign capital in Iranian commerce had created a rift between those harmed and those favored by the changes. On the other hand, foreign influence, international markets, and the beginnings of modernization had a unifying impact, as they broke down localism and barriers to communications and also reinforced a sense among many of the commonality of Persian interests.[33]

The strength of the merchants was not due to strong corporate organizations, for in the large cities the formal head of the merchants was appointed by the state and the organizational structure of the bazaars was rather loose. Rather, their influence was due to their position as a traditional class performing honored activities in a system of interlocking traditional elites. They had little power to act independently, but in conjunction with allied groups, particularly the ulama, they could effectively promote their ends.

[31] For a description of this system, see De Madariaga, *Russia in the Age of Catherine the Great*, 90–93.

[32] Julian Bharier, *Economic Development in Iran 1900–1970* (London: Oxford University Press, 1971), 180.

[33] Abrahamian, *Iran between Two Revolutions*, 58–60.

As compared with Russia, where the very concepts of townsman (*meshchanin*) and bourgeois carried negative connotations, the merchant has always enjoyed higher social status in Islamic societies. Muhammad is reported to have said that "merchants are the messengers of this world and God's faithful trustees on Earth,"[34] and much of the language and imagery of the Koran is commercial in tone, with Allah as the ideal merchant. Historically, too, the relative prestige and wealth of the mercantile classes have been the reverse side of the weakness of the landed elites, and have contributed to the distinctiveness of Islamic civilization over the centuries.[35] Together with the administrative buildings, the bazaar with its shops and mosques formed the heart of Moslem cities.

The religious sanction of trade, its economic centrality, and the physical location of the mosque at the nerve center of cities made the bazaaris central to Iranian economic, political, and social life. Through this strategic location multivalent links were formed with the other elites of Moslem societies. The bazaaris supported the ulama with taxes and endowments, and they frequently made loans to state treasuries in fiscal straits. In the mid-nineteenth century, for example, the Iranian state, in the absence of a modern fiscal apparatus, was financially dependent on merchants. The interconnections between the bazaaris and the ulama were particularly close, as the former meticulously observed a pious life-style, organized religious rituals, and conducted their trade in accordance with religious norms. The ulama, in turn, helped resolve disputes, conducted religious services, and contributed a general tone of legitimacy, even sanctity, to the bazaaris' activities.[36] Intermarriage between the two groups was frequent.

The relationship between the merchants and the ulama became even more symbiotic in the nineteenth century, as the tension between both groups and the fitfully modernizing state increased and as foreign influence threatened both groups' positions. The first great incident of mass popular protest against the autocracy, the Tobacco Rebellion of 1891–1892, was founded on an alliance between the merchants and the ulama. This same partnership was critical in the Constitutional Revolution and the Iranian Revolution of 1978–1979.

Reza Shah well recognized the obsolescence and potential danger of the merchants and ulama for his project of the creation of a powerful modern economy and nation-state conceived along Western lines. Industrialization required higher taxes, which aroused the hostility of many merchants. In addition, the government initiated new controls over foreign trade and established state-run monopolies, threatening the positions of many mer-

[34] Maxime Rodinson, *Islam and Capitalism* (New York: Pantheon, 1973), 16.

[35] Hodgson, *Venture of Islam*, 2:78–79.

[36] See Gustav Thaiss, "Religious Symbolism and Social Change: The Drama of Husain" (Ph.D. diss., Washington University, 1973), chap. 3.

chants, although a small merchant elite also benefited from these policies. Changes in the guilds' right to collect taxes undermined the power of the traditional guild leaders and weakened the bazaar organizations. No more palatable were the enforced changes in dress and the attacks on the position of the ulama, with whom the merchants had historically been allied.

The ulama, even more than the merchants, suffered from the effects of Reza Shah's commitment to modernization. Legal reforms undercut the shari'a courts; the number of ulama in the National Assembly was drastically reduced; and in 1939 the state declared that it would take control of all religious lands and foundations.[37] Protests in 1926–1927 and 1935–1936 revived the old ulama—merchant alliance. But, confronting a stronger state and without the support of the secularists (as during the Constitutional Revolution), the united opposition of these two groups failed to deter the shah, who earned the deep hatred of the traditional classes. It was symptomatic that Khomeini's first public political pronouncements, appearing in a 1941 book, reproached the recently deposed shah for his betrayal of Islamic law and criminal imitation of Europe. "What nightmare is this into which we are being plunged?" he asked. "These idiotic and treacherous rulers, these officials—high and low—these reprobates and smugglers must change in order for the country to change."[38]

Religious Hierarchies and Traditions

The sharply differing role of religious authorities and religious ideas is probably the most striking point of contrast between the Russian and Iranian revolutions. Although there had been many oppositional voices in the Russian Orthodox church in the last decades of the old regime, the church as an institution was largely cut off from the broad currents of social change in Russia. Even the flowering of theological thought in the same period took place largely outside the auspices of the official church. By contrast, it hardly needs to be emphasized that the Iranian clergy, including the hierarchy, were at the heart of the revolutionary events in 1978–1979, as they had been over the previous century. The role of Islamic ideas and leaders will be discussed at greater length in a subsequent chapter; here it will suffice to touch on some of the main historical contrasts between the two countries.

It is a commonplace of Russian Orthodox ecclesiastical history that the

[37] For a description of these and many related policies, see Abrahamian, *Iran between Two Revolutions*, 135–65.

[38] See *Islam and Revolution*, ed. Hamid Algar (Berkeley: Mizan Press, 1981), 169–73.

Eastern church was distinguished from the Western church in its otherworldly emphasis. In his work on the Papal Revolution in the West, Harold Berman claims that Eastern Christian theology was primarily centered on God the Creator and heaven; Christ has shown mankind the way to him. Western theology after the great changes of the eleventh and twelfth centuries emphasized Christ as the immanence of God; incarnation was the central reality of the universe.[39] In line with this fundamental distinction, Russian Orthodoxy tended to stress the cultic side of religion, with its ritual and aesthetic aspects. Extremely long and elaborate services came to predominate. Philosophy, theology, and canon law received much less development in Russia than in the Western church; mysticism, as contrasted with asceticism, was also less characteristic of the Russian religious tradition.

Because of the external pressure of the state and also due to Western influence on the hierarchy, notably by way of Kiev, the overall modernization of Russian society brought forth far-reaching changes in the Orthodox church. The rationalization and centralization of the Muscovite state in the sixteenth century found its parallel in attempts to order the doctrine and organization of the church. In the late seventeenth century, Western scholastic and rationalist ideas, including Port-Royal logic and natural law philosophy, began to make an imprint on Russian theological education.[40] So, too, acquaintance with early Greek liturgy led to reformist tendencies seeking to purify the Russian church of what were now regarded as its native distortions.

Foreign influence was thus central to the Nikonian reforms of the late seventeenth century. These formal changes in the liturgy fomented widespread opposition within the church, partly on the grounds of their foreign origin. The reforms were confirmed by the government, and so antiforeign and antistate discontent were fused with opposition to the church hierarchy. The Old Believers, who refused to accept the changes, and sacrificed themselves in large numbers rather than change their practices, became the defenders of Russia's past and a rallying point for overall political discontent.[41] Peter the Great's administrative reforms several decades later reinforced these connections between modernization, the state, and the church hierarchy, even if the changes on the local level were undoubtedly less pronounced. Consequently, religious searching and commitment often took

[39] Harold Berman, *Law and Revolution: The Formation of the Western Legal Tradition* (Cambridge: Harvard University Press, 1983), 178–79.

[40] Raeff, *Understanding Imperial Russia*, 21–22; James Cracraft, "Feofan Prokopovich and the Kiev Academy," in *Russian Orthodoxy under the Old Regime*, ed. Robert Nichols and Theofanis Stavrou (Minneapolis: University of Minnesota Press, 1978), 44–66.

[41] Robert Crummey, *The Old Believers and the World of Antichrist* (Madison: University of Wisconsin Press, 1970), 13, 15–16.

place outside Orthodoxy, either in the form of independent theological and philosophical inquiry or through the medium of popular religiosity.[42]

The fundamental traits of the Moslem religion place it at the other end of the spectrum from Russian Orthodoxy. As is well known, Islam places a great deal of emphasis on the this-worldly community of believers, who are enjoined to live their lives in accord with God's law. As Smith has pointed out, this is not legalism (as has often been charged), for the submission of the faithful to God's will is the foundation, and a sense of ethical responsibility the consequence, of this deeper religious commitment.[43] Nonetheless, it is true that obedience to religious law, both individually and collectively, is central to Islamic values. Law embraces not just religious practices directed toward salvation, but also all dimensions of everyday life. The Islamic law of contracts is thus a central part of religious education, a subject on which Khomeini gave lectures at religious schools.

No stratum of priests with a monopoly over ritual performance exists in Islam. Rational inquiry is of generally high repute, especially in the development of law; philosophy sometimes flourished but was often regarded with skepticism by the interpreters of the law. The vitality of Sufism, with its stress on direct experience and mystical training, should warn against oversimplification in this regard; but even Sufism and *erfan*, mystical knowledge, were compatible with a legal and ethical consciousness. Khomeini, for example, was a legal scholar as well as an adept in erfan. Finally, the this-worldly, communal orientation of Islam undercut the appeal of monasticism and ascetic withdrawal from this world. Muhammad is an entirely different religious type from St. Sergius of Radonezh, the great saint of Russian Orthodoxy who began his religious vocation as a monk in the forest.

The Shiʿite tradition in Islam somewhat blurs the overall contrast between Russian Orthodoxy and Islam. As compared with Sunnism, Shiʿism has a more chiliastic orientation, and Shiʿite doctrine exalts the knowledge of the spiritual elite over the mass of the community. Whereas Sunnism tends to be exoteric and centered on obedience to law in the everyday world as an expression of faith, Shiʿite teachings are more esoteric and the field of religious experience is more displaced to the world to come. Martyrdom in the face of the evils of the present world looms as more central in its ethic. The visible law was distinguished from the invisible truth, the former identified with the Sunni, the latter with the Shiʿa.[44] In these respects, Shiʿism resembles Russian Orthodoxy more than does Sunnism.

Whatever these similarities, it is striking how differently the Shiʿite hi-

[42] Raeff, *Understanding Imperial Russia*, 153–54.

[43] Wilfred C. Smith, *On Understanding Islam* (The Hague: Mouton, 1981), 108–9.

[44] Hamid Enayat, *Modern Islamic Political Thought* (Austin: University of Texas Press, 1982), 22.

erarchy responded to the challenge of modernization. Whereas the consolidation of the Muscovite state and Peter's state-building efforts entailed the creation of a formalized and hierarchical church organization, the religious hierarchy in Iran, though somewhat more structured beginning in the late nineteenth century, remained plural and somewhat amorphous. There was no single line of command, no authoritative decision-making body. The hierocracy never came to shape itself into a system of corporate bodies. Nor did the religious scholars permit the absorption of religious influences from the west. According to Arjomand, in Iranian Shiʿism "the revitalizing synthesis, therefore, does not entail the meaningful absorption of any Western beliefs and ideas through the reinterpretation of the sources of the Shiʿite tradition, but rather the mere adoption of the ideological frame of thought."[45] Indeed, the Shiʿite hierocracy became one of the main voices against modernization and Western influence; already from the late nineteenth century it based its opposition to the shahs on what it saw as their betrayal of Islam. In this sense, the Iranian clergy occupied a position parallel to that of the Old Believers in Russia, except that they were not a persecuted sect.

The sources of the Iranian clergy's independence from the state in the modern period are multiple. Here it will be sufficient to list some of the main contrasts with Russian Orthodoxy. First, beginning with the Petrine reforms, the Russian state imposed its bureaucratic controls over the church hierarchy. By the time of Nicholas I, the church somewhat resembled a state ministry, with its new offices located in St. Petersburg next to the Senate. The procurator general, a lay government official equivalent in rank to a minister and appointed by the tsar, supervised religious education and programs in the interests of social order and obedience to the state. "Religion was used to preach obedience to the emperor, the officer, and the landlord."[46] The procurator general's staff carefully controlled the content of preaching and enjoined local priests to report on subversive activities in their districts.[47] By contrast, in Iran the major religious centers were not located in the capital; no such bureaucratic hierarchy existed; and the shahs had very limited influence over the far-flung network of religious schools and mosques.

In addition, in 1763–1764 Catherine the Great deprived the Orthodox church of much of its property; throughout the nineteenth century the

[45] Said Amir Arjomand, "Traditionalism in Twentieth-Century Iran," in *From Nationalism to Revolutionary Islam*, ed. Said Amir Arjomand (Albany: State University of New York, 1984), 230.

[46] Nicholas Riasanovsky, *Nicholas I*, 95.

[47] According to Peter the Great's Religious Regulation, priests were obligated to inform against those who confessed evil intent against the state or the sovereign. John S. Curtiss, *Church and State in Russia* (New York: Octagon Books, 1965), 25.

clergy in Russia depended on state salaries. In Iran the religious establishment had substantial independent economic resources in the form of land and endowments. The clergy's close ties with the bazaar also ensured them continuing sources of support. Finally, in Russia the church certainly had its mass following of believers, but it had little mobilized mass support. Indeed, many people, including the great majority of the intelligentsia and a not inconsiderable number of priests, saw it as the compromised handmaiden of the state. For reasons that will be explored later, the Iranian clergy came to be seen at times of crisis as the embodiment of the Iranian nation and its culture, and so gained prestige even among groups otherwise alien to religion. In Russia the church establishment could not even count on the loyalty of believers, as lay and clerical voices demanding church reform and greater separation from the regime multiplied in the last decades of the empire.

The Patterning of Institutions

From a comparative perspective, western European institutions from the early modern period onward developed an unusual degree of corporate character. Their "corporativeness" was expressed in the following traits and tendencies: juridical personality; formal organization, including a hierarchy of offices; fixed membership; and a set of defined rights and duties. According to Berman the great transformation that established this Occidental pattern was the Papal Revolution of the eleventh and twelfth centuries, in which the Western church differentiated itself from the state and emerged with an independent corporate structure regulated by canon law. The state likewise differentiated itself as a secular institution with its own sphere of activity and body of law. Law became formalized and explicit, disembedded from custom, and specific in its jurisdiction.[48] Cities, guilds, universities, trading companies, and later industrial firms and trade unions would be established as corporate entities. Institutions of this kind proved to be internally dynamic, since formal organization permitted coordinated purposive action; and, possessing juridical personality, they also facilitated linkages among each other. Similarly, institutions could define their interests and act in order to maximize them over a long time horizon. It is perhaps not too much to suggest that the pursuit of "progress" is almost inherent in the nature of corporate institutions.

For very different historical reasons in each case, corporate social institutions were weakly developed in both Russia and Iran. In Russia the autocratic state sometimes substituted for, sometimes inhibited, and some-

[48] Berman, *Law and Revolution*, 85–88.

times encouraged—within strict limits—the development of corporate institutions. But even when it sought to nurture them, its own predominance in social life deprived them of the dynamism they showed in Europe. In Iran, as in other Islamic societies, there was historically a much richer and more autonomous associational life than in Russia, particularly in the cities. But associations seldom acquired that fixity characteristic of the corporation; they had more of the air of contract, even improvisation, a pattern that Hodgson has called "occasionalism."[49] In a sense, then, Russia and Iran were at opposite extremes from western Europe. The weakness of corporations in Russian life stemmed largely from the overbearing power of the state; associational life in Iran flourished in traditional patterns that were inimical to corporate organization. But whatever the differences, the consequences for the modernizing monarchs, limited in their ability to transform their societies because of the latter's very amorphousness, were similar.

The low degree of corporate structure and autonomy in Russian institutions stemmed from mutually reinforcing traits of state and society. As a general rule, the state distrusted all independent social initiative. In its place it elevated the logic of the absolute state, able to unify the nation and reconcile partial, conflicting interests for the benefit of all. Much of the educated public embraced this statist ethos, affirming that the state was the active and formative principle of Russian life, the basis of national feeling and unity. From such perspectives, independent social institutions threatened the overall welfare, the foundation of which was a dynamic autocratic state that overshadowed class groupings. Supporters of state centralism could point to the paucity and general helplessness of independent social institutions to buttress their belief in the primacy of state initiative. The very weakness of guilds, estates, or cities did indeed provide powerful evidence for the necessity of state initiative and control.

Yet it is one of the lessons of Peter's attempted reforms that autocratic command could accomplish little in the absence of institutions able to involve social groups. Cognizant of the limits of purely state initiative, Peter undertook reforms of local government on the Swedish model and of municipal government after the patterns of Riga and Reval. Both of these initiatives were stillborn. The latter, for example, envisioned the formation of three urban corporations, a town council, and a town assembly. None of these institutions took on any life of its own, and in 1717 the councils were formally subordinated to state officials.[50] The shortcomings of efforts to create social institutions *ex nihilo* through state initiative can also be seen in the establishment of artisan guilds by Peter in 1721. These were not

[49] Hodgson, *Venture of Islam*, 2:346.

[50] Michael Florinsky, *Russia: A Short History*, 2d ed. (London: Macmillan, 1969), 179.

closed, voluntary associations of the European type, with monopolistic control over their crafts, but looser associations with limited power. Their leaders served as administrative and fiscal agents of the government.[51] Not surprisingly, they were also unable to fulfill the important economic and social functions of the European guilds.

Fifty years later, German-born Catherine the Great clearly perceived the weakness of Russian social institutions and the limitations this placed on social progress and the capacity of the state to reform society. As noted earlier, Catherine embarked on a series of Westernizing reforms enacted by purely Russian methods of state direction. It was Catherine who defined the personal rights of the nobles and the collective rights of their estate, creating for them, on paper, a new role in local administration. Similarly, in the Charter to the Towns were listed the individual and collective rights of the urban estate, regulations for craft guilds, and norms of urban self-government. The charter "was very much Catherine's own handiwork," based, as were Peter's ill-starred urban reforms, on foreign models.[52] The attempt to create independent corporate institutions for the nobility and the towns seem to have borne little fruit. Just as these institutions were largely the product of state initiative, so after Catherine's death they withered with the waning of the tsars' enthusiasm for them. In addition, particularly in the towns there was a limited social foundation for them, including a lack of appropriate leadership. Finally, the new institutions had little capacity to defend themselves against the traditional provincial administration, and so found the range of their activities curtailed.

Russia's defeat in the Crimean War called into question the relationship between state and society as never before.[53] It was felt that the war had exposed the fundamental weakness of Russian institutions and that dramatic changes had to be undertaken. Public debates unprecedented in Russian history raged over the proper diagnosis and cure of the illness. Many publicists and officials were deeply influenced by Alexis de Tocqueville's recently published *The Old Regime and the French Revolution* and traced the weakness of Russian society to the dominance of the state and the correlative lack of initiative and independence of social groups. Proposals for local self-government achieved enormous influence among the educated public and even among local officials.

The most significant institution to emerge from this ferment was the *zemstvo*, legally created in 1864 as a new organ of local self-government. Zemstvo assemblies and boards were elected at district and provincial lev-

[51] Reginald Zelnik, *Labor and Society in Tsarist Russia* (Stanford, Calif.: Stanford University Press, 1971), 11–12.

[52] De Madariaga, *Russia in the Age of Catherine*, 299.

[53] The following discussion is based on S. Frederick Starr's *Decentralization and Self-Government in Russia, 1830–1870* (Princeton: Princeton University Press, 1972), chap. 2.

els, with the participation of the towns, peasant communes, and individual landowners on a basis proportional to the size of agricultural properties. Although many reformers had great hopes for the zemstvos as the basis of a new cooperation between state and society, their optimism was not fully justified. While many of the zemstvos' proponents both within and outside the government expected that they would have a broad sphere of activity and considerable autonomy, their responsibilities turned out to be quite limited and of an administrative nature. Although the services they provided in the areas of health and education were often quite valuable, they hardly constituted local self-government. In addition, no adequate financial base was provided for them. Finally, from the beginning they had aroused the hostility of some sectors of the government, who saw in them infringements upon the power of the central government. The surge of revolutionary activity against the regime and the attempt on the tsar's life in 1866 strengthened the position of these opponents, and the government curtailed the prerogatives of the newly formed bodies. The tenor of public debate and official discussion also changed: no longer was the key danger identified as the smothering of society by the state; instead it was now seen as the paralysis of the state by harmful social forces.[54]

The case of the zemstvos well illustrates the general dilemma of the Russian autocracy with respect to autonomous social institutions. Modernization and economic growth expanded the range of government in Russia, and the administration was hard pressed to cope with the myriad of tasks that fell upon it by default. In addition, many were aware that some form of partnership between state and society was called for by the new conditions of Russian life. By the late nineteenth century an educated public had emerged to shape public opinion, now a significant political force, and exert pressure in this direction. For their own reasons, the governments too were attracted to these ideas of greater social involvement, just as Peter and Catherine had perceived their rationale and the limitations of a state isolated from society. Thus, the state initiated reforms, but society's continuing lack of initiative and resources provided insecure protection in the face of government ambivalence, later turning to hostility. The zemstvos, as well as the new judicial organizations, scientific establishments, and other public bodies, survived. Yet their lives were racked with dilemmas and inconsistencies, and they proved unable to establish new bonds between state and society or provide the social support that the autocratic regime would desperately need in the period of rapid modernization. Indeed, zemstvo activism against the regime, led by nobles, would play a profound part in the emergence of the revolutionary crisis of 1905–1906.

The absence of corporate institutions in premodern Islamic society is a

[54] Starr, *Decentralization in Russia*, 346–47.

relatively recent finding in Western studies of Islam. The opposite viewpoint was enshrined in the influential work of Louis Massignon, who found in the medieval urban guild the same corporate traits as in Europe. Writing specifically of medieval Persia, Ann Lambton, also a highly respected scholar, described a series of urban "corporate" organizations. Key among these, the most organized and differentiated, she held to be the craft guilds, closed communities with collective responsibilities and a notable sense of corporate life.[55] Among other associational forms mentioned in her discussion are the *futuwwa* orders and the *ayyar* movements, both largely drawn from the urban underprivileged youth and often degenerating into roving gangs. These, too, she claims, had corporate organization similar to the guilds.

The contrary view of Albert Hourani, summarizing the more recent research of a number of scholars, merits direct citation:

> In the Islamic view of the world there was the individual believer and there was the whole community of believers, but in between there was no stable grouping regarded as legitimate and permanent. Islamic law did not recognize corporate personality except in a limited sense, and the whole spirit of Islamic social thought went against the formation of limited groups within which there might grow up an exclusive natural solidarity hostile to the all-inclusive solidarity of an umma based on common obedience to God's commands. Not only did corporations have no moral or religious basis, it is not certain that they ever existed.[56]

Hourani's emphasis on the cultural significance of the sense of Moslem solidarity should be supplemented by the contractual and individualistic elements of Islam stressed by Hodgson.[57] The Moslem's personal religious experience is not mediated by a church hierarchy, and the individual is not so constrained by doctrinal orthodoxy. Shiʿism does require the believer's choice of a "model" for emulation, so the individual's religious experience is not unmediated by claims to expertise. But even here, in the choice of an authority, a contractual element remains, since there is a wide choice of doctrines and teachers available. The same cultural matrix was expressed, argues Hodgson, in other social spheres: the Moslem principle stressed "egalitarian and moralistic considerations to the point where it ruled out

[55] Ann Lambton, *Theory and Practice in Medieval Persian Government* (London: Variorum Reprints, 1980), 7:19–20. The essay "Islamic Society in Persia," the source for this reference, was originally published in 1954.

[56] Albert Hourani, "Introduction: The Islamic City in the Light of Recent Research," in *The Islamic City*, ed. Albert Hourani and S. M. Stern (Oxford: Bruno Cassirer, 1970), 14. See also the papers by Stern and Cahen in the same volume.

[57] Hodgson, *Venture of Islam*, 2:344–49.

all corporate status and reduced all acts to the acts of personally responsible individuals."[58]

It was not only religious and cultural assumptions that worked against the development of corporate organizations in the Moslem Middle East. In the decentralized political systems of most Moslem societies, local emirs resided in cities and were naturally jealous of any corporate autonomy. Medieval European urban institutions arose in the interstices of feudal society in a context of urban autonomy. In patrimonial Moslem societies, as Lapidus notes for the Mamluk case, the fusion of social and political leadership was such as to give all social action political overtones.[59] Lower-class political organizations posed special threats, and the rulers made every effort to prevent the growth of independent associations.

Urban associations proliferated in traditional Iran, as elsewhere in the Middle East. There were a multitude of religious associations, generally organized as religious schools, Sufi brotherhoods, or other forms of discipleship. In such cases shared loyalty to a revered religious figure or to a legal school could give rise to very intense social bonds among the membership. The resulting sense of solidarity, though hardly corporate, facilitated collective action, and religious groupings of this type often had considerable political significance. The multiple poles of leadership, as in Iranian Shiʿism, imparted an amorphousness to the organizational structure and hindered centralized coordination. But the pluralism and contractualism of the associations rendered them voluntary even more than western interest groups, with their more exclusive representation and rigid rules and procedures. Their importance was magnified by their linkages to other key groups in the society, especially the bazaaris.

Communal solidarities of neighborhood, tribal or ethnic origin, craft or profession, or kinship also constituted powerful foundations for associational life. Indeed, it can be argued that communal identities in Moslem cities were so strong that only a combination of the overarching values of Islam, the integrative role of the ulama, and the authority of the emir imparted any cohesion to the society. Further, the strength of communal ties could work against the central criteria of membership in institutions such as cities, professional associations, or social estates. Communal energies were aggregated, not undermined, by religion, and it was for this reason that this older pattern of association, rather than modern forms based on profession or class, provided the basis for solidary action during the Iranian Revolution.

[58] Ibid., 347.

[59] Ira Lapidus, *Muslim Cities in the Later Middle Ages* (Cambridge: Cambridge University Press, 1984), 103.

The weakness of corporate organizations in Russia and Iran had two contrasting sides. On the one hand, it debilitated social groups in the assertion of their interests and viewpoints over and against the government and in their ability to pursue their goals in a dynamic way. They could not easily resist the encroachments of state power, which in turn found its justification in their lack of leadership. On the other hand, this very shapelessness of social groups made them in some ways less vulnerable to government control and less-ready instruments for the purposes of the ruler. Established leaders could not be held responsible for institutional misbehavior or shortcomings. Social ties were fluid and ever changing. Resources could not be so easily appropriated by the government. Finally, in urban Russia and Iran underground connections difficult to detect and control emerged to fill the gap left by corporate institutions in the West. Their weakness was also their strength, as they proved their resiliency in the face of persistent government efforts to undermine or eliminate them.

At this point some of the key historical differences between the two countries relevant for understanding social change during modernization may be summarized. A social anatomy of Russia and Iran taken during the early peaks of autocratic power, the roughly contemporaneous regimes of Ivan the Terrible and Shah Abbas I, might have led one to expect parallel historical developments in the future. After both societies had been delivered from Mongol rule, strong centralizing states seeking to control threatening centrifugal tendencies had made their appearance. The rulers of both countries had invested themselves with a semidivine status, claiming absolute authority over their subjects by the will of God. Yet in the succeeding centuries very different historical trajectories would be followed. The Russian state, subject to Western challenges and also Western cultural influence, would seek to modernize both itself and society in order to maintain its great-power status. On the most superficial level, modernization meant economic improvements, enforced cultural changes, and administrative rationalization, but as early as Peter the Great the autocratic rulers recognized that they had to establish social institutions that could translate their will into reality. Thus, Peter the Great and Catherine both experimented, on the whole unsuccessfully, with efforts to form estate organizations and organs of local government to provide a connecting link with and lever over society.

Despite the limitations inherent in such changes imposed from above, it is nevertheless true that by the late nineteenth century the Russian state had developed itself administratively and had established numerous interconnections with social elites, primarily the landed nobility, but also merchants and industrialists. The state had not voluntarily relinquished control over these social groups, as it sought to mobilize them for its own purposes. Nonetheless, the noble assemblies, zemstvos, and urban institutions demonstrated a degree of autonomy in pressing their own interests in the formulation of state policy. By the turn of the century they would also demonstrate a significant potential for open opposition to the autocracy.

The greater sophistication of the Russian state and its longer experience with social and political modernization thus had superficially contradictory consequences. On the one hand, the Russian state was able to regulate the activities of social elites and the church relatively effectively. Yet its attempts to control and make use of them also increased their participation in the state and gave them a degree of leverage over it. They could never be truly independent and oppose the state unconditionally, but they could exert pressures either for or against reform. Under Nicholas II at different times significant groups within both the landed gentry and the industrialists espoused reformist ideas against the autocracy, goals that were ultimately rejected by their own class and the state alike. Of even greater significance, both rural and industrialist elites, so interwoven with the state apparatus, proved to be extremely effective opponents of any reforms that might threaten their social positions and give the masses a greater stake in the systems.

By contrast, after its peak of development under the Safavids, the Iranian autocracy underwent over two hundred years of decay. It could not establish an effective state apparatus with which to control and modernize society. Large sections of the society, including tribal groups and the religious establishment, remained relatively impervious to its mandate. On the one hand, this meant that they enjoyed a much greater degree of autonomy from state regulation, though the arbitrary will of the autocrat could impose itself unpredictably to stunt too great an assertion of independence. On the other hand, it also implied that social elites and the state were much less interdependent than in Russia.

Consequently, starting from weak positions, the two Pahlavi shahs would not modernize through society, but largely over and against it. Since they had almost no social base among either the nobility or an urban merchant or industrial elite, they could impose programs of sweeping change impossible for the late nineteenth-century tsars. Nonetheless, what seemed like the superior position of the shahs had two major disadvantages. First, like Peter the Great they faced the dilemma of enacting policies in a largely amorphous society, in which the links between state and society were much more tenuous than in late tsarist Russia. Thus, their very autonomy limited their power to change society. Second, although they were not forced to bow to the interests of social elites with whom their own interests were intertwined, they did have to confront, unlike the tsars, the opposition of strong traditional groups that were certain that the regime was bent on their destruction.

Two

Autocracy in Russia and Iran

THE GENERAL CONCEPT of autocracy encompasses a wide array of historical variants; it is not a uniform or unchanging social phenomenon. The autocracy of Ivan the Terrible was as different from that of Nicholas II as Shah Ismail's (the first Safavid ruler) was from Muhammad Reza Shah's. In these different examples the claim to divinely sanctioned absolute rule was consistent with different mythologies, ideologies, institutional configurations, and relationships to society. For example, the autocrat could be conceived primarily as the protector and representative of the divine will, or even, as in the case of Shah Ismail, for some of his subjects the manifestation of God himself.[1] By contrast, Peter the Great secularized the mythology of the tsar in Russia, appearing as the sovereign emperor bringing progress to his people.[2] Similarly, the autocrat might be a visible presence among his subjects, through daily rituals and appearances reinforcing his supreme authority;[3] or he might isolate himself from his people out of a sense of limitless superiority or out of fear. In general, autocratic rulers could be energetic or listless; conservative or reformist; surrounded by personal retinues or by complicated bureaucracies; pitifully weak or unimaginably powerful. To say, then, that a ruler claims autocratic power tells us something of great importance, but it is far from a sufficient characterization. In many crucial respects the exercise of autocratic power was quite different in Nicholas II's Russia and Muhammad Reza Shah's Iran.

The Autocracy of Nicholas II

Nicholas II was the thirteenth Romanov monarch, the inheritor of a long tradition of ideological justification of autocratic rule. The authority of the

[1] Roger Savory, *Iran under the Safavids* (Cambridge: Cambridge University Press, 1980), 33.

[2] Michael Cherniavsky, *Tsar and People: Studies in Russian Myths* (New York: Random House, 1969), 72–100.

[3] Apparently Reza Shah was quite visible indeed to his subjects: "he dumped pots of inferior food on the heads of cheating army quartermasters in front of the recruits, and when horses defecated at parades, fear of his disapproval made great landowners and generals fall to their knees to clean the ground before he came." Roy Mottahedeh, *The Mantle of the Prophet* (New York: Pantheon, 1985), 85.

tsars also had deep roots in Russian cultural life and society. The autocracy was so fundamental in Russian society that many, including a whole school of historians, regarded it as the only creative force in Russian history, the foundation of all other social institutions. In this context, Nicholas II may perhaps be forgiven for a certain inability to conceive of the contingency of the autocracy. In his view, his own authority as tsar was consecrated by God; absolute rule over his people was his divine responsibility which he could not shirk; and autocracy was the immutable lodestar by which Russian society was guided. As a promonarchical Russian historian has written of Nicholas: "He believed that he alone was responsible for the destiny of Russia and that he would answer for this trust before the throne of the Almighty. Some might assist and others might obstruct him, but God would judge him alone for his custodianship of Russia. As the responsibility was solely his, so too was the power."[4]

The hallowed tradition of autocracy and the firm belief in divine sanction may help explain a certain passivity in Nicholas's style of rule. As will be seen, the shah's awareness of the fragile bases of his own legitimacy led him to develop an explicit apologia for his program and take an active role in managing political conflict. Nicholas II's initiatives in these directions were altogether more restrained. The ideological bases of his rule were not formulated in any sophisticated way. They were largely inherited from the past, as was Konstantin Pobedonostsev, the closest equivalent to an ideologist in the tsar's entourage. Similarly, although the complicated bureaucratic administration and delicate relationship of the regime to society required an energetic monarch to give organizational and policy coherence, Nicholas largely abdicated from an active political role. For him it appeared to be enough that the tsar set the basic direction of policy and acted as the final arbiter in disputes.

The passivity of the regime can be seen first of all in the ideological realm. Throughout the nineteenth century numerous writers—some hack publicists, others, like Dostoevsky, major literary or philosophical talents—had emerged to defend the Russian autocracy. In general terms, two strands of thought can be distinguished, a traditional brand of conservatism and a more expansive, nationalist ideology based on a romanticization of the Russian people. Both tendencies supported the autocracy, but for different reasons and with different implications.

The traditional conservative vision, represented by figures like Nikolai Karamzin, Mikhail Katkov (after the 1870s), and Konstantin Pobedonostsev, had as its starting point the baseness of human nature. For Pobedonostsev, for example, man in general was weak and vain. Russians were

[4] S. S. Oldenburg, *Last Tsar: The Autocracy, 1894–1900* (Gulf Breeze, Fla.: Academic International Press, 1975), 1:37.

even worse than the common lot, characterized, he said, by "decomposition and weakness and untruth." Russia was "an icy desert and an abode of the Bad Men."[5] The nineteenth century was an age of illusions, and its childish faith in the common man, education, and democracy undermined the state, the key source of order in human society.[6] The great reforms of the 1860s, in following European ideas, would bring catastrophe to Russia, and so had to be abolished. Russian subjects had not rights, but obligations. Conservatives of this stripe celebrated autocracy as the bulwark against anarchy and the guarantor of order. On the part of the subjects, they favored not commitment and belief, even in the monarch, but simple obedience. They distrusted abstract ideas and ideological rationalizations, justifying their own perspective on the basis of historical tradition and the common good.[7]

A second group of supporters of the autocracy was altogether more optimistic about the Russian people and their prospects for the future. As exemplified by Mikhail Pogodin, the first professor of Russian history at the University of Moscow, as well as by the Slavophiles, these thinkers praised the positive traits of Russian nationality and expressed trust in the people's judgment and reliability.[8] They favored the emancipation of the serfs well prior to its enactment and also the extension of public education. Influenced by romantic nationalism, they proclaimed the unity of tsar and people in the accomplishments of Russia's historical tasks. Through this partnership the people had a right to express their opinions openly, and the tsar had the obligation to consult with his people. Pogodin favored a classless society and inveighed against the aristocracy who stood between tsar and people.

The autocracy was not, then, simply the bulwark of order, but the embodiment of the people's political and spiritual unity. The Russian Orthodox church, too, had an entirely different significance for the two groups: whereas for Pobedonostsev it was the cement of society and so subject to governmental control, the Slavophiles opposed the political subjugation of the church and conceived of it as the embodiment of *sobornost'*, the spiritual community of all Christians apart from all purely formal institutions. These thinkers celebrated the unlimited, autocratic power of the tsar, but he was now a tsar who could inspire and lead an enthusiastic people, not just a protector of the people against their own incompetence and ignorance.

[5] Quoted in Robert Byrnes, *Pobedonostsev: His Life and Thought* (Bloomington: Indiana University Press, 1968), 292.

[6] For his attacks on the nineteenth century, see Konstantin Pobedonostsev, *Reflections of a Russian Statesman* (Ann Arbor: University of Michigan Press, 1965).

[7] For the views of Katkov, see Edward Thaden, *Conservative Nationalism in Nineteenth-Century Russia* (Seattle: University of Washington Press, 1964), 38–56, esp. 53.

[8] For an analysis of this tendency during Nicholas I, see Riasanovsky, *Nicholas I*, 124–67.

There was thus widespread, if far from unanimous, sentiment among the educated public in favor of autocracy. The shah of Iran would enjoy no such potential advantage. But Nicholas II did little to encourage or promote monarchical ideals. Indeed, his own ideas on the subject were seldom developed or even made very explicit. Fundamentally, his assumptions seemed to be close to those of Pobedonostsev, at least insofar as he never promoted an activist conception of autocracy. Just as the government of his father Alexander III had been suspicious of even promonarchical enthusiasm, disbanding the Holy Company—formed by aristocrats to protect the emperor and combat the revolutionaries—so the government of Nicholas II made insignificant efforts to organize or otherwise encourage social support for the monarchy. One of his most perceptive and creative officials, Sergei Zubatov, at one time head of the Moscow secret police, perceived the weakness of a purely passive autocratic conception in an age of industrialization and Western influence. He conceived of an activist strategy of dividing and ruling social forces through government-controlled mobilization of the workers: "For the above-class autocracy, 'divida et impera' is necessary. . . . The struggle of social forces unties the hands of the just autocracy unconditionally and guarantees its long life."[9] In line with these ideas, the Moscow secret police formed a network of monarchist worker organizations meant to inspire their members with a new enthusiasm for the tsar, somewhat along the lines of the Slavophile vision. But this was an isolated experiment, and one that was especially dangerous for the emerging capitalist class structure. Initial skepticism was reinforced by the painful experience of increased class conflict to cut short this effort at state-controlled mobilization.

The government of Nicholas II thus preferred divine sanction, not ideology, as a foundation for autocracy. It also pursued a conservative social and political strategy consistent with the basic premises of Pobedonostsev. Any manifestation of autonomy, either on the part of individuals or of groups, was suspect. Society itself had no sustaining principle of order in the view of the regime. Social groups pursued their own selfish interests, it was assumed, and it was the duty of the autocracy to balance them in accord with the general interest, thus protecting the weak against the strong. The autocracy conceived itself as an "above-class" entity, through its power and wisdom able to protect individuals and society against their own worst impulses. This paternalistic model, which likened social groups to willful children, remained the implicit ideological foundation of Nicholas II's regime. In its lack of vision and inability to provide a model of autocratic rule for a rapidly modernizing society, it provided no adequate rationale

[9] Quoted in A. P. Korelin, "Krakh ideologii 'politseiskogo sotsializma' v tsarskoi Rossii," *Istoricheskie zapiski* 92 (1973): 112–13.

for the regime's own policy of rapid change. If individuals and groups were so wicked, if initiative was to be distrusted, how could the autocracy justify its sponsorship of capitalism?

Muhammad Reza Shah's regime suffered from the opposite debility: by imposing an ideology of progress in tension with native traditions, he mobilized a powerful coalition against himself. Could there have been some intermediate step between the ideological sterility of Nicholas II and the shah's all-out commitment to an imposed vision of progress? Is an ideology conceivable that reconciles autocratic authority and popular participation, tradition and progress? The Slavophiles, in their conception of a messianic Russian people, united with their tsar in pursuit of a glorious future, provided such a synthesis, but it was based on a misreading of the past and wishful thinking about the present rather than on a realistic appraisal of Russian society. The question goes to the heart of the viability of modernizing autocracies: is the combination contradictory, in the ideological sphere as well as in other dimensions? Is there any way to make arbitrary personal authority compatible with modern social institutions and class relations in a convincing way?

The weakness of the regime's ideological foundations and its skeptical view of society underlie much of the practice of autocratic rule under Nicholas II. Here, too, the tsar's leadership was conventional, unimaginative, unable to deal with the challenges of politics and administration in the emerging Russia. More than this, it was in a profound sense reactionary. Nicholas II could not fully accept the Petersburg world of bureaucracies, nascent interest groups, and public opinion, much less that of the subversive organizations, whether liberal or radical, that directly challenged his rule. Like his father, but even more so, Nicholas's response was to turn his back on the capital and reaffirm the old Muscovite model of rule.[10] Moscow now seemed to him the purer embodiment of the Russian spirit, the expression of the mystical union of tsar and people, the image of which comforted him in his distress. The tsar read a great deal in Muscovite history and took great pleasure in visiting the old capital, certain that he was more warmly welcomed there. His appearances in St. Petersburg, whether in court society or at public functions, became rarer. The geographical symbolism corresponded to a contradiction in his conception of the nature of his autocratic rule: although he may have regarded himself as a Muscovite autocrat, his rule over an increasingly complex and independent society was mediated through a bureaucratic and administrative apparatus. His imperial will could be realized only through complex political and administrative procedures which he could ignore only at his own peril. As Wortman remarks, "the tsar, by depriving the capital of his personal aura, gave

[10] Wortman, "Moscow and Petersburg."

sanction to a historical and symbolic tradition that in many respects was at odds with the government through which he ruled."[11] In this context the autocracy, far from being the mainstay of order that Pobedonostsev proclaimed that it was, became itself a major source of disorder.

What, then, were the key institutions and methods through which Nicholas II sought to rule Russia as an autocrat? The most important organs of government were the ministries, especially, in domestic affairs, the Ministry of Finance and the Ministry of the Interior. The ministerial system had replaced the colleges established by Peter the Great as a result of Alexander I's reforms, which sought to establish one-man control and responsibility in government organs. The ministries grew into enormous bureaucratic agencies—not, of course, in the strict Weberian sense, for favoritism by social category was widespread—with professional staffs, formal hierarchies, and immense resources and responsibilities. It was Witte's Ministry of Finance, for example, that developed an industrialization strategy and vigorously promoted foreign investment and the growth of heavy industry. Without its sponsorship the industrial upsurge of the 1890s would not have occurred.

Although the ministries were not without their achievements, their effectiveness was undercut by the autocratic system of rule. The tsars tended to put their trust in men, not in institutions, a precept strongly endorsed by Pobedonostsev. They thus placed a great deal of weight on the personal bond between themselves and the high officials who served purely at their discretion. The implications of an appointment or a dismissal for the ministries as institutions was less significant than the tsar's favor, which was often unpredictable. In the last decades of Nicholas II's reign, ministerial turnover was astoundingly rapid, in some years taking on comic-opera proportions. It became difficult to find competent people who would serve; nor was competence always Nicholas's main criterion of selection.

The emperor's absolute discretion in matters of appointment led to instability and uncertainty, traits that were compounded by the weak development of administrative law in Russia. The eminent legal scholar Korkunov recognized the problem clearly: autocracy in the modern world, like other governments, depends on an administrative staff to execute the ruler's will. Without precise norms and fixed responsibilities, there can be no clear division of labor, and administrative agencies are likely to become "independent sovereigns, each acting in its own special interest."[12] Thus, for Korkunov, law—at least in the form of bureaucratic positive law—was a necessary complement to autocracy. Yet such a legal division of rights

[11] Ibid., 244.

[12] N. M. Korkunov, *Russkoe gosudarstvennoe pravo* (St. Petersburg: M. M. Stasiulevich, 1899), 1:204–13.

and responsibilities among the ministries never emerged. Nor was there, until the 1905 revolution stimulated administrative changes, any position corresponding to the post of prime minister. The tsar consulted ministers according to their spheres of competence and on an ad hoc basis. Even after the attempt to introduce an authentic cabinet system, with a prime minister responsible for leadership and coordination, the situation did not change in its essentials. As Witte, the first occupant of the new post, later remarked: "I knew that I was really without power, or with a power perpetually nullified by the cunning, not to say treachery, of Nicholas II."[13]

This legal and organizational chaos, combined with the ministers' need to compete with each other for the tsar's favor, led to administrative anarchy. The case was put strongly by V. I. Gurko, an official in the Ministry of Interior who has left us some of the most illuminating glimpses of the tsarist administration in the years before the revolution. "In the hands of Nicholas II, autocracy, conceived as a personal and independent direction of state problems, had ceased to exist. It was actually supplanted by an oligarchy of a dominant group composed of rival chief administrators, who were united by no common political opinion and therefore were in continual opposition to one another."[14] With Gurko's judgment that lack of ministerial coordination and the presence of competing oligarchies signified the end of autocracy, one must strongly disagree. Indeed, autocracy, undermining fixed rules, made administrative incoherence virtually inevitable. It is for this reason, as well as for others yet to be examined, that autocratic regimes can never be as powerful as they claim. But the power of the autocrat should never be confused with the existence of the institution of autocracy, which at a given time can be relatively weak or powerful.

The tsarist autocracy also depended on the police and the army for its power in internal affairs. The police, of whom there were roughly 105,000 in the general state administration in 1897,[15] were divided into a gendarmerie and a plain-clothes secret police, the famous Okhrana, successor to the Third Department. The police, and especially the political police, had exceptionally broad functions in the tsarist regime, with its mistrust of the individual and its comprehensive, though often ignored or violated, rules. Significantly, too, the police had the tutelary role of safeguarding the welfare of all sectors of the population, at least in theory. The local police often inquired into economic abuses or other kinds of social injustice, and sometimes took the part of the oppressed. This function was in line with the

[13] Quoted in Richard Hare, *Portraits of Russian Personalities between Reform and Revolution* (London: Oxford University Press, 1959), 323.

[14] V. I. Gurko, *Features and Figures of the Past* (Stanford, Calif.: Stanford University Press, 1939), 21. See also V. N. Kokovtsov, *Out of My Past* (Stanford, Calif.: Stanford University Press, 1935), 32, for similar comments from a former minister of finance.

[15] Teodor Shanin, *Russia as a "Developing Society"* (London: Macmillan, 1985), 39.

instructions to the Third Department given by its first chief, Count Benckendorff: "Every man will see in you an official who through my agency can bring the voice of suffering mankind to the throne of the Tsars, who can instantly place the defenseless and voiceless citizen under the protection of the Sovereign Emperor."[16] Despite these nobly expressed intentions, the Russian police, secret or otherwise, were in no position to right all injustices. Police supervision could be no substitute for the independent legal system and secure political rights that the regime refused to grant.

The Russian army underwent great changes in the course of the nineteenth century. From being an army of virtually lifetime serf conscripts, it became a peasant army with more limited, though still long, terms of service. The quality of the peasant conscripts was improved through literacy programs, and more humane discipline heightened morale. The officer corps was similarly transformed from a nonprofessional, mostly noble, elite to a reasonably professionalized cadre of diverse social origins.[17] According to the 1897 census, in that year there were 1,133,000 military personnel, of whom roughly 1 million were conscripts, overwhelmingly of peasant origin.[18]

The professionalization of the army suggests a possible lesser degree of noble dominance and greater independence from the personal will of the tsar. Certainly, both the nobility and the rulers were aware of this threat and took halting measures to ensure noble dominance in key sectors of the officer corps, with questionable success. Additionally, the last two tsars took great personal interest in military affairs and monitored the officer corps with great care, especially the elite units in the capital. The top officers were naturally selected by the tsar himself. Yet it was inevitable that the tsar's command could not be so authoritative in a relatively modern, technically more advanced army of so vast a size. In addition, the policy of using army troops to quell civil disturbances, including strikes and rural rebellions, called into question the loyalty of the troops, who often sympathized with the rebels. It also violated the sense of professional competence and dignity of many officers. For these reasons, the army was not necessarily such a trustworthy protector of the old regime. Indeed, according to one recent account the army's loyalty during the 1905–1906 revolution was extremely tenuous, and many soldiers mutinied when it seemed that the regime might collapse.[19]

[16] Quoted in P. S. Squire, *The Third Department* (Cambridge: Cambridge University Press, 1968), 78.

[17] Raymond L. Garthoff, "The Military as a Social Force," in *The Transformation of Russian Society*, ed. Cyril Black (Cambridge: Harvard University Press, 1960), 325.

[18] Shanin, *Russia as a "Developing Society,"* 39.

[19] John Bushnell, *Mutiny amid Repression: Russian Soldiers in the Revolution of 1905–1906* (Bloomington: Indiana University Press, 1985).

If observant members of the tsarist government were led to question the integrity of autocratic power on the basis of the workings of its key institutions, even more doubts arise when one examines institutions seeking to limit autocracy. As a result of the great reform period, zemstvos, municipal governments, and new legal institutions, such as civilian courts and trial by jury, had arisen as an expression of the burgeoning demands of many social groups for limits to autocratic power. In principle, and to some extent in practice, there were significant changes, but the regime managed to whittle down the scope of their authority, limit their independence, or, when necessary, bypass them entirely. We have already seen how the zemstvos became primarily administrative bodies with limited resources, jealously watched by the local authorities.

Of broader significance is the question of the limitations to autocratic power imposed by the formation of the Duma in 1906. According to some historians, the October Manifesto (1905), which guaranteed basic civil liberties and promised the formation of a duma with legislative responsibilities, transformed the autocracy into a constitutional monarchy.[20] Others are more circumspect. In his history the historian and leader of the liberal Kadet party, Paul Miliukov, writes merely that the manifesto "opened the first breach in the absolute power of the tsars," adding that it was precisely for this reason that Nicholas would never forgive Witte for forcing him to issue it.[21] Clearly, the manifesto and the Duma it authorized were fraught with ambiguity. The manifesto proclaimed changes that the tsar could not truly accept. Issued at a time of great danger for the regime, the period of the October general strike, in the course of late 1905 and throughout 1906 the somewhat vague promises were defined more precisely in terms narrower than the liberals had expected. The electoral law of 11 December 1905, was moderately restrictive. Most of the deputies were to be chosen through indirect elections, propertied groups were favored disproportionately, and the weight of the urban vote was grossly diminished.[22] Women, of course, were denied the vote.

Yet this was still not the epoch of universal suffrage in Europe, and the Russian law was not without parallel in its restrictiveness. Even more a disappointment to the reformers was the announcement during the first half of 1906 of the new legislature's limited rights. This is not the place to go into the details of the provisions, but some of the most important restrictions should be noted. First, the Duma did not have full legislative

[20] Riasanovsky, *A History of Russia*, 408; Michael Florinsky, *Russia: A History and an Interpretation* (New York: Macmillan, 1961), 2:1177.

[21] Paul Miliukov, *History of Russia* (New York: Funk and Wagnalls, 1969), 3:220.

[22] "The vote of one landowner was equal to that of 3.5 townsmen, 15 peasants, and 45 workers." Hans Rogger, *Russia in the Age of Modernisation and Revolution 1881–1917* (London: Longman, 1983), 218.

powers: its measures had to be approved by an upper chamber, the State Council, whose composition was weighted in the tsar's favor. Further, the tsar retained for himself an absolute right of veto. Vast areas of policy remained outside the Duma's competence, including foreign policy, the armed forces, and the imperial court. The ministers remained appointed by and responsible to the tsar alone. The tsar had the right to issue emergency decrees when the Duma was not in session (it was not required that it meet more than two months a year). Finally, although the adjective "unlimited" was deleted, the tsar retained the title of autocrat.

The resulting system was described by the Almanach de Gotha as "a constitutional monarchy with an autocratic Tsar."[23] Although this is a logical contradiction, it well illustrates the actual struggle of rival forces and institutions. The tsar never reconciled himself to any diminution of his authority. The interpretation of the October Manifesto and the tsar's reaction to it by the monarchist historian Oldenburg is no doubt faithful to the tsar's own view: "The irresponsibility of a constitutional monarch, as propounded in liberal doctrine, seemed to Nicholas a criminal washing of the hands. That was why he unfailingly reserved to himself the option to all final decisions. The October Manifesto did not violate that principle."[24] The proponents of a constitutional system saw in the new rules and institutions the betrayal of the promises of the October Manifesto, and resolved to struggle against their limits, but their efforts did not make of the Russian system of government a constitutional monarchy.

In this fundamental conflict of viewpoints was the source of the struggles between Duma and government of the following years. The First Duma was dissolved a few months after its convocation. The Second Duma proved no less hostile to the government. It was dissolved before six months had passed, and the electoral laws were revised to favor the election of a more pliant assembly. In the Third Duma, the right wing was indeed more preponderant, but the political divisions within the assembly deprived it of any of the slight potential for initiative it possessed. Those liberals who saw in the Duma the promise of constitutionalism continued to be disappointed.

On the formal institutional level, then, the Russian political system was a curious mixture of autocracy and constitutional monarchy. The Duma was not a matter of form only, concealing an entirely unreconstructed autocratic power, for it was the result of struggle, the expression of important social aspirations, and a sign of forced concession. Yet in content and style, Russian politics after the 1905–1906 revolution remained fundamentally autocratic. Although, as noted earlier, the tsar isolated himself from his

[23] Leon Trotsky, *1905* (New York: Random House, 1971), 350.

[24] Oldenburg, *Last Tsar*, 2:196.

capital and his government and the imperial command was often weak, it was still the autocrat who set the fundamental course of policy. For example, if he had decided that his God-given rulership were compatible with constitutionalism, the government's confrontation with liberalism would have been more muted. Similarly, although his will was not always firm or consistent, it was sufficient to hamper the nascent efforts of society to organize itself. Social groups might be consulted at the tsar's discretion, yet they had no acknowledged right of representation other than in a Duma crippled by restrictions. The tsar remained impatient with institutions and regularized channels of communication, preferring to depend on the right individuals in informal ways. The autocrat was still not bound by law, as was evident most clearly in the ruthless repression of the formally legal trade union movement.

In conclusion, although it is legitimate to divide the rule of Nicholas II into two distinct periods demarcated by the 1905–1906 revolution, the division does not correspond to that between autocracy and constitutional monarchy. Autocracy, with its distinctive institutions and style of rule, remained in force until the end of Romanov rule. Economic, social, and political modernization had certainly led to important modifications in the nature of autocracy. But it was still as an autocracy that the Russian regime pursued the rapid modernization of the country, with consequences fatal for itself.

Autocracy in Pahlavi Iran

By 1941 Reza Shah had managed to reverse a centuries-long decline in the position of the autocracy in Iran. For the first time since the Safavids, the Iranian monarch exercised effective control over the country, neutralizing the tribes and keeping foreign powers at a distance. A partially Westernized army of roughly 180,000 soldiers by 1941 guaranteed that the autocrat's will was more than a fiction, and that autocratic claims could be backed by effective force.[25] The onset of World War II dramatically altered the fortunes of the newly established dynasty. The allies forced Reza Shah into retirement and established Iran as a de facto protectorate, without, however, taking direct control of domestic affairs unrelated to the war effort. The removal of Reza Shah unleashed many of the social forces repressed during his reign. Domestic social and political affairs became highly confused, as class, ethnic, tribal, and religious antagonisms reasserted themselves. Political life lost its coherence, and it was often unclear whether the Majlis (the parliament established by the 1906 constitution), the cabinet,

[25] Arjomand, *Turban for the Crown*, 215.

the court, foreign powers, or one or another social group or movement held effective power.

It was under this threat of political disintegration and foreign domination that the young Muhammad Reza Shah acquired his first political experience. Unlike Nicholas II, he could not but have an acute sense of the many potential challenges to his authority from within and without. Perhaps it was this very sense of vulnerability that led him to assert his will much more vigorously than any Russian tsar since Peter the Great. His manipulation of political rivals, formation of pseudoparties to engage in a shadow play of politics, dramatic initiatives to transform Iranian society, attempts to propagate an official ideology, and his reliance on the power of the secret police all invited comparison with totalitarian regimes.

That the shah was more vulnerable and also more assertive than Nicholas II can be seen very clearly in the realm of ideology. The last tsars had no official ideology, but their reigns were surrounded by a vast penumbra of conservative thought, identification of the Russian people with the monarchy, and popular promonarchist sentiments that had developed over the course of centuries. During the nineteenth century many of these ideas became more systematized as a result of the challenge of foreign models and the growth of opposition to the autocracy, but the rulers kept a certain distance even from the promonarchical ideological tendencies with which they sympathized. The tsar did not identity himself with a program or an ideology, but with tradition and the nation.

There were certainly elements in the Iranian cultural tradition legitimating the absolute power of the monarch.[26] Some of these, such as the idea of the king's divine mandate to reenact the cosmic drama of order, derived from the pre-Islamic past and arguably still retained some of their force in modern Iranian culture through their transmission by such major thinkers as Nizam ul-Mulk, who combined ancient Persian and Islamic ideas.[27] From Islamic tradition came a variety of legitimations of kingship that were not always consistent with each other. For example, the Sufi idea of the philosopher king can conflict with the more orthodox idea of the king as guardian of the Islamic community and Islamic law. Finally, according to some Islamic interpretations appealing to Muhammad's leadership of the community of believers, there is no warrant for kingship at all. From

[26] These are discussed by Ann Lambton in "Quis Custodiet Custodes: Some Reflections on the Persian Theory of Government," parts 1 and 2, originally published 1956, reprinted in *Theory and Practice in Medieval Persian Government*.

[27] Lambton, "Quis Custodiet," part 1, 135; also see Gholam Reza Afkhami, "The Nature of the Pahlavi Monarchy," in *Ideology and Power in the Middle East*, ed. Peter Chelkowski and Robert Prager (Durham, N.C.: Duke University Press, 1988), 36–37, for an assertion of the relevance of Zoroastrianism to contemporary views of the monarchy.

earliest Islamic times, some Moslems have held out for the idea of an egalitarian community of believers.

No matter what their particularities, Islamic legitimations always implied limitations on kingship much more clearly than in the Russian tradition. The king had to rule according to the sacred law and he had to defend, or better promote, the integrity and welfare of the community. Granted that these obligations allowed for a wide latitude of interpretations, it is still the case that rightful kings could not violate tradition. There was no warrant for the kind of rupture with the past envisioned and promoted by the two Pahlavi shahs, particularly the second and last. In this respect the modernizing tradition of the Russian state was comparatively more favorable for an active state role in social change. Except for his father, the shah could not convincingly appeal to the example of other Iranian rulers since the time of Islam, and he could not but have been aware of the tradition of Islamic pronouncements and protests against the encroaching West and Iranian governments that compromised with it.

The shah was thus forced to establish the ideological foundations of his regime, with its commitment to change, *ab initio*. Ideologies, by their redefinitions of social life, their often activist conception of elites, and their utility in inspiring loyalty and enthusiasm, have proved their indispensability in rapid social change in the twentieth century. But a comparison between tsarist Russia and the shah's Iran suggests that the efficacy of ideologies for autocrats is much reduced. Autocracy is a traditional institution that depends upon a set of diffuse loyalties and ideas. The shah's identification of his rule with progress and his specification of its content increased his own vulnerability, for the appeal to progress undercut many of the traditional ideas on which the autocracy was based[28] and the ideology became eclectic at best, and a contradictory and cynical hodgepodge at worst.

The shah claimed to have been chosen by God to bring progress to his people. The idea of divine election goes back to the Safavid shahs, and even further, but to this old pattern the shah added the element of idiosyncratic personal vision. Muhammad Reza Shah liked to speak of his mystical experiences, the sign, to him, of special divine protection and favor:

> I believe in God, in the fact of having been chosen by God to accomplish a mission. My visions were miracles that saved the country. My reign has saved the country and it's saved it because God was beside me. I mean, it's not fair for me to take all the credit for myself for the great things that I've done for Iran. Mind

[28] There is a parallel, I think, with contemporary religious ideologies, such as liberation theology or Islamic socialism. With the specification of ideological content they lose the authority derived from the more diffuse aura of religion as tradition. Khomeini's regime was undoubtedly not free from the effects of this dilemma.

> you, I could. But I don't want to, because I know that there was someone else behind me. It was God.[29]

It was perhaps these experiences that isolated the shah from his country's religious traditions and gave him the confidence to attack the Shiʿite hierarchy.

Just as the shah was cut off from his country's religious culture, yet claimed to be deeply religious and participated in religious rituals in a symbolic way, so his upbringing and his education in Switzerland had separated him from his own people, especially the common people, yet he claimed an extraordinary degree of communion with them, always in the collective. "There exists today," he claimed, "indissoluble spiritual ties and emotional ties between my people and me the equivalent of which perhaps exists nowhere else." This reciprocal attachment finds its justification "in the sovereign's elevated spiritual level."[30] On the basis of this special relationship, the shah claimed that his was a populist government and, because of government control and solicitude, a classless society.[31] Populist measures ranged from the reception of citizen complaints in special suggestion boxes to the agrarian reform and the other policies proclaimed as the White Revolution. Such so-called welfare-state programs permitted the shah to claim that Iran was more socialistic than England or Sweden, and to add that it had transcended the limitations of both capitalism and socialism.[32]

The alleged special character of Iranian institutions, especially the unique ties between monarch and people and the concern for popular welfare, at times led the shah to scoff at the West.[33] This attempt to construct an independent political identity, though it did not go nearly as far as comparable efforts by, for example, the Slavophiles in Russia, was one dimension of the shah's effort to devise a usable nationalist rationale. Other initiatives included his fanciful efforts to link his monarchy with the ancient Persian past, which culminated in the infamous celebration of twenty-five hundred years of Persian monarchical tradition through the liberal dispensation of Western champagne and other delicacies. The strategy was not a new one: already in the nineteenth century Iranian nationalists had begun to appeal to the ancient glories, implying or even stating that Islam was the root of backwardness. But the shah was much more brazen in his efforts to

[29] Oriana Fallaci, *Interview with History* (Boston: Houghton Mifflin, 1976), 268.

[30] Quoted in Kazem Radjavi, *La revolution iranienne et les moudjahedines* (Paris: Editions Anthropos, 1983), 54.

[31] In January 1972 he claimed that "we eliminated classes in our state and we do not wish to reestablish them." Quoted in M. S. Ivanov, *Iran v 60–70-kh godakh XX veka* (Moscow: Nauka, 1977), 167.

[32] For the former assertion, see Parviz Radji, *In the Service of the Peacock Throne* (London: Hamish Hamilton, 1983), 101; for the latter, see Ivanov, *Iran v 60–70-kh godakh*, 167.

[33] See, for example, Fallaci, *Interview with History*, 274–75.

revive a very distant and unreal past, going so far as to impose a new, non-Islamic calendar on his people. Nicholas II also appealed to past customs, those embodied in the pristine Muscovite autocracy, and tried to shelter himself from the social and political changes that made the image of the past a mirage. But the shah's demarche was much more radical: in his struggle against tradition, he sought to invoke a past without authentic traces in Iranian society. In essence, his goal was the creation of a non-Islamic nationalism consistent with his ideas of progress.

The revived national identity, which would contribute to the recovery of Persia's greatness, was to be buttressed by a "positive nationalism" in foreign affairs—as opposed to Mossadegh's "negative nationalism." Authentic nationalism, stressed the shah, meant an independent policy that would denounce all forms of imperialism and shape relations with foreign countries to Iran's best advantage. It also required a positive program to develop the country, with specific guidelines on how change was to be brought about.[34] This, the gift of progress to his backward people, was the key ideological element in the shah's "mission for his country." However much he may have proclaimed the glories of the pre-Islamic heritage, in fact for him the past and the present were both obsolete, to be transcended through the creative act of the monarch.

The appeal to progress entailed a corollary belief in the capacity of a rational elite to understand and transform the society on the basis of a superior vision. One form of this ideological elitism was the stress on the shah's own superior vision, but this was supplemented by a strong technocratic ethos of planning and expertise appropriate for the new bureaucratic elite in charge of administering the country. The celebration of progress also evoked a revolutionary rhetoric rather out of tune with the fundamental traits of the regime. Prime Minister Hoveyda declared in 1967 that "the old structure must be completely destroyed. Only then can a new system be built. You cannot build the new on the foundation of the old."[35] Statements of this kind reveal that the shah's nationalist ideology was purely normative, based on a vision of the future rather than a celebration of the historical and cultural uniqueness of an existing human society. It did not issue in measures such as the creation of institutes for the study

[34] Mohammed Shah Pahlavi, *Mission for My Country* (New York: McGraw-Hill, 1961), 127.

[35] Quoted in James Bill, *The Politics of Iran* (Columbus, Ohio: Charles E. Merrill Publishing, 1972), 141–42. The shah asserted that "Iran needed a deep and fundamental revolution that would, at the same time, put an end to all the social inequality and all the factors which caused injustice, tyranny and exploitation, and all aspects of reaction which impeded progress and kept our society backward." Quoted in George Lenczowski, "Political Processes and Institutions in Iran: The Second Pahlavi Kingship," in *Iran under the Pahlavis*, ed. George Lenczowski (Stanford, Calif.: Hoover Institution Press, 1978), 455.

of popular culture, but in the construction of massive agricultural complexes.

In a fundamental sense the shah judged his country and his people by the standards of the West, his own nationalist claims notwithstanding. Undoubtedly decisive here were his Swiss education and his lack of roots in his own society. This Western frame of reference also explains the moral tangles and contradictions of his declarations. He, too, was a defender of freedom and democracy: "Let us say that we [Iran and the West] have a common philosophy concerning the respect for the individual and other fundamentals of what you call the open society of Western civilization."[36] Rhetoric about himself as constitutional monarch, about the two-party system, about the deeper traits of Iranian democracy abound in his public statements. These liberal concepts, too, found a place in his melange of ideas. Perhaps they were mainly aimed at foreign consumers, but they also had their domestic impact and became embodied in the formal appearance of a parliamentary system.

What, then, can be made of the shah's ideological pronouncements? First, the obvious should be stressed: they came from the autocrat himself and so his was the responsibility. No parallel for this surfeit of ideas, plans, and opinions exists for Nicholas II. Second, it is evident that the shah's declarations were rife with inconsistencies, contradictions, and even falsifications. For example, he used the traditional authority of monarch to attack tradition; and he denied the fundamental role of Islam in Iranian nationalism. As a consequence, it is fair to conclude that the official version of Iranian nationalism remained devoid of any authentic cultural resonance. Finally, it is clear that the shah's outspokenness had its costs: he and his enemies could easily recognize each other; and the weaknesses and inconsistencies of his ideas were painfully clear. An autocrat claiming to represent the whole people on the basis of twenty-five hundred years of tradition should have shown more caution.

Tsar Nicholas II abhorred the very concept of a constitutional monarchy and maneuvered to reverse the concessions forced from him by his enemies. The shah was more hypocritical: claiming to be a constitutional monarch, he made a mockery of the constitution and ruthlessly dominated Iranian political life. As in the ideological sphere, he was a much more active monarch than Nicholas, creating and dissolving political parties, pursuing an active strategy of divide and rule, and manipulating, co-opting, or repressing potential opponents in ways unimaginable to the last Russian tsars.

[36] E. A. Bayne, *Persian Kingship in Transition: Conversations with a Monarch Whose Office Is Traditional and Whose Goal Is Modernization* (New York: American Universities Field Staff, 1968), 206.

The Iranian constitution had many parallels to the new political norms worked out in Russia after 1905. Both involved compromises between a monarchical system and a constitutional framework based on law and representation. However, the Iranian constitution went further in the direction of a parliamentary system through making the ministers responsible to the legislature, the Majlis. In addition, the religious authorities were empowered to judge the admissibility of new legislation according to its compatibility with Islamic law and custom. In both these senses, and in others as well, the Iranian monarchy was in principle more limited than its Russian counterpart, for the Iranian constitution was more clearly based on Western models. Yet under Reza Shah, and even more so under his son, constitutionalism was a sham, except in the important sense that it was embraced as a goal by important social currents and political movements. Under Muhammad Reza Shah, civil and political rights were far more vulnerable even than in Russia, where the autocracy had not yet learned to use more up-to-date methods of repression. The party system was entirely controlled and manipulated by the shah. Majlis deputies passed through a careful process of screening by the political police, and then were personally approved or denied by the shah himself. No true oppositional force could emerge from the parliament, nothing equivalent to the liberal or socialist parties in the tsarist Duma. Nor were there leaders of the stature and independence of men like Paul Miliukov in Russia. If Russia could be plausibly seen as taking halting steps toward constitutional monarchy, in Iran it is fair to conclude, with a leading political scientist, that constitutionalism was "a farce." Indeed, Binder's diagnosis is even bleaker and probably exaggerated: he claimed that the concocted party system and counterfeit parliament actually discredited liberal ideas and made the whole question of constitutionalism irrelevant to the majority of Iranians.[37] One wonders what must have been thought of the shah's claims to rule as a constitutional monarch. Given the sorry history of constitutionalism, what can have been the effect of the shah's 6 November 1978 promise to stop oppression, which declared that "I am the guardian of the constitutional monarchy which is a God-given gift entrusted to the Shah by the people."[38] Words and symbols, though malleable, are not infinitely so, and may ring hollow or even have the opposite of the intended effect. Could not one conclude, for example, that the promise to end repression had the same worth as the reference to the God-given constitutional monarchy?

Observers are in agreement that the shah took an extraordinarily active part in Iranian political life. His was a dynamic autocracy, bent on chang-

[37] Leonard Binder, *Iran: Political Development in a Changing Society* (Berkeley: University of California Press, 1962), 85.

[38] Quoted in Robert Graham, *Iran: The Illusion of Power* (New York: St. Martins Press, 1980), 232.

ing the very shape of Iranian society. In matters of significance he ruled largely by decree, unrestrained by any formal checks or institutional counterweights. Formal law was dispensable if it stood in the way of progress and what he regarded as substantive social justice.[39] As was the Russian tsars', his independence was grounded in control over the agencies of repression as well as over the bureaucracy. In addition, the court itself, with its vast wealth derived from oil, was a significant underpinning of the autocracy.

Like Nicholas II, Muhammad Reza Shah had a deep interest in the army. Not only did the condition of the armed forces occupy an enormous portion of his time, understandable in the light of the fragile social base of his rule, but he seemed to have had an enormous emotional investment in it as well. His remark to an American interviewer that "I am the army" is symptomatic.[40] His ambassador to London claimed that he was at heart a military man, with Spartan habits and tastes.[41] His solicitude for the army took two basic forms. One priority was to transform the Iranian military into one of the world's greatest, an essential part of his design to make of Iran one of the great powers. To this end he solicited and for the most part obtained vast quantities of technical advice and advanced equipment. Second, he took great pains to ensure the army's loyalty to his person and prevent any possibility of independent action on its part. The natural sensitivity of an autocrat to potential rivals was heightened in the shah's case by the revelation of significant Communist party influence among the officers in the 1950s.

His mechanisms of control were multiple and extremely effective.[42] Highly trusted individuals, often family members, were put in the top posts. The army as a whole was treated as an extremely privileged caste, cut off as far as possible from the rest of society and enjoying the special favor of the monarch. Yet the shah did everything possible to discourage a sense of solidarity and mutual trust within the hierarchy, since a cohesive officer corps posed potential political dangers. The highest ranking officers were seldom allowed to communicate among themselves directly; as a result, the three services had few links other than through the person of the shah. In addition, he created a multiplicity of offices and agencies and purposefully played them off against each other. The military apparatus became unwieldy, with unclear lines of authority and a poorly defined structure. Whatever drawbacks this shapelessness may have had for administrative

[39] See Lenczowski, "Political Processes and Institutions," 454–55.

[40] Bayne, *Persian Kingship*, 186.

[41] Radji, *In the Service*, 200.

[42] They are described in Bill, *Politics of Iran*, 42–44; Marvin Zonis, *The Political Elite of Iran* (Princeton: Princeton University Press, 1971), 112–17; Graham, *Illusion of Power*, 176–91; and Paul Balta and Claudine Rulleau, *L'Iran insurgé* (Paris: Sindbad, 1979), 132–35.

rationality were offset for the shah by its political advantages, unless the military forces were ever required to act cohesivelly. As their lack of political independence in the fall of 1978 demonstrated, the shah's manipulative strategy had worked only too well.

Until that crucial juncture, the shah's military had proved its reliability and effectiveness in repressing internal rebellion. Declarations of martial law at times of crisis enabled it to quell popular unrest, most notably in the 1963 demonstrations, with their combined tribal, religious, and antiautocratic protests. In addition, the regime resorted to the expediency of trying many political cases before military tribunals, thus reducing their visibility and ensuring harsh punishments. These repressive functions, combined with the military elite's American training and connections and the persistent corruption among the officers, deprived the army of its potential character as a national army independent of the regime.[43]

The shah pursued many of the same policies with regard to his secret police, SAVAK (National Security and Information Organization). On the one hand, this infamous agency was allowed to act with all the ruthlessness and arbitrariness characteristic of the regime as a whole. It penetrated all aspects of Iranian life, infiltrating organizations through its network of fifty-three hundred full-time agents and a large number of paid informers.[44] Iranians, particularly urban Iranians, lived with the permanent fear that they were under surveillance. SAVAK's functions were manifold: it gathered information on individuals and groups; infiltrated or directly controlled many organizations, such as trade unions; exercised influence over many aspects of government social and economic policy, which could easily be construed as relevant to security; and pursued and punished enemies of the regime without limitations on its power. The cruelty and scope of its activities far exceeded those of the infamous prerevolutionary Russian secret police, whose budgets were quite restricted and whose activities were restrained by norms of conduct that would appear naive by later standards. Yet even with all its power, SAVAK was subject to the same set of controls and instruments of surveillance of which it was a part. It was set off against the military security organization and monitored by a still more secret, independent organization, the Imperial Inspectorate, whose last chief had known the shah since the latter had been a student in Switzerland.[45] No doubt this flowering of the coercive apparatus intimidated many of the dictator's potential opponents and destroyed a significant part of the opposition, but it did so at enormous cost to the shah's domestic and international reputation. His mastery of the instruments of autocratic

[43] See the remarks in Balta and Rulleau, *L'Iran insurgé*, 132–35. The authors call the army the "colossus with feet of clay."

[44] Abrahamian, *Iran between Two Revolutions*, 436.

[45] Graham, *Illusion of Power*, 142–43.

rule proved their limitations in the actual governing of a modern society, which depends on more than the public's fear of the ruler.

The court, with its own organization and its immense wealth, was an additional instrument of autocratic rule in Iran.[46] Different branches of the court apparatus organized the shah's daily schedule, and thus controlled access to his person, and promoted the extensive economic interests of the ruler and his family. There was an extremely powerful executive arm of the court, the Special Bureau, whose task was to ensure that the shah's policies and orders were carried out and to serve as an overall filtering and coordinating mechanism. Perhaps the most distinctive court institution was the Pahlavi Foundation, established in 1958 allegedly as a charitable organization financed from the shah's personal wealth. However, the foundation received enormous subterranean funds from the government and also extended its influence throughout the economy, owning a major bank as well as stock in 207 companies. Although the foundation did sponsor charitable and cultural activities, its resources were also used to extend the influence of the court over the economy and society. It was a visible segment of the overall pattern of corruption and venality, contributing to the general sense of the regime's moral decadence. More generally, no exact figures on the wealth of the royal family are available, but estimates place the figure at somewhere between five and twenty billion dollars.[47] Much of this was gained through the illegal channeling of oil funds into the family's personal accounts. Aside from the corrosive effect of this immense wealth on the regime's image in society, it undoubtedly contributed to the shah's sense of his own omnipotence and thereby undermined his ability to comprehend the world around him.

The governmental bureaucracy was the final basic support and conduit of autocratic power. With its long history of centralized government, Iran, like Russia, had witnessed many different administrative experiments that provided the basis for further systematization.[48] The Safavids, for example, had introduced a rudimentary form of council of ministers. Throughout their rule the Qajars attempted to further the administrative rationalization of the government, enhancing the power of the prime minister and defining functional responsibilities more clearly. Nonetheless, much remained to be done to reduce arbitrariness and favoritism and to fashion a coherent machinery with clearly demarcated lines of responsibility. Halting steps toward a parliamentary form of government with cabinet supremacy were taken after the adoption of the constitution, but the political chaos in the years before the rise of Reza Shah prevented much progress.

[46] See Graham, *Illusion of Power*, 140–42, 157–67; Abrahamian, *Iran between Two Revolutions*, 437–38.

[47] Abrahamian, *Iran between Two Revolutions*, 437.

[48] This account is based on Binder, *Iran*, 99–107.

In the 1920s and especially the 1930s Reza Shah adopted significant new measures to improve the quality and the efficiency of the administration.[49] The first civil service code, influenced by European models, was enacted in 1922 to regularize the qualifications and benefits of civil servants. The education and training of officials were improved to permit them to respond to the more active role of the state in social life. For the first time, a partially Westernized class of bureaucratic technocrats emerged as a significant social and political force in Iran. All these tendencies toward expertise, specialization, and predictability were sponsored by the very autocratic power whose arbitrariness hindered their further development.

The development of the state apparatus under Muhammad Reza Shah was similarly filled with ironies. Challenging new demands were placed upon it, and the administration grew rapidly in size and in technical expertise. For example, in the years from 1963 through 1977, the number of ministries expanded from twelve, with 150,000 employees, to nineteen, with 304,000.[50] The nature of their responsibilities changed just as rapidly, for they were now charged with the rapid modernization of virtually all aspects of the nation's life. Highly placed technocrats, many of them trained abroad, were urged to use their advanced techniques to model, plan, and transform the economy of this ancient land.

Despite the growing size and responsibilities of the ministries, the institutional traits of the bureaucracy still bore the marks of the autocratic system. Observers agree that the administrative system was completely unintegrated and lacked independence.[51] Lateral communication was weak, as each agency looked only to the center for direction. As with the security agencies, the shah intentionally created overlapping and competing jurisdictions in order to limit the powers of any one institution and to set each off against the others. Networks of informal ties based on clientelism generally predominated over and against the formal administrative structure. Cooperation, trust, and initiative were discouraged by the all-encompassing fear of the arbitrary power of the ruler. "Fear rather than rationality, fear rather than common sense, fear rather than patriotism, seems the governing force in the life of an Iranian public servant."[52]

Through the agency of such an administration cut off from the Iranian people by its training and its high position, and constantly circumscribed in its autonomy by the reality of arbitrary power, the shah sought to realize his civilizing mission.

[49] These are briefly described in Amin Banani, *The Modernization of Iran 1921–1941* (Stanford, Calif.: Stanford University Press, 1961), 58–61.

[50] Abrahamian, *Iran between Two Revolutions*, 438.

[51] See, especially, Khosrow Fatemi, "Leadership by Distrust: The Shah's Modus Operandi," *Middle Eastern Journal*, 36, no. 1 (Winter 1982): 48–61.

[52] Radji, *In the Service*, 51.

These, then, were the fundamental traits of the autocracies bent on bringing their countries into the modern world. They brought much from the past: traditionalist political ideas, repressive political institutions, shapeless bureaucracies, a suspicion of any individual and social initiative, and hostility to the realities, if not always the appearances, of representative political institutions. The rulers often claimed that these legacies would provide continuity and order to the process of modernization, and so avoid many of the negative phenomena visible in the West. Both exulted in the deep ties of love and affection that bound their people to them, claiming that devotion to the autocrat was at the core of the national psychology. As will be seen shortly, the reverse turned out to be the case: the autocratic heritage and practices undermined many of the potential advantages of modernization, and modernization sapped whatever life was left in these already outmoded ideas and institutions.

Three

Dimensions of Modernization

THE PREVIOUS CHAPTER examined the nature of autocracy in the two countries and described the main institutions through which the autocrat sought to maintain his power and promote his goals in society. The present chapter and the one to follow pose the analytical problem of the viability of a modernization process spearheaded by this type of regime. The analysis presupposes that the nature of political authority is one of the fundamental determinants of the traits and outcomes of any path of development, which cannot therefore be reduced to economic or class variables alone. In all modernizing societies there is a tendency toward the rationalization of state power and its extension into new areas of social life, as older institutions decline or become more specialized and economic development poses new social and political challenges. Yet autocratic modernization is surely distinguished within this overall pattern by the importance of state initiative and control. In this respect it is parallel to modernization led by one-party mobilizational states, with the difference that autocratic regimes are unwilling and probably unable to organize and mobilize the population.[1] Modernization and economic growth are not spontaneous phenomena rooted in the goals and actions of social groups, but state projects determined upon and directed by the regime. If the greater weight of the state in economic development is a general tendency for latecomers, as Gerschenkron has taught us,[2] only in autocratic regimes does it have the institutional structure already outlined.

It is this political structure, based on the will of the autocrat and the institutions that protect and promote it, as well as the patterns of social relations that it encourages, that gives such a distinctive cast to autocratic modernization. The regime's decisions are hardly subject to the approval even of the social elites, and the pace and timing of change can be defined, if not realized, without consultation or consent. But the apparent independence of the political structure proves illusory, for the weak links between state and society put their own limits on the ability of the state to transform

[1] Stalin's Russia shows that party-based mobilization regimes are compatible with virtually autocratic power. As noted in the introduction, the Stalinist pattern of modernization is of a different sociological type, however, precisely because autocracy is combined with mass mobilization and modern ideology.

[2] Alexander Gerschenkron, *Economic Backwardness in Historical Perspective* (New York: Praeger, 1965).

society. In addition, the political institutions of autocracy coexist uneasily with fundamental tendencies, perhaps even requirements, of industrial society, and so lead to contradictions that are perhaps insurmountable. The fact that the only two experiments in autocratic modernization both culminated in revolution at the very least suggests an unusual vulnerability. It is a debatable question whether, if given more time, modernizing autocracies could have developed into something along the lines of a constitutional democracy. The matter of immediate concern here is less speculative and more sociological: the nature of the key tensions and limitations in this path of modernization.

The darker and more pessimistic side of the questions will occupy the majority of our attention. Both the limits to effective state action in a modernizing autocracy and the deleterious effects of this action on the society as a whole will be discussed at some length in chapter four, which presents the core of the overall argument. But it is well to begin here by analyzing in brief compass what the regimes aimed to do and in what senses they attempted and succeeded in modernizing the societies. It will become clear that, whatever their limitations, these were dynamic regimes able at least to initiate a significant process of transformation, even if at great cost. Indeed, in both cases their very dynamism was one source of their downfall, as time-honored legitimations lost their force and traditional social groups were either weakened or pushed into opposition. This is not to repeat the familiar cliché that these regimes were too progressive, that they sponsored more "progress" than their benighted people could bear. The kind of "progress" was if anything more decisive than the amount, though these categories cannot in practice be separated from each other. Thus, after a short review in this chapter of some of the most important economic and social changes in Russia and Iran, in the following chapter we will inquire into the more difficult qualitative dimensions of change and trace their consequences.

The Modernization of Russia

We have seen that government-sponsored and -induced economic and social change was much more a tradition in Russia than in Iran, but that it was in the latter country that the autocratic regime would take the boldest leaps in its modernization effort. In Russia the tradition of government activism and the deeper involvement of social groups in economic change and political reforms, including the development of the modern bureaucracy, led to a more restricted set of policies and more ambiguity in the fundamental directions of change. In addition, the conceptual models available to the Russian state at the time did not include economic planning, nor was there a technocratic elite confident of its ability to manipulate social reality.

The state's primary motivation for economic change in Nicholas II's Russia was the same as at the time of Peter the Great: to enhance national strength in order to be able to compete with the West. Because of the industrial revolution, which was in Europe already at a more advanced stage based on new organizational methods and applications of science to technology, the gap between Russia and the West was without doubt far greater than it had been under Peter. Liberal thought traced Russia's backwardness to the restrictions on individual initiative and the market, and so one conceivable model of change would have entailed drastic changes in the nature of the regime. Fortunately for the ruler, by the time of Nicholas II's accession, there was another historical model of development available, as adumbrated theoretically by Friedrich List and as embodied historically in the experience of Germany. Indeed, List's theories and Germany's modernization provided the inspiration for Sergei Witte, Alexander III's and Nicholas II's minister of finance, the man primarily responsible for the policies followed in the crucial decade before the 1905 revolution.

Witte's "system" has been expertly analyzed elsewhere[3] and need not be discussed in detail here. Witte accepted from List the idea that the strength of a great power in the modern world depends on industrialization. Through his influence, too, he became convinced of the need for an active state role in promoting modern industry, a role, he also believed, that corresponded to the traditions of the Russian state. Witte's appeals for a dramatic upturn in state sponsorship of industrialization gained the tsar's favor and became the central goal of government policy in the 1890s. The program of railway construction provided the necessary demand for industrial goods, and the treasury was generous with loans and financial incentives. Peasant demand was not only not central to the industrialization effort—many populists had argued that the weak Russian domestic market made industrialization impossible—but was actually reduced through heavy taxation of the peasants to provide the necessary funds for industrialization.[4]

Despite its indispensability, the state's role in Russian industrialization seems rather limited by contemporary standards. Although the government protected, subsidized, and rewarded private entrepreneurs, it was they ultimately who had to respond to the incentives and organize production. The wager, then, was on private capitalists and the market; overzealous historical comparisons with the command economy of Stalin are en-

[3] Theodore Von Laue, *Sergei Witte and the Industrialization of Russia* (New York: Atheneum, 1963).

[4] For a good description, see Alexander Gerschenkron, "Problems and Patterns of Russian Economic Development," in Black, *Transformation of Russian Society*, 47–48.

tirely misleading. Yet there was necessarily grave doubt whether Russia had a sufficient potential supply of entrepreneurs to respond to the government's favors. It was here that the third element of economic policy came to the fore: the encouragement of foreign capital and foreign entrepreneurship. As Witte himself stated in his famous 1899 memorandum, "The inflow of foreign capital is, in the considered opinion of the Minister of Finance [i.e., Witte], the only way by which our industry will be able to supply our country quickly with abundant and cheap products."[5] Lured by the prospect of high profits because of protected markets and weak competition, foreign entrepreneurs did indeed invest in Russian industry in massive amounts in the 1890s. According to the most thorough study of the subject, foreign investors accounted for 55 percent of new industrial capital formation in Russia from 1893 to 1900.[6] The impact of foreigners was especially pronounced in mining and metallurgy, but it was widely distributed throughout the economy, including both light and heavy industry.

The industrialization of the 1890s achieved considerable successes. Specialists estimate the annual rate of industrial growth at approximately 8 percent, and the industrial base now included a technologically advanced metallurgical sector created largely by foreign capital in the Ukraine. Yet doubts about the wisdom of the policy were understandably persistent. Virtually nothing was done to modernize agriculture, and heavy taxation and the commune reduced potential peasant initiative. The favor given to industry signaled a further decline in the fortunes of the nobility, the regime's main social base. Added to this was the charge that Russia was merely copying foreign models, even mortgaging itself to foreign interests. A great power, it seemed to many, was turning itself into an economic colony of the Europeans. The economic crisis at the turn of the century in both industry and agriculture seemed to vindicate the claims of Witte's opponents and induced a reversal of government economic policy.

The economic crisis, the government's turn toward agriculture, and the onset of war with Japan and then revolution interrupted Russia's industrial progress, but rapid growth was resumed between the end of the 1905–1906 revolution and the outbreak of World War I, this time at an annual estimated growth of about 6 percent. Scholars have noted significant differences between the two periods. In the latter interval the importance of state subsidies and foreign investment was reduced. Russian bankers, entrepreneurs, engineers, and foremen were now more able to work on their own, by their own efforts recapitulating the earlier patterns of emphasis on

[5] John McKay, *Pioneers for Profit* (Chicago: University of Chicago Press), 11.

[6] Ibid., 29.

heavy industry and a high level of industrial concentration.[7] By 1914 Russia was a great industrial power, though it was not an industrial country and in industrial growth per capita it ranked below Italy and Spain.[8]

The central question about Russian industrialization before World War I concerned its future course, not its reality. On the basis of its achievements, could Russia have repeated the experience of Germany and become an independent industrial society, as Gerschenkron suggested? Or did its overwhelmingly rural economy, foreign dependency, weak entrepreneurial class, and dominant state invalidate such European parallels, forcing one to conclude that it represented a qualitatively distinct pattern of development?[9] In purely economic terms the answer may be equivocal; but when one considers the social and political underpinnings of the industrialization program, doubts inevitably multiply.

Economic development brought a host of other social and economic changes in its wake. It was in large part responsible for the explosive growth of Russian cities in the decades before the revolution. Although the urban population as a proportion of the total population did not increase markedly, the size of the urban population grew from 14.6 million in 1897 to over 21 million by 1913.[10] Within this overall pattern, the capitals underwent especially tumultuous population growth, the great bulk of it due to internal migration from rural Russia. St. Petersburg added an average of 50,000 people per year to its population between 1890 and 1914;[11] Moscow at the turn of the century was one of the world's ten largest cities, and the fastest growing among them, with a growth rate of roughly 4 percent per year.[12]

The social structure of the cities was also transformed. Although the percentage of factory workers in the work force as a whole remained small, they came to be a significant social and political presence in the cities. In St. Petersburg, for example, the number of factory workers increased from 35,000 in 1867 to 200,000 by 1913; between 1890 and 1914 industrial employment in the city nearly tripled, while total population doubled.[13] This did not mean that the capital, or any other of the large Russian cities, had become primarily industrial. In fact, the petty craft and commerce sec-

[7] McKay, *Pioneers for Profit*, 232–41; Gerschenkron, "Problems and Patterns."

[8] Alec Nove, *An Economic History of the U.S.S.R.* (Harmondsworth: Penguin, 1976), 14.

[9] This possibility is suggested by Teodor Shanin in *Russia as a "Developing Society."*

[10] Rogger, *Russia in the Age*, 125–26.

[11] James Bater, *St. Petersburg* (Montreal: McGill–Queen's University Press, 1976), 310–11.

[12] Joseph Bradley, "Moscow: From Big Village to Metropolis," in *The City in Late Imperial Russia*, ed. Michael Hamm (Bloomington: Indiana University Press, 1986), 13.

[13] Bater, *St. Petersburg*, 385, 213.

tors remained vital, giving the urban economic and social structure a notably dual character.[14]

The urban middle class also underwent a notable expansion. Industrial growth increased the demand for white-collar workers such as clerks and accountants, and the overall process of social and economic transformation augmented the need for the services of professionals such as physicians, lawyers, and journalists. Clearly, a new Russia was in the process of being born, but the implications of these changes for the country's political future were less evident. How would the new groups fit into the old patterns of Russian social and political life? Which of the new groups would be able to organize and press their demands for social recognition and political rights? What ideas would appeal to them? All of these questions inspired vigorous debates within the government as well as among the intelligentsia.

Partly as a result of economic growth, momentous changes also occurred within the sphere of education. The government, social elites, and masses all came to place greater emphasis on the importance of literacy and secondary education. Aspiring to maintain Russia's great power status, political elites came to understand that they could not move forward if the majority of the population was illiterate. Economic progress, social order, and public health were inconceivable when, in the words of a Ministry of Education magazine, "millions of people who produce the wealth of modern society are wallowing in a mental world lower than that of the primitive."[15] Although some suspicion remained that education might raise unrealistic aspirations and hasten the spread of subversive ideas, in the mid-1890s the government embarked on an impressive campaign of primary-school creation. Central government expenditures on primary education "doubled between 1896 and 1900, doubled once more by 1907 . . . and then soared from slightly over 19 million [rubles] in 1907 to 82.2 million in 1914—more than fourfold in seven years."[16] The increase in the number of teachers, number of primary schools, and percentage of the peasant population exposed to school was impressive, although the country still lagged far behind European societies. Government initiative was matched by newfound popular enthusiasm, as industrial development and the exposure to urban life put a new premium on skills and knowledge. Educated Russians were also learning to judge their country by European standards, finding the country's educational backwardness scandalous and joining the crusade for improving popular education. Many of them looked to education as

[14] See Daniel Brower, "Urban Revolution in the Late Russian Empire," in Hamm, *The City*, 325.

[15] Quoted in Ben Eklof, *Russian Peasant Schools* (Berkeley: University of California Press, 1986), 115.

[16] Ibid., 90.

the cure for the country's many ills, hoping that it would improve work habits and even provide a cultural basis for popular political participation. These new attitudes and efforts gave significant dividends. To take the simplest and far from the least significant indicator, literacy rates nearly doubled from 1897 to the eve of World War I, rising from roughly 20 percent to about 40 percent.[17]

Some of these changes were the direct result of government policies, some were desired indirect effects, and others, such as the development of new political identities among emerging social groups, were neither intended nor advantageous for the regime. In general the Russian state's stance toward social change was less activist, more ambiguous, than was that of the shah's regime. It was committed to modernization in a rather narrow sense, hoping to keep much of the social structure and culture intact, even, at times, seeking to protect them from the inroads of modernization. It had no sense that it had the power or the right to reshape society from top to bottom according to the criteria of a vision imposed from above.

Certainly the most significant experiment in social engineering for the sake of modernization during Nicholas II's reign was the agrarian reform sponsored by Prime Minister Peter Stolypin beginning in 1906. Voices had long been raised against the communal structure of land tenure set up after the 1861 emancipation of the serfs. The emancipation had legalized the peasant commune as the dominant institution of rural Russia and had tied the individual peasant to it in a multitude of ways. Communes had title to the great majority of lands allotted to the peasantry, and indeed to roughly half of the arable land of European Russia. Land within the commune was periodically redistributed to its members according to family size and laboring ability, a policy that did not prevent but surely limited the emergence of inequality among the peasants. Peasant families were assigned separate strips of land, often at considerable distance from each other, a practice that clearly inhibited efficiency. In general there was limited incentive for agricultural improvements, for the land belonged to the commune in any case.

It is often claimed that the majority of peasants favored the relatively egalitarian practices of the commune, but reformers criticized its inefficiency and restrictions upon individual initiative. For the individual peasant was tied to the commune not just economically, but also legally. He was responsible for his share of the collective taxes and had to receive permission to leave the commune from the village authorities. Further, some authors give a most unflattering picture of the peasant leadership of the

[17] Jeffrey Brooks, *When Russia Learned to Read* (Princeton: Princeton University Press, 1985), 4.

commune, arguing that it replaced the tyranny of the landlord with its own strict forms of control and that it was manipulated by the political authorities.[18]

The reformers of the 1860s had intended the commune to be a temporary fiscal expedient for the collection of taxes and redemption payments, but in the last decades of the century a number of laws strengthened its power and it became surrounded by an aura of sanctity for many traditionalists and populists. The debate over the peasant commune and the desirability of government reforms was one of the most heated political issues of the early years of the century. The reform program that came to bear Stolypin's name (but was in fact a dilution of his own program) was a complicated set of measures whose impact upon Russian agrarian relations is still controversial. In essence, the reforms sought to facilitate the consolidation of communal land into individual private property and to weaken the hold of the commune over its members. In one sense, then, the reform envisioned the breakdown of traditional peasant society and was to that degree a revolutionary measure. In comparison to truly radical programs of agrarian change, however, its fundamentally moderate character stands out. Stalin's and the shah's policies, for example, represented much more revolutionary breaks with the past.

In 1906–1914 Russia the administrative apparatus for highly ambitious imposed change simply did not exist. For example, the official in charge of the reform in its early stages, the land captain, could encourage private ownership, but could hardly oppose a peasant community unwilling to permit individual consolidation.[19] In addition, although the government could legalize and promote the changes, the reforms depended on the willingness of individual peasants and the communes to cooperate. When it became clear that more peasants petitioned for rearrangements of communal patterns rather than outright individual ownership, the government was willing to accommodate them, showing a surprising responsiveness to peasant preferences.[20] This tendency toward reform, not abolition, of communal patterns, called group land resettlements, may have strengthened internal village unity and cohesiveness in many cases, as the peasants worked together to shape their own tenure relations.

The agrarian program was but one part of Stolypin's overall project for economic and political reform of the empire. His plans also included administrative rationalization, rebuilding the army and navy, the improvement of public education, social welfare measures for the workers, and tax reform. Taken together, these changes might well have constituted a "rev-

[18] See Lazar Volin, "The Russian Peasant: From Emancipation to Kolkhoz," in Black, *Transformation of Russian Society*, 295–96.

[19] George Yaney, *The Urge to Mobilize* (Urbana: University of Illinois Press, 1982), 305.

[20] Ibid., 358.

olution from above" had they been enacted, but the land reform was the only significant aspect of the program to be realized. Some scholars have argued that even by itself this change might have transformed the major part of Russia's society and economy. It is estimated that by the beginning of 1916 somewhat less than half of the peasant households in European Russia belonged to communes,[21] and one can suppose that this slight majority of independent peasant proprietors might have provided the basis for a dynamic capitalist agriculture in the future. In the short run, however, the economic achievements of the reform were limited and the vast majority of the rural population remained land poor, partly because of rapid demographic growth in the countryside. In addition, after Stolypin's political defeat and then his assassination, Nicholas's regime displayed a notable lack of boldness and imagination. The incoherent tsarist government, so closely tied to the nobility and so frightened by the threat of revolution from below, was incapable of pursuing a more profound revolution from above.

In both its economic and social aspects the tsarist model of modernization exhibited deep inner tensions. The autocracy decided to wager on the private capitalist entrepreneur and, with less energy, on the prosperous independent peasant. The dynamic socioeconomic structure that they would dominate would provide the necessary underpinnings of a modern great power. In theory, too, these changes were to be compatible with the maintenance of the autocratic political system, for these new social groups would define themselves not ideologically but in terms of their own economic self-interest. Economic modernization would thus be compatible with political quiescence, as the flourishing classes would trust in the above-class state to adjudicate claims and control conflict.[22] Yet, as will be argued in the following chapter, private initiative and a functioning civil society were not as compatible with the autocracy as this idyllic image would suggest.

The Modernization of Iran

The shah combined an appeal to the realities of great power politics a la Witte with a Third Worldist rhetoric to justify urgent state initiatives in the economic, social, and cultural modernization of Iran. The first type of argument was not without its own irony, for Iran was a world power only

[21] Riasanovsky, *A History of Russia*, 433.

[22] For a most illuminating description of the logic of this political model, see Iu. Martov, *Sovremennaia Rossiia* (Geneva: Tipografiia soiuza russkikh sotsial'demokratov, 1898), 2–3.

potentially, if at all. Paradoxically, too, the shah's image of a powerful modern society was modeled on the West, and it was by this standard that his own society was deficient; yet this assumption collided with the anti-colonialist and populist rhetoric that was very likely an authentic response to his own country's humiliations. It was on the fusion of the glorious Persian heritage with modern accomplishments that the shah sought to stake out a uniquely Iranian path to the modern world, but the real fusion seemed to be of the worst features of advanced capitalist and socialist societies, with few of the advantages of either.

The shah married the autocratic to the technocratic ethos. This combination was responsible for many of the frightening elements of his vision of progress. Statements such as the following are simply unimaginable from Nicholas II:

> I looked at Iranian society, recognized its weaknesses, needs and potentialities; I studied the structure of other societies and saw how they had progressed; I analyzed the various philosophies and programs which had been advocated or implemented. The realization came to me that Iran needed a deep and fundamental revolution that could, at the same time, put an end to all the social inequality and all the factors which caused injustice, tyranny, and exploitation, and all aspects of reaction which impeded progress and kept our society backward.[23]

The shah's revolution was to be an alternative to extremisms of both the left and the right, and it was to synthesize the Iranian past and Western-style progress. In economic terms, his program commingled government planning of ever greater scope and scale; state ownership and management of strategic industries; private Iranian industrial investment, frequently through state stimulation; and the encouragement of foreign investment, especially in more technologically advanced sectors. Specialists disagree on virtually all aspects of this program of economic development. To a German economist and former technical advisor to the shah's government, "the history of planning in Iran is an exciting chapter in Iranian national development."[24] To a well-known Iranian economist working in England, the "main purpose was to keep up with the Joneses of comprehensive planning. And the plan was never adhered to, either in the letter or in spirit."[25]

Similarly, on the achievements and prospects of economic development as a whole the Princeton economist Issawi wrote in the mid-1970s that

[23] Quoted in Lenczowski, "Political Processes and Institutions," in Lenczowski, *Iran under the Pahlavis*, 455.

[24] Harold Mehner, "Development and Planning in Iran after World War II," in Lenczowski, *Iran under the Pahlavis*, 167.

[25] Homa Katouzian, *The Political Economy of Modern Iran 1926–1929* (London: Macmillan, 1981), 231.

"there is every reason to envisage the future with confidence."[26] The historian Ervand Abrahamian, hardly sympathetic to the regime, is willing to recognize that the last fifteen years of the shah's rule witnessed "a minor industrial revolution."[27] For Katouzian, again, the regime of "petrolic despotism" could produce only pseudogrowth and development, particularly in the form of an inflated service sector expert in consumption rather than in production. Thus, if in Russia legitimate questions arise about the permanence and capacity for further evolution of the tsarist industrial economy, for Iran deeper and more troubling uncertainties emerge about the significance and even reality of the surface achievements. Was the industrial growth of Iran merely an artificial, ineffective, and impermanent consequence of the vast oil revenues available to the government in the late 1960s and especially the early 1970s?

These doubts are connected to the general analytical question of how to conceptualize the process of Iranian economic development. Clearly the liberal model of development based on the market and private entrepreneurship is an inappropriate model, no matter how appealing its normative elements may be in some quarters. Gerschenkron's model of late development is also not fully adequate, for it still presumes that the mainspring of development is internal to the country, in private banks or in government accumulation policy, for example. Perceiving the lack of fit between these previous models and the Iranian experience, scholars have applied conceptual frameworks derived from the experience of contemporary developing countries, especially the models of import-substitution development and dependent development.[28] As conceived by scholars working on Latin America, these theories sought to interpret a pattern of industrial development dominated by a triad of actors. In the major Latin American countries, protectionist tariff policies and state encouragement had given birth to a native industrial class oriented around the production of consumer goods in a protected market. Foreign capital dominated highly productive economic enclaves, such as oil or copper, and also the high-technology modern industrial sector. The relationship between native and foreign entrepreneurial sectors, as well as between both of these and the agrarian elites, was complicated, a mixture of both interdependence and considerable tension. The state mediated among these conflicting elites, forging

[26] Charles Issawi, "The Iranian Economy 1915–1975: Fifty Years of Economic Development," in Lenczowski, *Iran under the Pahlavis*, 166.

[27] Abrahamian, *Iran between Two Revolutions*, 430.

[28] See, for example, M. H. Pesaran, "The System of Dependent Capitalism in Pre- and Post-Revolutionary Iran," *International Journal of Middle East Studies* 14 (1982): 501–22; and Robert Looney, "Origins of Pre-Revolutionary Iran's Development Strategy," *Middle East Studies* 22 (January 1986), 104–19.

compromises and ensuring that all elites would benefit from the system of dependent capitalist development.

The general consensus among scholars in this tradition is that this pattern of development had a number of serious and insurmountable weaknesses, including the inability to create an independent national advanced industrial sector; the weakness of the industrial export sector, and consequently limitations on the ability to import, which constrained further development; limited employment opportunities in industry, and thus the weak development of a domestic mass market; weak and divided social elites; and increasing income inequality and widening urban-rural gaps. In this context of a limited though developing economic system, social fragility and fragmentation, and greater inequality, the state had to intervene in order to protect the system from internal challenges, thus sacrificing democracy in favor of "bureaucratic-authoritarian" regimes.[29]

Many of the traits ascribed to dependent development appear to fit Iran, especially the increase in inequality and the widening economic gap between the cities and the countryside. But in my view, the nature of the Iranian state and the oil wealth at its disposal call into question the applicability of the model to Iran, particularly in the 1970s. Foreign capital and technicians flooded into Iran, and sometimes entrepreneurs, competing for the government's largess. In general the latter were forced to meet terms dictated by the government, even if extraordinarily high profits were assured.[30] The Iranian government did not have to induce investment because of a shortage of domestic funds, but could concentrate on encouraging investments in advanced sectors where there was a shortage of Iranian skill and technology. In addition, the "national" bourgeoisie did not have the social and political weight of its Latin American counterparts. In general, Iranian entrepreneurs were simply the conduits of government investments, not independent actors in their own right. The shah's industrialization policy thus created what the Soviet scholar Agaev calls a "state-monopolistic social structure"[31] quite different from the fragmented and stalemated social structures characteristic of Latin American dependent development. The Iranian state was not at all mainly a mediator among competing elites.

[29] The literature on this model is immense and diverse. Probably the best-known expositions can be found in the work of Fernando Enrique Cardoso and Guillermo O'Donnell. Dependency theory has frequently been criticized for its economic determinism and its failure to analyze domestic social and political actors. This schematic view does not pretend to do justice to the variety of perspectives and debates.

[30] Fred Halliday, *Iran: Dictatorship and Development* (Harmondsworth: Penguin Books, 1979), 155.

[31] S. L. Agaev. *Iran mezhdu proshlym i budushchim* (Moscow: Izdatel'stvo politicheskoi literatury, 1987), 9.

Indeed, the oil wealth "separated the state from society so much so that it would be difficult to find parallels anywhere in human history."[32] Precisely from this separation and autonomy derive the artificiality of the whole process. The Iranian state could initiate massive petrochemical development and programs of dam building and land resettlement, but there was no assurance that these were rooted in the needs, aspirations, and skills of the Iranian people, which were hardly taken into consideration. By contrast, systematic planning takes into account the needs and resources of a country. Planning in Iran amounted to directives from above in the virtual absence of the kind of knowledge and information that could have led to its successful implementation.[33] Thus, although in Iran the industrial growth rate was "of a magnitude almost unmatched in history,"[34] it lacked a foundation in social reality. Implemented from above, the newest forms of capitalist development could not reshape the traditional social structure and so create an authentic bourgeois society and capitalist economic system, although they could threaten and in part displace the older economic classes and structures.[35]

With this larger context in mind, it is worth citing some of the quantitative indices of economic development.[36] Their very magnitude suggests that, whatever the levels of waste, conspicuous consumption, useless investment, and corruption, much of value must have been accomplished. With the immense increase in oil revenues, from $555 million in 1963–1964 to $1.2 billion in 1970–1971 and almost $20 billion in 1975–1976, substantial economic growth could almost have been taken for granted. First, the increase in gross national product (GNP) progressed at the following rates: 1962–1970, 8 percent; 1972–1973, 14 percent; and 1973–1974, 30 percent. Much of the investment in the earlier part of the period was devoted to infrastructure, greatly increasing electrical output, the road network, port facilities, and the like. Considerable investments were also made in agriculture, especially in fertilizer production, irrigation projects, the reform of land tenure, and the creation of large agricultural corporations, with fairly modest results. The most likely estimates for agricultural growth seem to be around 3 or 4 percent per year, although the statistics are judged unreliable. Specialists agree that agriculture did not keep pace with the demand for food, necessitating substantial imports; per capita

[32] Katouzian, *Political Economy*, 255.

[33] For a contrast between planning as state directives, often labeled "voluntaristic," and planning based on economic calculations, see Moshe Lewin, *Political Undercurrents in Soviet Economic Debates* (Princeton: Princeton University Press, 1974), 97–124.

[34] Issawi, "The Iranian Economy," 150.

[35] Agaev, *Iran mezhdu*, 9–10.

[36] The following information is taken from Abrahamian, *Iran between Two Revolutions*, 426–31.

growth in agriculture lagged far behind the leading sectors; and the gap between rural and urban living standards augmented considerably, thus stimulating rural to urban migration on a vast scale.

Industry was, of course, the main beneficiary of state investments, particularly in the 1970s. The state industrial sector itself grew enormously, absorbing in the mid-1970s two-thirds of overall investment and accounting for more than half of industrial production.[37] The private sector, mainly centered on the production of import-substitution consumer durables, also expanded significantly. Overall, manufacturing increased its weight in the GNP from 11 to 17 percent between 1968 and 1977, and annual industrial growth increased from 5 to 20 percent.[38] Goods not previously manufactured in Iran, like paper and telephones, came into production, and the output of sophisticated items like tractors and metal sheeting skyrocketed. Until the mid-1970s the rate of growth could partly justify the regime's euphoria, at the same time dangerously inflating its sense of accomplishment. It was during this period that the shah began to regard the Western democracies with an air of condescension.

The shah knew what he wanted for his country and clearly perceived that his people were not in their present state fit vessels for the national mission. He thus embarked on a program of social transformation of breathtaking scope. The most dramatic of his initiatives was the famous White Revolution, as distinguished from the red variety and also from "black" (clergy) reaction. Approved in 1963 through an almost unanimous referendum, the White Revolution originally consisted of a six-point program to break up the old "feudal" structure and create the foundations for a modern industrial society. Land reform was the cornerstone of the program. Its implementation and implications will be discussed more fully in a later chapter. At this point it should be noted that it had both an economic purpose, an increase in rural output and productivity, and a political goal, the neutralization of the landed elite as potential rivals for power and the creation of a grateful independent peasantry. In its political dimensions it went far beyond the Stolypin reforms, which did not dare touch the remaining noble property. There can be no doubt that the land reform dramatically changed the lives of millions of tenant farmers, who now received title to their land. It also left a residue of landless laborers free to make their way to the rapidly growing margins of the cities.

Additional principles of the White Revolution, some of them announced in the following years, included the nationalization of forests and pastures; a profit-sharing scheme for industrial workers; creation of a corps to reduce illiteracy, especially in the rural areas, and a health corps; the

[37] S. L. Agaev, *Iran v proshlom i nastoiashchem* (Moscow: Nauka, 1981), 166.

[38] Abrahamian, *Iran between Two Revolutions*, 430.

establishment of village courts of law; and large-scale administrative reorganization.

The White Revolution, like the shah's regime in general, embraced different, sometimes opposing, elements and motives. Its inspiration was in part political, in part social and economic. The reforms were announced partly for domestic considerations, but also because of pressure from the Kennedy administration. Their tone was both technocratic and populist, dictatorial and democratic. In part, too, the White Revolution was pure demagoguery, and its achievements often bore little resemblance to the exaggerated claims made for them. Yet, as in the industrialization program, there can be no doubt that Iranian society witnessed major changes, many of them positive. School enrollments and health facilities expanded impressively. Literacy among young people increased, although the overall literacy rate remained rather low (estimated 37 percent in 1972).[39] Women entered the universities and professions in unprecedented numbers, partly because of the labor shortage, but also because of government efforts to incorporate them despite opposition from some sectors of the clergy. Whatever one may think of the methods of change, it was clear that many Iranians were being prepared for new roles in a more modern economy and society.

The cult of modernity also had its drawbacks, which could be observed in all their clarity in the realm of culture. All non-Western societies have confronted the imposing challenge of Western culture, with its clear superiority in technical and scientific knowledge and its capacity to project its high and mass culture throughout the world. Many intellectuals both within and outside the West have raised the question of whether greater Western mastery of the material world does not somehow correspond to some deeper cultural or religious wisdom; or at the least they have wondered whether modern technological society does not require some version of Western culture to support it. In Russia rulers like Peter and Catherine had attempted to adopt many Western cultural patterns, and throughout the Petersburg period a significant portion of the Russian intelligentsia was committed to the cultural Westernization of the country. However, the last tsars were quite passive, if not reactionary, in this respect, following the designs of Pobedonostsev to restore the most conservative ideals of the Russian autocracy. Despite government indifference or even hostility, however, imperial Russia in its last decades witnessed an indigenous modernist cultural outpouring, the sign of a flourishing elite culture as well as of a deep division between the educated classes and the masses.

[39] F. Aminzadeh, "Human Resources Development: Problems and Prospects," in *Iran: Past, Present and Future*, ed. Jane Jacqz (New York: Aspen Institute, 1976), 189. Katouzian presents his usual bleak picture of the attainments of the regime in education in *Political Economy*, 286–90.

The rapid modernization of Iran and the enormous Western cultural influence posed the question of the meaning and vitality of Iranian national culture in an especially dramatic way. The government itself took a much more active role in cultural change than had been the case in Russia, eventually having to assume the blame for the ill effects of what came to be called in many circles "Occidentosis," a term coined by the writer Al-e Ahmad. But the regime was not committed to cultural Westernization in any simple sense. Certainly the shah's modernization program led him to attack much of the Shiʿite heritage as black reaction and to undermine the influence of Islam in education, law, and economic life. Yet he did not proclaim the superiority of Western culture in principle. Rather, he claimed allegiance to Shiʿite Islam while seeking a return to pre-Islamic cultural values of ancient Persia, primarily those connected with national greatness and political absolutism. In theory, the past wonders of Iranian culture were to be synthesized with the requirements of a modern industrial society to create a uniquely great civilization.

In practice there is every reason to suppose that the new cultural synthesis not only failed to emerge, but also that the grandiose claims only reinforced the general sense of the regime's hypocrisy. For while the regime talked of the past, it silenced contemporary cultural expressions, creating what two authors called "an incredible cultural impoverishment."[40] Major Iranian writers were censored or prohibited; the national cinema withered, largely replaced by anodyne foreign imports; and the number of book titles published actually shrunk in absolute terms, to a number significantly smaller than that in Turkey or Egypt.[41] Meanwhile, Iranian culture, especially classical Iranian culture, was propagandistically promoted abroad and modern Western culture, often of an avant-garde persuasion, was ostentatiously imported into Iran. The Shiraz arts festivals, Teheran film festivals, and the newly built museum of modern art in Teheran (inaugurated in 1977) were showcases for Western culture, not in any sense expressions of national achievements, and, apart from the enthusiasts in the new middle class and the cosmopolitan elite, the borrowings often alienated or shocked Iranians, especially those of more traditional inspiration.

An ex-minister of the shah, Houchang Nahavandi, concluded in retrospect that under the shah the promotion and development of culture was remarkable, and that Iran was "in all respects at the forefront of cultural progress among the developing nations."[42] Yet the examples he gives are either quantitative (how many theater troupes) or dubious expressions of national cultural achievements (opera companies, symphony orchestras,

[40] Balta and Rulleau, *L'Iran insurgé*, 254.

[41] Graham, *Illusion of Power*, 203.

[42] Houchang Nahavandi, *Iran. Anatomie d'une revolution* (Paris: S.E.G.E.P., 1983), 58; also, see his discussion on 57–58.

museums of modern art). The popular perception of the regime's cultural policy can doubtlessly better be gauged by the title of Al-e Ahmad's enormously influential book, *Occidentosis*. Clearly, large segments of Iranian society became convinced that their country was becoming culturally Westernized by force, and for this they blamed the shah. SAVAK repression of national culture and, even more ferociously, of the cultures of the non-Persian minorities, as well as the regime's enthusiastic embrace of Western imports made a mockery of its pretensions. In the words of an important Iranian writer, "The shah's alienation from both the East and the West became the dominant pattern of the culture of his reign. If there is something called colonial culture in Iran, it is the Shah who is responsible for it."[43]

The sterile claim to promote a new cultural synthesis, which could not mask the reality of repression and cultural dependency, exemplified the regime's hubris. Whatever was lacking, whatever was desirable, could be supplied or manufactured from above. Just as the regime's voluntarism extended into the realm of culture, where its claims lacked credibility, so it also led to a comic-opera experiment in political modernization, perhaps the most absurd expression of the regime's conviction that it could get away with anything. For it should have been obvious that if there is anything an autocratic regime cannot do, it cannot sponsor and initiate authentic popular participation. Yet in the early 1970s a number of American-trained social scientists, citing Karl Deutsch, Samuel Huntington, and David Apter (not, like the mid-nineteenth-century Russian reformers, Alexis de Tocqueville), came to the realization that political participation was a necessary component of modernization, and that Iran was sadly deficient in popular political enthusiasm and initiative. But perhaps the deputy minister of interior and a professor of political science at the National University can better explain the dilemma:

> In order to increase the level of performance with respect to rising expectations, the Iranian political system requires increasingly greater supportive capacity. Polity capacity does not only mean greater bureaucratic and technological efficiency. Rather, we are referring to a special capacity of the socioeconomic and political infrastructure to respond, innovate and adapt to a wide range of demands. In short, society must develop the machinery to manage continuous change. Perhaps the key point about the special capacity required here is the advantage of a political culture of participation. Through the institutionalization of political participation, the new elite is in a position to significantly increase its legitimacy and thereby increase polity capacity. In fact, it is the new elite in var-

[43] Reza Baraheni, *The Crowned Cannibals* (New York: Vintage, 1977), 108.

ious ministries, government organizations, and the Rastakhiz-e-Mellat-e-Iran that are trying to implement the plans for participation and decentralization.[44]

One wonders what this passage would sound like in Farsi, or, indeed, whether it could be translated at all.

The regime's attempt to create a mobilizational one-party system on the basis of these ideas will be discussed briefly in later chapters. Here it will suffice to point out, first, that once again the shah's regime sought to impose a much more far-reaching model of modernization on the Iranian people than anything attempted by the last tsars. Lacking the necessary historical models and not swayed by grandiose dreams, Nicholas II never conceived of an official one-party system or of any other form of government-sponsored mass mobilization. The closest parallel, the Zubatov experiment, ranks as a schoolyard exercise by comparison. Second, the experiment in political modernization was an unqualified and embarrassing failure, as even the shah himself recognized. The Iranian people greeted the invitation, or order, to participate with the cynicism it deserved, as well as with fear. The discrepancy between promises and reality and, perhaps even more, the clear evidence of a fundamental lack of sound judgment could not but weaken the prestige and legitimacy of the regime.

In conclusion, historical judgments on both regimes should recognize their ambiguous successes in the modernization of their societies. That there was "progress" in many areas of the nations' life—in industry, education, the growth of cities—is undeniable. In both countries, much of this transformation was clearly stimulated or directed by the state. Yet aside from the obvious questions of whether the changes were positive and, if so, whether they might have been accomplished more efficiently or humanely, two serious sets of reservations about the process of autocratic modernization necessarily arise. The first cluster concerns the coherence, efficacy, consistency, and ultimately the justice of the governments' efforts to modernize society. The second set centers around the disarticulation of society produced by the hasty and often coercive drives to modernization. As we shall see shortly, both political incoherence and social disorientation reflected back on the regimes, whose claims to superior wisdom and monopolization of political initiative compelled them to bear the costs of all failures. The pattern of state action and the incoherence of society characteristic of autocratic modernization made both societies unusually vulnerable to the threat of revolution.

[44] Amin Alimard and Cyrus Elahi, "Modernization and Changing Leadership in Iran," in Jacqz, *Iran: Past, Present, and Future*, 223. See this article and the equally astonishing following two articles by other government technocrats and bureaucrats for insights into the regime's strategy of political modernization. Here we are truly in a "through the looking-glass" world.

Four

Dilemmas of Autocratic Modernization

A COMPARATIVE STUDY of two revolutions, it was claimed in the introduction, can move back and forth between historical particularities of the cases and more general analyses. So far the emphasis has clearly been on the historical contrasts, as I have sketched out fundamental differences in historical backgrounds, the nature of the two autocracies, and the modernization processes sponsored by the regimes. With the present chapter the discussion moves to a more abstract level, presenting the core of the argument about the shared traits of the two experiments in autocratic modernization. The general implications of this specific route to the modern world for the regimes and the societies will be spelled out, thus clarifying the unusual vulnerability of this pattern to social revolution.

Not all of these dilemmas are unique to autocratic modernization. Many of them emerge, in one form or another, in all modernizing dictatorships; others are probably inherent in the very process of modernization itself. I do contend, however, that this route holds more perils for social and political elites than do the alternatives discussed in the introduction.

Some examples and evidence will be presented here in order to clarify the propositions. However, this chapter is primarily analytical, and so set out rather abstractly. The following three chapters—on urban affairs, rural patterns, and the cultures of revolt—will return to the level of historical comparison, thus supporting and specifying the more general points argued here.

The Inherent Limitations of Autocratic Government

The impotence of the despot was a classical theme of the Enlightenment. Thinkers and men of affairs like Montesquieu, Condillac, and Turgot emphasized the dependence of the autocratic ruler on his staff and the stubborn resistance of subjects compelled to act without their consent. They concluded that rulers must be "enlightened" for their will to resonate with the purposes of others and so be translated into effective policy.[1] Either the ruler recognized the limits to his own power and acted appropriately, or

[1] Leonard Krieger, *An Essay on the Theory of Enlightened Despotism* (Chicago: University of Chicago Press, 1975), 37–39.

his power would be limited by the tacit or active resistance of others. The wise absolute ruler issued commands in accordance with law, custom, and social opinion. By contrast, absolute rule without regard to tradition, what Weber would later call "sultanism," is in their view self-limiting and self-defeating. The sultanisms of Nicholas II and Muhammad Reza Shah introduced a further political dilemma into absolute rule: through their sponsorship of social modernization they undermined the traditional rationale upon which autocratic rule was based and created a hybrid social and political model satisfying neither conservatives nor modernizers.

This contradiction between the principle of autocracy and the actual place of the monarch in modern life could be clearly seen on the symbolic level. Nicholas II, retrenching himself in a renewed Muscovite ethos, regarded himself as a traditional patriarch in direct communication with his people, and he attempted to invest himself with the sanctity of the Muscovite tsars. Yet his return to Muscovite political symbols and attempts to associate himself with Moscow rather than Petersburg added up to very little in modernizing Russia. His government was highly bureaucratic and, like it or not, his subjects included an intelligentsia and incipient modern social classes rooted in a capitalist economy, and not merely estates ranked by a patriarchal regime.

The events surrounding the massacre of 9 January 1905, remembered in history as Bloody Sunday, testify to the hollowness of the tsar's patriarchal poses and to the confusion it brought into being in the minds of the workers. The idea of a march to the Winter Palace to present the workers' demands to the tsar had originated among the leadership of the Gapon societies, a movement that had emerged from police sponsorship of religious and cultural activities to become increasingly class-oriented and political. Nonetheless, the workers (from fifty to sixty thousand strong) who marched to deliver the petition to the tsar surely regarded themselves as loyal subjects presenting legitimate grievances to their protector. However, their "little father" did not even bother to be present at the palace, much less receive the workers either in person or through a high official. If the workers had been indulged, even if nothing had been granted, it is almost certain that bloodshed would have been avoided.[2] As it was, the workers were stunned to be met by gunfire, resulting in numerous deaths and serious injuries. This, for many, was the demise of the image of the tsar as patriarch of his people. Nicholas's response to the tragedy also speaks volumes. Two days later, at the urging of the governor general of St. Petersburg, he received a hand-picked delegation of workers, justifying the bloodshed through references to the malign influence of traitors to the

[2] Abraham Ascher, *The Revolution of 1905* (Stanford, Calif.: Stanford University Press, 1988), 92.

country. Nonetheless, he assured them that he believed "in the integrity of the workers and in their unflagging devotion to me, and therefore I forgive them."[3] Nicholas had apparently forgotten that patriarchal relations implied some form of mutuality.

The shah's claims to patriarchal guidance of his people were equally difficult to adjust to his actual role in political life. First, like Nicholas, he isolated himself from his people, abandoning the old palace in the city for a new fortresslike complex in the Elburz foothills.[4] He seldom made public appearances, withdrew from any routine contact with the populace, and traveled throughout the city by helicopter. Although he cast various of his policies, such as the land reform and the profit-sharing program for workers, in the rhetoric of autocratic paternalism, this style resonated poorly with his ice-cold demeanor, his frequent expressions of contempt for his own people, and his regime's ruthless use of political violence. Further, his outlandish manipulation of the symbols of Iranian monarchy, culminating in the infamous celebration of twenty-five hundred years of Persian kingship, probably bred more cynicism than awe. How powerfully this ceremony evoked the spirits of the past for many Iranians can be inferred from this account by a dissident writer:

> We watch the event on television. The Shah is the master of ceremonies. He walks to Passargadi where the tomb of King Cyrus is located. The celebrities follow him at some distance. We hear the Shah's weak and childish voice: "Cyrus! You rest in peace, I am awake!" When the Shah speaks in this ludicrous manner, Agnew touches his nose and the king of Denmark squints his eyes as if to say: "Adieu, adieu; remember me, I've sworn it." Dust rises from the wind in the desert, disturbing the eyes of the rulers of this world. Several delicate princesses cough into their handkerchiefs. A storm may rise and cleanse the surface of the earth from these rulers who have shown they are the representatives of the thieves of the world or will be so later. I can easily imagine the wind lifting the frail Haile Selassie on its wings, his black chihuahua chasing him, Spiro Agnew trailing behind. The masters and mistresses of the world leave this part of the desert for the slopes of Persepolis and an encampment of luxurious tents—all made in Europe and flown along with a thousand other items via Teheran and Shiraz to Persepolis.[5]

This superb passage, with its pointed contrasts between the shah's grandiose pretensions and his diminished presence, and between the pseudonationalist rhetoric and the foreign audience and provenance of the event,

[3] Quoted in ibid., 97.

[4] Gerard de Villiers, *The Imperial Shah* (Boston: Little, Brown and Company, 1976), 265.

[5] Reza Baraheni, *The Crowned Cannibals*, 100–1.

underscores the emptiness of traditional monarchical symbolism in the Iran of oil and SAVAK.[6]

In both Russia and Iran the tensions of modernizing autocracy also found expression in a general uncertainty about the overall goals and direction of change. Many adhered to a neotraditionalist vision opposed to an independent civil society. They played upon the ancient themes of the ruler as benefactor and as guardian of order. For Russian conservatives, society had no principle of cohesion other than the autocracy, the very foundation of social relations; private initiative and democracy produced the rule of the strong over the weak and anarchy. Better that order and progress be the responsibility of the autocratic ruler. Iranian apologists for autocracy, including the shah himself, were more likely to accept the desirability of democracy in principle but to plead that the Iranian people lacked maturity and must be tutored like children in political affairs. This argument was endorsed by many American advisors and officials so they could reconcile themselves to U.S. support for a blatantly nondemocratic regime.[7]

In both countries, however, this traditionalist perspective had to confront aspects of a more liberal view, expressed even within the governments. Indeed, the very same official could embrace liberal ideas at variance with his own deeply held autocratic beliefs. Sergei Witte, who combined a deep commitment to the Russian monarchical world view with a belief in private initiative, exemplifies how this tension could play itself out within the same individual. More generally, in both regimes, some government officials favored the development of a more autonomous civil society with its own mechanisms of self-regulation. Referring to the successes of Western society, they agreed that excessive government tutelage hindered social and economic progress by crippling individual initiative and inhibiting contract and the development of trust among social groups and between them and the government. Modern society, they argued, should be based not on authority and coercion but on consent and the free flow of information.[8] These views did not add up to an appeal for democracy, because

[6] This is not to deny that the shah's ceremony and pretenses may have been convincing to many Iranians, even if such people were not in evidence by late 1978.

[7] An instructive example of this attitude is the following statement by an O.S.S. advisor at the end of the war: "Iran, like a small child, needs a strong governing hand until education has done its work, political consciousness has developed, and a group of properly trained public officials has been established." Quoted in Habib Ladjevardi, "The Origins of U.S. Support for an Autocratic Shah," *International Journal of Middle Eastern Studies* 15 (1983): 225–39.

[8] In Russia many of these ideas were most fully worked out in the Ministry of Finance in the period around 1905. A good source for the imprint of liberal ideas on Iranian officials is the set of previously cited articles in Jacqz, *Iran: Past, Present, and Future*. For example, M. Bagher Namazi, undersecretary of state for regional affairs in the Plan and Budget Orga-

a more autonomous civil society was held, rightly or wrongly, to be consistent with autocracy; but they did conflict with the rival view that the regime should superintend social life in all its dimensions.

These contrasting images—for it would be too much to call them ideologies, for different elements of each could be combined in unpredictable ways—played themselves out in political life, generating conflicts and abrupt changes of direction in public affairs. Institutions became subject to debate and open to contrasting interpretations; they lost any clear-cut meaning in the political struggle over their significance. In Russia, for example, what was law? Many traditionalists opposed it without qualification for the limits it set upon autocratic rule and for its enshrinement of procedure over substantive justice. For some conservatives it was a mechanism for ordering the administration and the estate society according to the wishes of the sovereign—in this view law meant bureaucratic positive law. For those of a more liberal persuasion, law should recognize and define the rights of individuals and different social groups in order to allow them to act independently within a defined framework.[9]

Nor was there consensus on the significance and desirability of the peasant commune. Conservatives favored the preservation of the commune because they saw it as the foundation of a traditional social order in the country and the guarantee of stability. In addition, they believed that the practice of repartition ensured a minimal standard of living for everyone, thus securing a degree of social justice. By contrast, reformers believed that private property and independent peasant households should be encouraged in order to maximize initiative and efficiency.[10]

Debates over labor organizations were equally intense. Many conservatives adhered to the traditional view that independent organizations threatened social peace and the integrity of the divinely inspired social order headed by the tsar. Other conservatives, including Minister of Interior V. K. Plehve, favored them as a means for organizing and disciplining the workers: "the power of the strong military leader completely depends on the organization of his soldiers. . . . Thus, in essence, I cannot react negatively to the thought of representation."[11] From a different perspective, many officials in the Ministry of Finance advocated independent trade

---

nization, criticized the hypercentralization of decisionmaking in Teheran and advocated the formation of democratically elected bodies to decentralize power and make it more responsive to the public will. "Iranian Approaches to Decentralization," 243–45.

[9] For examples of these views, see McDaniel, *Autocracy, Capitalism, and Revolution in Russia*, 92–93.

[10] For a summary of these views, which are more complex than I have indicated, see Geoffrey Hosking, *The Russian Constitutional Experiment* (Cambridge: Cambridge University Press, 1973), 57–60.

[11] Central state historical archive, Leningrad, f. 1153, g. 1903, op. 1, d. 153, ll. 97–98.

unions as a way of ensuring a balance of power between workers and industrialists and encouraging worker moderation. Perhaps most telling of all was the conflict over the meaning of the Duma. After Nicholas II was forced to accept its existence, he chose to interpret it as an advisory body not fundamentally limiting the autocratic will. For reformers, the Duma was a representative body with political rights in a constitutional monarchy.

These conflicting views were not the accidental product of individual personalities or circumstances. The different positions in the debates reflected in one way or another the dilemmas and alternatives inherent in autocratic modernization. The overall tensions in this project could not but be reflected in the perspectives and programs of the different actors. Their conflicts, in turn, had enormous political consequences. In many areas, most notably labor policy, the Russian government was simply immobilized, unable to chart new policies capable of dealing with the social and political issues that had emerged with industrialization. In addition, even when the government did act, its policies were often unclear or indecisive, subject to changes of interpretation or reversals of policy. The promises of the October Manifesto could be reinterpreted after the defeat of the revolution; the legalization of trade unions could be construed narrowly as authorization of purely economic organizations without ideological or political goals. Although to one party these revisions may have been legitimate reinterpretation in accord with the authentic spirit of Russian political life, to the other they were both hypocritical and the betrayal of a commitment. In this process of polarization, social life lost its aura of givenness, institutions their penumbra of permanence. Little could be counted on for either side, as the most fundamental questions could never be finally resolved.

In Iran it is more difficult to identify the inner tensions in the regime wrought by the combination of autocracy and rapid modernization. The policy process was much less fixed and coherent than in Russia. Stable bureaucratic points of view and interests could hardly be articulated, and even more than in Russia key social groups had little opportunity to press their claims on the regime in an organized and consistent fashion. Far more than in Russia the meaning of policies and institutions is elusive, based not on shared rules and understandings but on the changeable and often shadowy will of the ruler. One can nonetheless identify incongruities arising from the overall pattern of social change parallel to those found in Russia. For example, in the land reform, which was the central issue of Iranian domestic politics in the 1960s, one finds an admixture of discrepant logics. The desire to neutralize the landed elite as a potential source of opposition can be read as a classic tactic of autocratic regimes, ever jealous of any possible elite independence. From this logic, too, flowed the luxuriant populist rhetoric about the close and direct bonds between the ruler and his people, unmediated by the corrupt elites. The reform, then, was not intended as a purely rational response to economic challenges, but also an expression of the reaffirmation of an age-old political model. In his address to a national congress of rural cooperatives in January 1963, the shah declared:

> By virtue of my responsibilities as Shah and those [vows] I took to protect the rights and honour of the Iranian nation, I cannot remain a neutral onlooker in the struggle against the forces of evil, but have taken up the banner myself. So that no power can reinstate the regime of slavery among the villages and plunder the nation's wealth for the benefit of a minority, I have decided, as executive, legislative and judicial head of the state to refer these reforms to a referendum.[12]

Casting himself as the representative of good, the shah claimed to stand for "class equilibrium" and the "equal distribution of wealth."[13] The myth continues:

> The Congress was to be a constituent assembly of the people with the Shah presiding over it. Four thousand peasants, elected by villages all over Iran, had come to attend the Congress as its delegates. They saw their king for the first time, without guards and attendants, far from the conservative minority, sitting under the same roof with them. The delegates found their king to be their leader. Their joy at this turn in their fate was equalled only by their sense of loyalty to him. . . . Confident and happy under the Shah's leadership, they eagerly awaited his call.[14]

Yet this very congress showed that the shah had no monopoly on the interpretation of the land reform. It was organized by Minister of Agriculture Hassan Arsanjani, who in fact had been the major architect of the 1962 land reform law. Arsanjani was already well known for his adherence to rather vaguely defined socialist ideas and his commitment to agrarian reform in his writings of the late 1940s and early 1950s. If the shah temporarily sided with him for purposes of his own, it is nonetheless true that Arsanjani and his officials were able to give the land reform an authentically popular tone for a time. Indeed, it was the threat of popular mobilization, as well as the swelling popularity of Arsanjani among the peasantry, that prompted the shah to dismiss him from his post. In later years yet another dimension was added to the land reform as economists and agronomists sought to create a large-scale mechanized agriculture and rural settlement patterns somewhat reminiscent of Nikita Khrushchev's ill-fated proposals for agrocities in the Soviet Union. The outcome of these latter proposals

[12] Quoted in Ramesh Sanghvi, *Aryamehr: The Shah of Iran* (London: Macmillan, 1969), 283; the quotation is from the shah's book *The White Revolution*. Sanghvi's work is mainly valuable for the compilation of many of the shah's statements.

[13] Quoted in ibid., 280.

[14] In the account of Sanghvi, in ibid., 281–82.

will be described in chapter six, on rural affairs. For present purposes, it is sufficient to note that the addition of this state capitalist market logic further confused the issue. After all this, what was the agrarian reform and what was rural Iran supposed to become? The mixture of logics and visions, rooted in the incoherence of the overall model of change, created conflicting policies and made all rural social patterns contingent, lacking a sense of permanency.

An equally striking expression of the fundamental political contradictions of the regime was the antiprofiteering campaign of 1975–1976. In the context of the high inflation and economic bottlenecks brought on by the increase in oil prices, the regime once again began to speak of the small minority of exploiters, this time in the guise of "industrial feudalism." Once again, the shah resolved to solve all class contradictions in Iran, claiming special solicitude for his loyal subjects, the downtrodden workers, with whom he shared the closest of bonds. The earnest of the autocrat's commitment to his people was a campaign against merchants and industrialists who charged unreasonable prices and earned excessive profits. The government fixed prices, closed shops, and even arrested a number of prominent figures. Yet the logic of the autocrat as protector of the poor clearly contradicted the shah's and the regime's basic strategy of capitalist industrialization based on private industry. The minister of the interior, Hushang Ansari, a businessman himself, led a wing of the nominal one-party system in opposition to the populist strategy. By 1977, due to a severe flight of capital and a lack of willingness to invest, which exacerbated the economic problems, the shah changed cabinets and economic strategies, moving toward the protection of private property once again.[15] Given these contradictory logics, what constancy and predictability could there be in government policy? Indeed, the very concept *policy* seems inappropriate as a label for this conflicting welter of motives and purposes.

In both Russia and Iran, then, the very project of autocratic modernization generated deep conflicts of purpose and interpretation within the regimes. The pressures stemming from the imperatives of a modern industrial society clashed with the logic of the autocratic assertion of power. The odd assortments of top officials in both regimes bear witness to the seriousness of these tensions. In Russia the most powerful ministers in the last decades of tsarist rule included the reactionary Plehve, the more conciliatory Sviatopolk-Mirskii, and the enigmatic Witte, torn between his devotion to the principle of autocracy and his commitment to the modernization of Russia. Nicholas II was compelled to appoint Witte head of the government entrusted with the creation of a constitutional regime despite

[15] For a brief account, see Hossein Bashiriyeh, *The State and Revolution in Iran* (London: Croom Helm, 1984), 93–104.

his reported distaste for the count. In Iran, an equally odd assortment of former oppositionists, such as Amini and Arsanjani, occupied key posts, together with Western-trained technocrats with little conception of the political implications of their programs. (The political scientists seemed particularly otherworldly.) The shah himself also seemed to be genuinely divided: although he violated both the letter and the spirit of the constitution, in late 1978, when his regime was in peril but might have been salvaged through a display of force, the shah rejected the hard-line military option with the objection: "This is against the constitution." He reportedly believed that a king could not massacre his own people as a dictator could, and therefore refused to sanction the bloodshed that others were willing to tolerate.[16] How much of the shah's rhetoric about constitutional monarchy and the paternal responsibilities of the king was authentic, how much a pose?

Such ambiguities were rooted in the very model of change, giving to policies and institutions their note of contingency and impermanence. The lack of stability and the changes in basic direction that resulted led many to charge the rulers with hypocrisy. The Russian law legalizing trade unions had been used to repress trade unions, it was charged. The Rastakhiz party's experiment in mobilization appeared to be nothing more than a more sophisticated set of controls. But in a regime so divided and beset by fundamental contradictions it is difficult to distinguish between hypocrisy and incoherence. In a political sense the distinction was of little significance, for in both cases it could justly be concluded that the regime was not to be trusted.

It is a defensible thesis that all societies have their internal contradictions. Marx, Schumpeter, and numerous recent theorists of the capitalist state have identified tensions between the ideological presuppositions of capitalist democracies and their institutional realities; between the social framework required by capitalism and capitalism's corrosive effect upon it; between the imperatives of "legitimation" and "accumulation." Similarly, in modernizing military dictatorships in Latin America economic and political contradictions surfaced between the requirements of nationalist development policies and the advantages of foreign economic ties, deeply dividing the military rulers and threatening the integrity of the armed forces.

The dilemmas inherent in autocratic modernization, however, were sharper than in other cases precisely because of the incompatibility of arbitrary, personal rule and modern institutions. First, autocracy undercuts the predictability born of laws and stable institutions fundamental to a

[16] William Shawcross, *The Shah's Last Ride* (New York: Simon and Schuster, 1988), 22, 24.

modern society, and this key weakness of the political model inevitably divided the regimes and weakened their ability to change society. In Russia, divisions within the government tended to lead to paralysis; in the labor question, for example, fifteen years of intensive effort yielded virtually no government measures to soften labor conflict. In Iran the relative weakness of bureaucratic institutions, especially the ministries, shifted the dilemma onto another plane—not so much bureaucratic paralysis, as shifting rhetoric and plainly contradictory policies rooted in a more voluntaristic autocracy.

Second, autocracy ruled out the resolution of these conflicts in any permanent way. In political systems in which interests and institutions have a fixed weight, political conflicts can lead to decisions enacted in law that are binding upon the actors involved, including the machinery of state. Administration can be influenced and decisions can be modified through further political conflict, but decisions nevertheless have objective significance and imply predictable patterns of action, whether in the form of government policies or social reactions to them. In autocratic systems, laws and policies have no such significance, for any compromise is contingent upon the will of the ruler. Compromise, therefore, has no real significance, and conflicts within the government cannot be resolved in any fixed and satisfactory way. All autocracies face this limitation, but in relatively stable societies neither the pressures for change nor the policy conflicts are so acute. Modernizing autocracies are especially prone, therefore, to irremediable conflict and decay within the regimes themselves.

These contradictions of policy were reflected in and even exacerbated by the administrative process, which had no fixed integrity to insulate it from political struggles. The classical distinction between politics and administration could not be maintained in a system without stable law and independent institutions. Administration could not simply be the enactment of previously determined policies, for the administrative apparatus reflected the higher level conflicts and also provided none of its own mechanisms for resolving them. In Russia the dilemmas of autocratic administration are well illustrated in the domain of labor policy. First, the policy itself was inconsistent and unclear. The two most powerful ministries, those of Interior and Finance, tended to defend competing principles in industrial relations—government tutelage and freedom of contract respectively. Further, each ministry had its own corpus of officials active in factory affairs, local and factory police employed by Interior, factory inspectors under Finance. In the absence of clearly defined laws, both sets of officials were free to enunciate their own norms, which at the local level were frequently in conflict with each other. Police officials often criticized the factory owners' exploitation of their workers, at times threatening to fine the owners or close the factories until justice was done. The idea of police-controlled worker organizations to counter the "impudent bourgeoisie" (in Zubatov's phrase) took the Ministry of Interior's protectionist outlook to an extreme. By contrast, the factory inspectors frequently criticized police interference in industrial relations and appealed to the market, and occasionally to the logic of the balance of opposed social forces, to resolve disagreements. The weakness of administrative law and the lack of accountability of all officials to an organized public permitted these conflicts to rage unresolved throughout the last two decades of tsarist rule. In this context, administrative policy was necessarily inconsistent and unpredictable, further exacerbating the larger political conflicts. Workers came to believe that the government was unwilling or unable to honor its word. Some may even have suspected that it could not even develop a consistent enough policy to give meaning to the idea of stable commitments.

We do not, to my knowledge, have the kind of detailed studies of the Iranian bureaucracy and its administrative functioning that exists for Russia. Yet with the plethora of overlapping agencies one expects that the most salient political conflicts penetrated throughout the administrative apparatus. The pronounced personalism of the Iranian bureaucracy, much more conspicuous than in Russia, surely served to heighten bureaucratic incoherence. It has also been suggested that rentier states—states that do not have to rely extensively on domestic taxation because of external financial resources, such as revenues generated by oil—are not under the same kind of pressure to develop an orderly and efficient bureaucracy.[17] The independence of the state apparatus from the local elite would also encourage the arbitrariness and high-handedness often ascribed to Iranian officials.

Some of these phenomena were clearly visible in the Iranian land reform. The first stage of the land reform, which lasted until mid-1964 when new regulations were passed by the Majlis, favored the peasantry, especially in its encouragement of individual peasant ownership and the formation of cooperatives. Even in this early period, however, the land-reform officials' success depended to a large extent on the convictions of the local officials, whether they personally favored land reform or not. Consequently, the success of the program varied widely by region, with the greatest successes registered in the North and Northwest.[18] In subsequent stages the government's commitment to the development of an independent peasantry weakened in favor of the presumed advantages of large-scale commercial farming. Administrative reorganizations undermined the original land reform agencies and conflicts developed between the Central Organization

[17] Hossein Mahdavy, "Patterns and Problems of Economic Development in Rentier States: The Case of Iran," in *Studies in the Economic History of the Middle East*, ed. M. A. Cook (London: Oxford University Press, 1970), 466–67.

[18] Ann Lambton, *Persian Land Reform 1962–1966* (Oxford: Clarendon Press, 1969), 124.

for Rural Cooperation, in charge of organizing the cooperatives, and a number of other government departments, often manned by Western-educated technocrats who favored massive private investments in agriculture.[19] One can easily imagine the administrative conflicts, the reversals of grass-roots policies, and the peasants' skepticism about the intentions of the government. One also begins to understand why the agrarian reform had so little success in its proclaimed aim of modernizing Iranian agriculture.

The capacity of the autocracy to reshape society was thus partly limited by the inner political and administrative dilemmas posed by the very project of autocratic modernization. To these contradictions derived from the nature of autocratic rule was added a further paradox stemming from the imperatives of modernization: this latter process requires the active participation of society and the forging of new links between state and society, but political autocracy inhibits independent social initiative and creates a nearly unbridgeable gap between state and society. This dilemma is clearly visible in the weaknesses of social organization in a modernizing autocracy. European history offers two models of social organization and corresponding modes of connection between state and society. The first type, which might be termed status-based organization, has been masterfully sketched in classical social theory: society is hierarchically organized in organizations with unequal and prescribed rights and duties. As Tocqueville has shown, this model of organization embodies both hierarchy and participation, for even the subordinate ranks have a voice in matters concerning them. Hierarchical status-based organization is one mode of linking state and society as well as elites and lower orders. It ensures that authority and decisions can reverberate throughout the social system and also that feedback from below can find expression. We recall that Catherine the Great favored the formation of this kind of hierarchical society to resolve the dilemmas of autocracy in eighteenth-century Russia.

The alternative form of organization may be termed, adapting the usage of Reinhard Bendix, *plebiscitary*.[20] Plebiscitary organization is premised on individual rights, not corporate membership, and it presumes a direct relationship between the state and the individual relatively undiluted by the inequalities of corporate group membership. In the French Revolution, we recall, there were calls to limit all forms of organization that would mediate between the individual and the state. Because all organizations do this, and because they could hardly all be eliminated, such proposals were utopian.

[19] Ibid., 280–82, 345, 355.

[20] See Reinhard Bendix, *Nation-Building and Citizenship* (Berkeley: University of California Press, 1977).

Instead, new types of organizations emerged—political parties, interest groups, trade unions—based on more egalitarian and individualistic principles even as they embodied functional differences in modern society. For present purposes, what is important is that these organizations entailed new forms of participation and new ways of linking state and society. Coordination and feedback were made compatible with each other, as the strictly defined rights of state and social organizations, of leaders and rank-and-file members, ensured a degree of both authority and participation. State policies emerged as the result of a political process involving society, and they were enacted through and by means of social organizations as well as through government administration.

In crucial respects, state-society relations in Russia and Iran departed from both these models. Indeed, they resembled the intermediary stage between aristocratic and democratic societies analyzed by Tocqueville—that stage, he argues, that gave birth to the revolution. In neither country was there, or ever had there been, a network of status-based organizations to link state and society, elites and masses. Naturally, the autocratic state was unwilling to permit the kind of plebiscitarian organizations that might have fulfilled a parallel function in the context of modern institutions. As a result, the state was suspended in a void, unable to count on an organized society for cooperation with its plans. The weakness of society in an autocratic system thus, in its own way, weakened the state as well. Its policies could not resonate through society; it could not benefit from the feedback essential for sound policy making and administration. In a modern society, the social base must be not only the object but also the subject of change.

In the abstract, another model of linking state and society was available: the radical plebiscitary principle of the one-party state. Minister of the Interior Plehve's references to the model of society as an army and the Iranian theorists' invocation of the mobilizational one-party state indicate that such ideas had their appeal, but they were clearly incompatible with the survival of traditional autocracy and with the demands of capitalist modernization. In Russia the state made no serious attempts to mobilize the population on plebiscitarian principles; in Iran the brief experiment of a one-party state to lead and penetrate society quickly turned into a fiasco. Both states remained quite limited in their capacities to penetrate and also learn from, and thus modernize, their societies. As for the governments, so for the rulers themselves: Nicholas II and Muhammad Reza Shah had little appreciation of the nature of their societies or the aspirations of their people. Insulated by the court, and able to ensure that they heard only what they wanted to hear, they nurtured illusions that blinded them to the fundamental political challenges facing their regimes.

The Weakness of Society

The weakness of society in an autocratic regime is not nearly as paradoxical as the weakness of the state. It is really the corollary of the state's attempt to concentrate all initiative and power of decision in itself. Unsurprising as our conclusions may be, it is yet essential to review some of the ways in which the state debilitated society, thus hampering its own modernization program and depriving itself of any significant bulwark of social support.

The crippling of society by the state is perhaps most clearly visible in the position of social elites in both modernizing autocracies. A distinguishing feature of autocratic modernization, as compared to other patterns of development, is the political frailty of both traditional and modern social elites. Even if we consider only those countries with a strong state role in industrialization, such as Germany, Japan, or contemporary Brazil, we note that neither the agrarian elites nor the nascent industrialist classes were so controlled by the government or so weakened in their capacity for social leadership as in Russia and Iran. These, indeed, were the two key dimensions of the social elites' debility in the latter countries—their dependence on an often-unreliable state for their welfare and their lack of leadership over other social groups.

The decline of the Russian landed nobility in the face of state-induced social modernization is one of the fundamental themes of Russian history after the period of the great reforms. The greatest blow was undoubtedly the emancipation of the serfs, to which was added the almost equally traumatic effect of the government's industrialization program later in the century. Numerous tsarist reformers also offered proposals to replace the provincial gentry by government officials in local affairs, somewhat along the lines of the French pattern of monarchical centralization. Although these reforms were by and large resisted, that they were seriously proposed already indicated the overall decline of the gentry in Russian society. The roots of this decline were socioeconomic, as the nobility proved generally incapable of adapting to the economic modernization of the country. Corresponding to their economic decline was a dramatic reduction in numbers, as more and more sold their ailing estates in order to enter securer areas of activity, such as industry or the professions.

In a significant sense, of course, the Russian landed nobility had always been weak when compared with the established aristocracies in other countries because its political and social independence had been sacrificed in the formation of the service state. Ironically, it was precisely this historical weakness that allowed them to salvage a degree of legitimacy in modernizing Russia, for it allowed them to claim privileged status as the social foundation of the tsarist state, thus returning to the archaic political model of the Petrine state. Nicholas II, with his own archaic ideological vision and his tenuous legitimacy among other segments of society, did not hesitate to embrace their claims, partly supporting them through economic subsidies, but even more by affirming their special political preeminence in the affairs of the empire. This political alliance between the regime and the landed gentry was strengthened after the 1905 revolution, when members of the gentry consolidated their political position after both they and the autocracy had been shaken to the depths. From a narrow point of view, this political rejuvenation appeared beneficial, but it was at the cost of further weakening their ties to the rest of society, especially isolating them from the peasants even further.[21] In seeking refuge in an autocracy whose social and economic policies were undermining their position, members of the gentry sacrificed any claim to independent leadership over other social groups. Probably their dilemma was unsolvable: before 1905 many of the landed nobility had embraced liberal ideas in opposition to the autocratic state, but 1905 had shown the great majority of the gentry that their class and the autocracy could not survive without each other.

The weakness of the Russian industrialists had different causes but similar consequences. By their very nature, the industrialists were something of a pariah class, with motley social origins and no fixed place in Russia's estate society. But it was precisely upon this heterogeneous category, engaged in economic activities largely deprecated by the rest of society—even workers frequently saw them as foreign to the Russian community—that the Russian state had to wager in its promotion of capitalist industrialization. As a result they were showered with loans, subsidies, protective measures, and the like, and with the rapid growth of capitalist industry their relative economic position was correspondingly enhanced. Yet by an odd parallel, just as the landed gentry's economic decline was compensated by a greater political role, the industrialists' economic prosperity was controverted by their continuing political debility. Just as the contradiction led some of the gentry to embrace liberalism, so the tension in their position led a sector of industrialists in the same direction. Yet the 1905–1906 revolution demonstrated to the majority of them, as to the gentry, that their own survival depended on an accommodation with the autocracy, and factory-owner liberalism declined accordingly. Their general acquiescence in the autocratic system underlined their political dependence even as their economic interests as a class continued to prosper. As a result the aspirations of some industrialists to assume a greater and more independent po-

[21] Leopold Haimson, "Conclusion: Observations on the Politics of the Russian Countryside (1905–14)," in *The Politics of Rural Russia 1905–1914*, ed. Leopold Haimson (Bloomington: Indiana University Press, 1979), 290–91.

litical role in Russian society foundered. Further, because of their implicit bargain with the autocracy—political quiescence in exchange for order in the factories—the industrialists were in no position to exercise influence over the workers. In the eyes of many of the latter, the industrialists and the state were both implicated in the associated injustices of autocracy and capitalist exploitation. Like the gentry, then, the industrialists took refuge in the autocratic regime, remaining in essence a closed and defensive caste unable to assume leadership.[22]

Historically the Iranian landed elite had been as much a threat to as a bulwark of the autocracy, a fact that helps explain Muhammad Reza Shah's aggressive attack on their social and economic position. His program of land reform led to a much more dramatic decline in the social position of the gentry than had taken place in Russia through more indirect causes. The shah's motives for the land reform were complex, as we have seen, but central among them was certainly the goal of attacking the social and political position of the landed elite. And in this, if not in a number of other targets of the agrarian reform, he was clearly successful. The reform, especially its first stage, forced the elite to liquidate a good part of their rural holdings; they invested much of the government's compensation abroad rather than in domestic industry, as was intended by the reform.[23] Deprived of much of their land, the transformed landowners could become privileged members of the shah's new elite assembled through court and government patronage. In this motley social context, the quondam landowners lost their identity; nor did the shah make any special efforts to incorporate them in his bureaucracy, preferring new men of indeterminate social origin. Having neutralized the landed elite as a political force, the shah made it clear that there was no potential role for them as a key social base of the regime.

The traditional merchants of the bazaar had also proved themselves to be potential opponents of autocratic power in times past, particularly in alliance with the ulama. In addition, their cultural conservatism, social traditionalism, and, in the eyes of the government, economic backwardness clearly marked them as potential victims and opponents of the shah's modernization campaign. In the 1970s the regime undertook a number of initiatives to weaken their position, including urban redevelopment programs that sought to deprive the bazaar of its former role as nerve center of urban life; the modernization of the banking system and the entry of the state

[22] For analyses of the industrialists' position in late tsarist Russia, see Thomas Owen, *Capitalism and Politics in Russia* (Cambridge: Cambridge University Press, 1981), and Alfred Rieber, *Merchants and Entrepreneurs in Imperial Russia* (Chapel Hill: University of North Carolina Press, 1982).

[23] Afsaneh Najmabadi, *Land Reform and Social Change in Iran* (Salt Lake City: University of Utah Press, 1987), 203–5.

into distribution; and the antiprofiteering campaign and price freezes of the mid-1970s. More generally, the whole tenor of the modernization program and the rise of new elites dependent on the court removed the bazaaris from center stage in Iranian society. However, they retained a good deal of their economic significance, accounting for more than two-thirds of domestic wholesale trade and at least 30 percent of imports.[24] This economic vitality gave them the resources to play a key role in the traditionalist opposition to the Pahlavi dictatorship, supporting the ulama and, at the time of the revolution, financing urban unrest. In general, however, the bazaaris played a subsidiary, if indispensable, part in social protest. Although they formed a vital link in the network of urban relations in opposition to the shah, they were incapable of independent leadership of society and had no program of their own. Yet despite these limitations, the Iranian bazaaris stood out as the only social elite in either Russia or Iran to play a significant political role in the revolutions, either for or against the regimes.

The Iranian industrialists were of much less social and political weight than even their Russian counterparts. They had only emerged as a visible social group in the late 1950s, and their heterogeneous origins and positions in the economy prevented their emergence as a cohesive social and political actor. In general, the industrialist was not an entrepreneur with a distinctive identity as a captain of modern industry but was a civil servant, ex-landowner, or merchant able to benefit from state patronage or ties with foreign corporations. Oil money and the dominance of the autocracy deprived the Iranian industrialists of the political significance enjoyed by their equivalents in Third World countries like Brazil or India. One author has gone so far as to write of them that "this was not a private sector; and the people who enjoyed its fruits were not industrial capitalists."[25] Nor did they have a common stance toward the regime: many supported it out of self-interest, but a good number also bridled at the restrictions and arbitrariness to which they were subjected.[26] But, during the crucial test, neither their support nor their opposition was of much account in Iranian social and political life.

Despite the diversity of relations between the states and the various social elites in Russia and Iran, two general conclusions hold. First, no social elite in either country was able to help sustain the regimes upon which their privileges depended. In this respect, the Russian and Iranian elites played a quite different role than have their counterparts in other countries facing revolutionary threats, whether in industrial societies, such as Ger-

[24] Graham, *Illusion of Power*, 224.

[25] Katouzian, *Political Economy*, 278.

[26] Behrang, *Iran: Le maillon faible* (Paris: François Maspéro, 1979), 15–16.

many after World War I, or developing nations, such as the relatively industrialized Latin American countries. Second, just as the social elites proved politically impotent during the crisis of the old regimes, so they were incapable of providing leadership in the creation of the new societies. Their weakness guaranteed that the revolutions would be distinguished by their radicalism. With respect to both the Russian and Iranian revolutions it would be difficult to apply Tocqueville's argument for France that the revolution only accelerated changes in French society and politics that had been under way for decades. In the context of societies so debilitated by autocratic modernization, the revolutionary elites in Russia and Iran were free to play a much more independent role than was the case in the French Revolution, leading their societies in directions that were far from the inevitable outcome of long-term historical forces.

The weakness of social elites during autocratic modernization suggests a more general contradiction in this pattern of development: both regimes staked the success of their modernization programs on private initiative, but by their very nature they stifled it. In the case of some groups, the regimes smothered their initiative quite consciously out of a fear of overt opposition. For example, the tsarist regime had no intention of permitting an independent trade union movement even if its suppression entailed worker disaffection both in the factory and in society at large. The Iranian regime's imposition of new controls on the religious establishment was likewise a consequence of a perfectly comprehensible fear of opposition. In another sense, government controls over social groups emerged from a general hostility to autonomous collective action no matter what its inspiration. Thus the tsarist regime wanted to incorporate industrialists into the policy process but not as an organized interest with guaranteed rights. They were permitted to participate in deliberations by invitation, and their input was regarded as information to be filtered and acted upon by the state in its higher wisdom. In Iran, too, there was a suspicion of horizontal ties based on shared interest and hostility toward collective action not dominated by the state. For example, the Iranian government initiated a state-controlled guild structure parallel to the older bazaar associations. The government dismissed the leaders of the newer organizations if they did not do its bidding and coerced their support for the regime's policies.[27]

Finally, both regimes discouraged social initiative out of a general suspicion of what in Russia was called "spontaneity"—actions arising from private interests unconnected with any higher (from the government's point of view) rationality. In the place of such spontaneity, both regimes preferred blueprints, rules, and plans expressing the superior wisdom of the state. Following this logic, both governments evinced considerable

[27] Thaiss, "Religious Symbolism and Social Change," 27–32.

hostility to market forces in practice, even if ideologically industrialization was to take place through private enterprise.[28]

Just as significant for the discouragement of private initiative as the direct controls over independent action were the many subtler, more indirect effects of the autocratic system. If people are to take risks, they must be able to calculate and predict likely outcomes to some degree. Such predictions imply regularized procedures of decision making and law. They also require respect for contract and private property. In an autocratic system all of these procedures and institutions are to some degree insecure, both from the impact of the regime itself and also because of the effect of their tenuous foundation in public attitudes. How could the necessary trust and predictability develop within society if it was not nurtured by the legal system and state policy? In Iran, for example, Islam had a well-developed system of contract law and certainly stressed the moral foundations of private property, but its ideal principles could not pervade society and give a sense of predictability on their own. One of the most influential contemporary Iranian writers described the contradiction thus:

> With all the present feudal organization and welter of wandering tribes, God knows how long we shall be faced with the consequences: insecurity, rootlessness, pessimism, despair about the future—and all this in an age when the machine not only is itself the greatest feudal lord, sitting on the throne of the Great Khan, but demands security, open doors, open borders, as well as naïveté (or rather credulity), obedience, trust in others, and confidence in the future.[29]

The consequences of these direct and indirect limitations on initiative, both individual and collective, should not be exaggerated. In both countries, the state could compensate for the uncertainty and lack of autonomy through subsidies and guarantees that could also elicit action. We must remind ourselves once again that state initiative was a dynamic force in both countries and that the complicated intertwining of state and private action could rightfully claim its share of achievements. Yet the limitations of this model are also evident: it bred inefficiency, mistrust, apathy, and weak motivation to innovate. Its continuation also depended upon the persistence of state resources and encouragement that could by no means be taken for granted. If the transition to modern industrial society implies a self-perpetuating process of change and the institutionalization of innovation in the society itself, the project of autocratic modernization was self-

[28] For Iran, see Grace Goodell, *The Elementary Structures of Political Life: Rural Development in Pahlevi Iran* (New York: Oxford University Press, 1986), 250–55. For Russia, a good example is the Ministry of the Interior's ambivalence toward private enterprise and market relations.

[29] Jalal Al-i Ahmad, *Occidentosis: A Plague from the West*, trans. Robert Campbell (Berkeley: Mizan Press, 1984), 68.

contradictory, for economic and social dynamism cannot be simply implanted by fiat.

Lack of initiative was a particularly important dimension of a larger complex of deformations in society generated by the autocracy, for, as should be clear by now, in both countries the effects of autocracy extended far beyond the political realm proper. Repression and the direct dependence of all social groups on the state weakened the bonds among social groups that should have been based on contact and interdependence. Different social groups had little mutual comprehension and could not predict the attitudes or behavior of other segments of the society. In Russia, for example, the peasants considered themselves to be a caste apart from the landowners and granted the latter's interests and aspirations no legitimacy whatsoever.[30] The landowners, for their part, were astonished by the weak electoral support they received from the peasants after 1905, unaware that the peasants no longer felt a great deal of filial gratitude toward them. Much the same pattern of isolation, mistrust, and lack of acceptance of the legitimacy of the other was characteristic of relations in the factory.[31] More generally, mistrust rooted in lack of open and routine contact generated doubt and suspicion throughout Russian society. As Konstantin Kavelin remarked in his famous reply to Dostoevsky's speech on Pushkin, Russians faced one another "ever on guard, with a stone hidden in the bosom. Therefore our arguments nearly always turn to personalities, and our business relations are so vague and indefinite that they constantly lead to lawsuits and litigation. The objective meaning of words and things has little importance in our eyes."[32]

In the shah's Iran, rural and urban, lower and upper, traditional and modern social groups were equally compartmentalized, isolated from each other not just by their social differences, which were of course formidable, but also by the fact that the Pahlavi state discouraged contact and understanding. Society was an agglomeration, not a tissue of overlapping and interdependent groups, and it had no principle of cohesion internal to itself.[33] Autocratic modernization undermined solidarity based on shared identities and traditions as well as the more modern form based on interdependence and shared commitment to law. In one sense, this pattern of atomization was functional for the regime, for it militated against the emergence of a cohesive opposition. It also vindicated autocracy in the eyes of many, for if society had no internal principle of cohesion, was not autocracy necessary to protect individuals and groups from the threat they

[30] Haimson, "Conclusion."

[31] McDaniel, *Autocracy, Capitalism, and Revolution in Russia*, 96–97, 115–16, 128–29.

[32] "A Letter to F. M. Dostoevsky," in *Russian Intellectual History: An Anthology*, ed. Marc Raeff (Atlantic Highlands, N.J.: Humanities Press, 1978), 303–4.

[33] For Iran, see the comments in Goodell, *Elementary Structures*, 324.

posed to each other? "Given the isolation of individuals and the lack of cooperative, responsible interpersonal relations in the society, Iranians argue that only an authoritarian relation between strong leaders and unwilling followers, who resist discipline, can accomplish anything."[34] But however much mistrust and fragmentation may have buttressed autocratic power in normal circumstances, such a society displays its ultimate fragility in crises. Suspicion and mutual recriminations abound; cooperation is impeded; and irritated social groups press their own interests in uncoordinated, if not contradictory, ways. When crises erupt they tend to escalate, for the societies have few mechanisms of social equilibrium.

The resulting lack of social cohesion is especially visible in the weak legitimation of social inequality characteristic of autocratic modernization. Because the social interdependence between lower and higher strata is weakened by the predominant role of the state, there is little sense of mutual obligation based on reciprocity. In rural Russia and Iran the peasants felt no sense of obligation based on benefits derived from hierarchical relations. There was no perceived community of interest in the rural areas of either country. In urban areas, factory owners were regarded as parasites or clients of the state or foreign corporations more than as benefactors of the workers (see the following chapters).

Just as the hierarchical underpinnings of social inequality were weak, neither was social inequality buttressed by meritocratic or individualistic assumptions. With their dependence on the state and its clientelistic policies, the industrialists' claims to privilege based on their individual contributions made little sense. Social inequality thus had weak moorings in social beliefs. Further, because of the centrality of the state and the fragility of traditional hierarchy, the system of stratification was unstable. Scholars of both Russia and Iran have frequently commented on the unusual degree of social mobility in both societies. In Iran under the Pahlavis, in particular, money and the shah's favor became the universal social solvents, reducing the claims of the old elites to nullity.[35]

Lack of knowledge of and contact with other social groups, the weakness of law and institutions, and the tentativeness of the system of social inequality all produced a notable lack of solidity in the very texture of social life, which was to a large degree deprived of its objective and taken-for-granted character. Personalism, fiat, and government control could not compensate for the fundamental lack of social cohesion that threatened the individual's bearings. Certainly rapid social change is always unsettling, as

[34] N. Jacobs, quoted in Bayne, *Persian Kingship*, 60.

[35] Amin Saikal, *The Rise and Fall of the Shah* (Princeton: Princeton University Press, 1980), 189; Graham, *Illusion of Power*, 154–55; Hamid Enayat, "Revolution in Iran 1979: Religion as Political Ideology," in *Revolutionary Theory and Political Reality*, ed. Noel O'Sullivan (Brighton, England: Wheatsheaf Books, 1983), 196.

old social identities are undermined, new social groups come into being, and new demands are made on the individual and society. But political autocracy constitutes an especially strong hindrance to individual adjustment and new forms of social cohesion because of the imposition of strict controls over social life. As the state's claims become more grandiose, its actual inability to define and control social change becomes all the clearer.

Particularly devastating in this respect was the state's unwillingness to permit society a degree of self-organization. We have already seen that the lack of stable organizations inhibited the state's efforts to penetrate society and extend its policies into the social fabric. Because there were no organizations mediating between state and society, the state's own capacity for action was surprisingly limited in both countries. The weakness of modern organizations had equally significant effects upon the ability of social groups to articulate and act upon their interests and decisively shaped the patterns of collective action that did emerge. We recall that in both Russia and Iran the corporate organization of society had traditionally been weak. In Russia the state had limited or prohibited autonomous social organizations, whether representing the elites or the lower orders of society, for centuries. In Iran, traditional forms of social organization were much better established, but they were naturally weak among modern social groups, were not generally centered around economic interests, and tended to take the form of lattices of personal relationships rather than corporate bodies. For all these reasons, they could not answer to the organizational needs of modern social groups. In both countries, then, political parties, trade unions, professional associations, and the like were seldom vital in the lives of the various social groups and were unable to reshape collective action. Many individuals remained in what has been termed a "mass situation": that is, because of a lack of organizational commitments and representative institutions, they were "available" for new forms of action.

In addition, in the absence of organizations to diffuse knowledge and impart a more realistic sense of the limits and possibilities of collective action, people could not develop a rational calculus of the means and ends of social action. Knowledge of constraints, of the limits to action, and of the nature of opposition could not discipline aspirations according to realistic appraisals of the situation. Miscalculations and illusions could flourish in this relative vacuum of knowledge and organizational experience, adding to the overall unpredictability of social and political life. Nor, in the absence of organization, could there emerge moderate leaders with the authority to restrain social militancy when it emerged. Robert Michels's analysis of the oligarchic and conservative effects of organization on social movements is thus inapplicable to both Russia and Iran. Once again, by failing to permit the self-organization of society, both regimes temporarily suppressed social activism at the cost of exacerbating long-term dangers.

For when protest began to emerge, few mechanisms internal to society existed to moderate it. In the absence of established leadership with some commitments to the status quo, the autocratic regimes were forced to confront underground leaders and organizations uncompromisingly committed to their overthrow—only such organizations had authority in the atmosphere of mass unrest.

We have now reached the point where the main argument of this chapter can be summarized; many of its elements will be further explicated and illustrated in the following chapters. We have seen that, stimulated and guided by the autocratic governments, Russia and Iran in the decades before the revolutions were dynamic societies experiencing rapid social and economic modernization. During the modernization of many European countries, the development of intermediate associations and political democratization allowed social groups, albeit not without conflict and strain, to adapt to these changes. In addition, society gradually acquired new mechanisms of cohesion and new modes of conflict resolution, as well as more effective methods of influencing political life. Throughout the autocratic modernization of Russia and Iran, however, social groups individually and society as a whole were blocked from this process of inner transformation in the senses described previously. As a result, there were severe limits to the state's ability to energize and transform society. This very dilemma was reflected in the state apparatus, which lost its coherence in the face of conflicting recipes for change. Further, the autocratic state, unable to turn itself into a modern administrative apparatus based on fixed rules, clearly demonstrated its own weaknesses as an instrument of change. Consequently, despite its dynamism, autocratic modernization was self-limiting.

It also generated a growing breech between announced policies and outcomes, between ideology and accomplishments, between appearances and reality. The above-class regimes promised to protect the lowest of their subjects from the ravages of the market and the exploitation by elites, but they could not deliver on these promises. They also committed themselves to allow greater participation and the beginning of democratization but never renounced the prerogatives of autocratic power. Finally, they reversed their policies and violated previous commitments as the dilemmas of any fixed course of action within the contradictory system made themselves felt. Social life acquired a surreal quality, the product of social change relatively untempered by law and by fixed social institutions, whether traditional or modern. The regimes, too, inevitably suffered from this lack of grounding in a taken-for-granted social world with a predictable future and so, when challenged, seemed to many both impermanent and dispensable.

Five

The Cities in Revolution

THE SEARCH for a general theory of revolutions has led scholars who believe in its feasibility to identify a set of fundamental causes of revolution and, in accordance with these, to single out certain critical revolutionary agents. I suppose that if one were to count heads, the leading candidates for revolutionary credentials would be the urban intelligentsia and the peasantry. It is especially striking how many specialists have identified the countryside as the decisive locus of revolutionary action in the contemporary era, whether their studies focused on the significance of the structural transformation of agrarian economies and social relations or on the attitudes, culture, and resources of the peasant community itself. Skocpol and Trimberger have put the case the most baldly: the success of social revolutions from below has been determined by "the class struggles of peasants against dominant landed classes and/or colonial or neo-colonial regimes."[1]

Generalizations of this scope—about all modern social revolutions—have little hope of hitting the mark. The decisive revolutionary actors will vary with the nature of the old regimes and with variations in the process of modernization. Ideal types such as "autocratic modernization" ought to be able to impart greater specificity to the prerevolutionary pattern of change and allow more accurate, if limited, generalizations. And, contra writers such as Barrington Moore and Theda Skocpol, who emphasize the decisive role of the countryside everywhere, in this pattern of development urban centers are the critical locus of revolutionary mobilization. The validity of this conclusion is incontestable for Iran: the villages certainly played some role in the revolutionary events of late 1978 Iran, even if the local militants were often workers who commuted to the cities from the villages. But there can be no doubt that the vital forces of the revolution—the leading clergy, the bazaaris, the urban poor, students, the nationalist opposition, the workers—were rooted in the cities. For Russia the case is more complicated, though only slightly so. Peasant revolutionism was clearly a necessary foundation of the eventual Bolshevik victory, as was the militancy of nationalist groups in the periphery, but the tsar was overthrown and the Bolshevik regime established in the capital. The momentous events of 1917, from the February revolution to the April and July

[1] Theda Skocpol and Ellen Kay Trimberger, "Revolutions: A Structural Analysis," in *Revolutions*, ed. Jack Goldstone (San Diego: Harcourt Brace Jovanovitch, 1986), 61.

crises and on to the October seizure of power, all took place in the cities. The Bolshevik party and its major social base, the workers, were both overwhelmingly urban. Indeed, the later course of Soviet history is incomprehensible without an appreciation of the extreme isolation of the revolutionaries and their social base from the countryside.

As a rule, two factors explain the relative weight of urban or rural politics in revolutions. First, there is the degree of political centralization: the more centralized the polity, the more likely that the cities, and especially the capital city, will be decisive in the revolutionary struggle. Thus, there is no equivalent to the predominance of St. Petersburg, Moscow, or Paris in the Chinese, Vietnamese, or Mexican revolutions. Second, urban affairs will increase in significance with the degree of industrialization. Here one need only contrast the revolutions in relatively industrialized Russia and Iran with those in Mexico, Vietnam, or China to understand the crucial impact of economic development, which shifts the demographic, social, and political center of gravity from the countryside to the cities. Either factor alone operates to increase the salience of the cities, as the importance of lower-class urban unrest in the European absolutist monarchies indicates, and in the nineteenth-century European revolutionary crises as well, but when both converge, as they do in autocratic modernization, the combined effect is all the stronger. As compared with the situations preceding the English, French, Mexican, Chinese, and Vietnamese revolutions—indeed, all other major social revolutions—the immense weight of social, economic, and political power in prerevolutionary Russia and Iran was located in the cities.

Alongside this key similarity between Russia and Iran, there are also manifest differences that will require discussion. For example, because of European influence and the presence of more significant European-style social movements—of the professional classes and of industrial workers—democratic demands for equality and participation were stronger in Russia than in Iran. Similarly, in Russian cities modern class conflict between the industrial working class and the industrialists was much more visible and distinguishable than in Iran, where the class element was weaker and where urban protest was dominated by groups involved in traditional urban social networks.

This is not to deny that urban politics in the last two decades of tsarist rule involved a wide variety of social groups. Crucial to the 1905 revolution was the mobilization of a broad segment of the urban, as well as rural, populations, including students, professionals, and even an important segment of industrialists, against the tsarist regime. Until the early fall of 1905 urban unrest had enough of an all-national character to buttress the hopes of liberals and moderate Marxists that the revolution was in essence a bourgeois revolution against the autocracy rather than a proletarian revolution against capitalism. The episodes of worker militancy in the fall of 1905 convinced such people that the proletariat had betrayed the bourgeois revolution and, learning from the revolution's failure, it should reconcile itself to the creation of an organized labor movement within the context of a developing capitalist society. But one major problem with this diagnosis was that after its taste of worker radicalism, the bourgeoisie also abandoned the bourgeois political revolution, seeking refuge in an autocracy that could protect it from the threat of worker insurgency.[2] In addition, after 1905, the failure of the revolution and the expanding economy encouraged many students and professionals to reintegrate themselves into society, leading many workers to feel that the intelligentsia and middle classes had abandoned them. The defeat of the revolution could not give birth to a revitalized autocracy, or bridge the immense gulf separating state and society, but it complicated urban politics by heightening the class gap between privileged Russia and the lower classes, and between workers and employers. Consequently, as would become evident in 1917, workers increasingly identified the political oppression of the tsarist state with the class oppression of the industrialists.

The salience of class conflict in urban Russia was linked to a complex of traits with few parallels in Iran. In Russia, popular interpretations and versions of Marxist ideas had considerable impact on the workers through the influence of underground circles and worker activists. In 1905 even nonproletarian groups often used basic elements of a Marxist conceptual apparatus to interpret their experience. The term burzhui, for example, became a general lower-class term of opprobrium toward their betters. Further, though largely isolated from the workers, socialist leaders had been able to establish significant ties with workers during periods of protest and the socialist intelligentsia had acquired considerable experience in guiding mass protest. Finally, traditions of radical labor protest had established themselves within the working class, and even if they became dormant during times of repression, they could be reawakened when conditions changed.

These phenomena, then, require interpretation: how did class conflict between workers and employers become the dominant note of social unrest in urban Russia; why did it overshadow other possible forms of urban conflict; and why did socialist leaders and ideas acquire a considerable degree of influence among the workers? The explanation of these patterns of conflict will be seen to lie in an understanding of the relationship between the state, the industrial elite, and the labor movement, as these were conditioned by autocratic modernization.

In Iran, none of the traits just enumerated had central significance. There

[2] McDaniel, *Autocracy, Capitalism, and Revolution in Russia*, 124–34.

were workers and there were Marxist intellectuals, but these groups never interpenetrated each other to the extent that they had in Russia. The Iranian labor movement possessed little coherence or sense of identity, and it certainly was not permeated with implicitly and explicitly socialist ideas. There were workers and industrialists, but their self-definitions and perceptions of each other lacked the clarity of those of their Russian equivalents. A proletariat and a bourgeoisie were far from the key actors in urban unrest that they were in Russia, and there is little evidence that they came to conceive of themselves in sharp class terms. Nor was either modern class able to originate visible social movements demanding reform and democratization.

Although by no means absent from Iranian society, the significance of these modern sectors was overshadowed by another roster of groups: the ulama, the bazaaris, the urban poor, and students, whose interrelations could not be defined in class terms and whose opposition was primarily directed against the shah. When considering the major episodes of political rebellion against the regime in the 1960s and 1970s, one does not think primarily of massive industrial strikes spreading through whole regions of the country (although these occurred) but of religious protests, student demonstrations, and the closing of bazaars. Iranian workers came to play their part in 1978, but as auxiliaries who did not even seek to define the major issues on their own terms. The resiliency of traditional groups and forms of protest in the face of rapid modernization and the relative faintness of class conflict in the modern sector sharply distinguishes Iranian urban unrest from the Russian pattern and requires investigation into the chief variations within a similar pattern of development. Autocratic modernization weakened both regimes internally, called into question their relations with society, and also undermined the inner cohesion of both societies, but it was compatible with distinct patterns of social change. As was suggested in chapters one and two, differences in historical experience and in the patterns of modernization must be brought to bear in shaping an explanation for these differences.

The Roots of Class Conflict in Urban Russia

The key to urban politics in Nicholas II's Russia is the unique combination of political autocracy and rapid capitalist development.[3] For its own reasons the autocratic regime resolved, however halfheartedly, to sponsor the

[3] This is the argument of my book *Autocracy, Capitalism and Revolution in Russia*, from which I have drawn for the present discussion and in which the thesis is spelled out in much greater detail.

capitalist industrialization of the country. The state played an undeniably crucial role in stimulating and guaranteeing private investments, but economic progress depended on private initiative and entrepreneurship. Yet by their very nature the autocratic state and the political culture that had formed around it undermined the legitimacy and independence of the capitalist class. The results of this tortured relationship were paradoxical, for the industrialists' very weakness threw them into the arms of the state that was so much the source of their debility. To add to the irony, the frailty of the capitalists did not facilitate an above-class, statist approach to industrial relations, for the regime was forced to favor the capitalists precisely out of a concern for their weakness and inability to survive without government protection. The strategy of autocratic capitalist development thus conditioned a highly conflictual but ultimately indissoluble linkage between the autocratic state and the capitalist bourgeoisie.

An extreme version of the ubiquitous conflict in capitalist economies between "legitimation" and "accumulation" thus took shape in tsarist Russia. The state socialist measures that might have given weight to the state's claim to be the above-class protector of all social groups were virtually impossible in a capitalist economy with a weak capitalist class. Thus, despite its claims the government accomplished almost nothing in the realm of labor legislation and even less in the actual alleviation of the harshness of early capitalism. Yet the threatened industrialists were also able to impede liberal legislation authorizing strikes and trade unions, which would have given the workers the capacity to defend themselves. The regime was also not overly anxious to grant the workers more independence, and so they remained essentially rightless—even if, after 1905, the rights to organize and strike existed on paper.

The distinctiveness of this pattern of development must be stressed. In the major European nations the position of the industrialists was undergirded by a historical development legitimating private property, the market, civil law, and the pursuit of personal gain. Further, governments were constrained by law and the countervailing power of established elites. Without assigning to these historical patterns an undeserved idyllic quality, it is still clear that they imparted to the emerging capitalist class a degree of legitimacy that could be translated into power and independence. With these resources at their disposal, the industrialists did not have as much to fear from the workers. Nor could the imposition of government regulations over industrial life dramatically threaten their overall social positions. Neither the French nor the English industrialists fought the legalization of trade unions or protective labor legislation as tenaciously as did their Russian counterparts. Ironically, the English and French states thus had considerably more de facto independence from the capitalist elites than did the above-class Russian state, tied to the industrialists largely as an unintended consequence of its above-class claims.

A more consistently statist approach relying only marginally on a private capitalist class also avoids the dilemmas of the Russian model. It is to this category that the Iranian pattern of industrialization belongs, for despite the shah's avowals that he was following the Western capitalist model, in fact the oil wealth at the disposal of the Iranian state conditioned an entirely different relationship between the state and private capitalists—one in which the state had considerably greater independence and the industrialists much less visibility than in Russia. This contrast, which will be developed in the discussion of Iranian urban politics, is introduced here to highlight the comparative distinctiveness of the Russian attempt to pair up an autocratic state and a relatively self-sufficient capitalist bourgeoisie.

These general assertions must now be elaborated through a discussion of the major actors, beginning with the tsarist state in its role as arbiter of industrial class relations. It has already been pointed out that the regime was officially committed to capitalist industrialization through the agency of a class of private industrialists. But the implications of this commitment were not always fully understood or accepted by government officials, who very often continued to cling to ideas and practices inconsistent with the overall policy. They did not regard the factory owners as a modern social class capable of autonomous and responsible action either in the political life of the nation or in the narrower sphere of industrial relations. Instead, government policy was in general guided by the assumption that the industrialists were a narrow and self-interested estate whose egoistic impulses must be evaluated and regulated by the above-class state. In this view, they were incapable of speaking for the interests of industry in general, much less of society as a whole.

It followed that the government should consult with the industrialists in order to gain insight into their particular estate perspective, but it should not grant them a decisive voice in government deliberations over industry. Minister of Finance Kokovtsov expressed these assumptions with unusual clarity in explaining to the factory owners their role in the government commission called to revise labor legislation in 1905: "Appealing to your experience and knowledge, I invite you, dear sirs, to help the Ministry of Finance by illuminating all questions designated for our discussion by order of the Tsar, and I am completely certain that you came here in order to give this help"—help not in drafting legislation, but merely in clarifying "the conditions of everyday life."[4] In a later conference the director of the Ministry of Trade and Industry's Department of Industry declared that

[4] *Rabochii vopros v kommissii V. N. Kokovtsova v 1905 g.* (Moscow: Voprosy truda, 1926), 200.

"we, the government, are obligated to stand for general state interests. We must protect the interests, not only of the workers and employers, but also of the population."[5] It was thus perfectly acceptable to encourage the industrialists to organize themselves and to invite their representatives to express the interests of their estate, but these organizations must not acquire the autonomy of strong class institutions, nor should the representatives have a direct policy-making function.

Similarly, in factory affairs it was widely assumed that the industrialists would act according to their own narrow interests and exploit the workers if unchecked by the government. Government officials evinced remarkably little trust in the paternalistic goodwill of the employers toward their workers. Many concluded that the interests of the two sides were contradictory, and that the government had the responsibility to protect the weak against the strong. According to an influential Ministry of the Interior report from March 1898, employers take advantage of the workers' helplessness to "exploit their labor for their own benefit." In phraseology that might easily be found in Marxist propaganda, the report condemned this exploitation as especially unjust because it was the workers who were the source of industry's prosperity.[6] The autocracy, like the socialists, distrusted civil society and sought principles of justice that would restore order to the chaos of selfish interests.

Given these assumptions, it was logical for government officials involved in factory affairs to advocate what was sometimes called the "management of labor." In this view, the government should take responsibility for the detailed regulation of factory life, making sure that it conformed to standards of justice higher than those of the selfish contending sides. Report after report proposed detailed rules and regulations for factory life and the formation of government agencies to make sure that they were enforced. Many of these proposals were remarkably advanced—and probably unrealistic—even by the standards of European labor legislation, including obligatory old-age, sickness, and accident insurance and criminal punishment for employers who violated the labor contract. These suggestions give insight into the mentality of government officials even though they were seldom enacted and, when enacted, indifferently enforced. Nonetheless, the claim to government supervision was frequently made, to the acute dissatisfaction of most industrialists, and as a result government officials of various kinds—local police, factory police, and factory inspectors—became highly visible fixtures in factory affairs. These promises and declarations, and the officials employed to oversee compliance with them, all served to underscore the government's distrust of the factory owners

[5] Central State Historical Archive, Leningrad, f. 150, g. 1905, op. 1, d. 492, l. 17.

[6] Central State Historical Archive, Leningrad, f. 1282, op. 1, d. 696, l. 3–4.

and give legitimacy to the workers' discontent. Government ineffectiveness in actually "managing" labor did not so much weaken the force of the promises as discredit the government, which could not honor its own commitments.

For in fact the government was in no position to regulate industrial relations or protect the workers. It had neither the administrative capacity to enforce its will nor, even more, the political ability to formulate a coherent policy. Its impotence was due partly to internal administrative and organizational weaknesses, but especially to the contradiction between government tutelage and the requirements of capitalist industrialization—a prime example of the underlying dilemmas of autocratic modernization working themselves out in concrete policy divisions. Every Ministry of the Interior proposal to curb the excesses of the industrialists was met with Ministry of Finance arguments based on a contrary model. Industrial life had its own logic, the latter ministry argued, one embodied in the laws of the market and the balance of power between the two opposing classes. Its complexity could not be regulated by government fiat, for this would only weaken the authority of the industrialists and create unrealistic aspirations on the part of the workers. Sometimes such arguments were merely a ploy to prevent government intervention, but they were also used to support a more liberal policy toward industrial relations, including the legalization of strikes and trade unions. As a government commission argued in 1906:

> Factory life is extremely complicated, and the regulation of it in no case can be accomplished only through government interference by means of factory inspection and police. In this matter it is essential to place both sides in such a situation so that neither of them can outweigh the other. From this flowed the necessity to allow the workers themselves to organize with the goal of self-defense and the improvement of their situation.[7]

The arguments against attempts to "manage labor" turned out to be much more effective than appeals to free the contending sides, as trade unions were never allowed to gain a real foothold in industrial relations. Yet these proposals were tendered by serious and influential officials and institutions, and though they could not reshape class relations in urban Russia, they did prevent the emergence of a coherent traditionalist strategy within the government.

Just as the logic of capitalist industrialization ruled out a consistently tutelary role for the government in industrial relations, so it implied a greater role for the industrialists in political life than did the above-class model of autocratic politics. The industrialists were not simply another estate with the right to inform and petition the government in matters of

[7] Central State Historical Archive, Leningrad, f. 1276, g. 1906, op. 2, d. 116, l. 27.

concern to it, but an elite emerging in difficult circumstances entrusted with tasks vital to the survival of the empire. It was therefore natural that a special relationship would develop between the industrialists and the tsarist state, in particular with the Ministry of Finance. In the first decades of the postemancipation period the government acted largely on its own to enact measures in the industrialists' favor, but it soon came to encourage and even help create industrialist organizations that could promote their interests more effectively. For matters vital to industry it called conferences to which industrialist representatives were invited for consultation. At first the participation of the industrialists was quite uncoordinated, but by the 1890s, and particularly after 1905, there had emerged a significant network of industrialist organizations well able to press their members' views.[8] The government continued to accord industrialist representatives privileged access to policy making, as in the Kokovtsov and Filosofov commissions of 1905–1907. Called to revise government labor policy and develop a body of labor legislation, these conferences had immense potential political significance. Industrialist representatives were invited to participate; workers were excluded. The justification given was that the workers were too immature and their organizations too young to participate responsibly, but their exclusion also gives testimony to the inability of a government sponsoring rapid capitalist industrialization to follow an above-class policy of state tutelage.

Government policy toward the industrialists was thus filled with contradictions, as it both undermined their legitimacy and accorded them special privileges in economic and political affairs. This contradictory stance decisively shaped the position of the industrialists in class relations and in Russian society and politics more generally. On the one hand, the Russian factory owners were never able to achieve the unity of purpose, legitimacy, or organizational coherence necessary for an authentic industrial bourgeoisie. In important respects, they failed to overcome the obstacles to social prestige and political power inherent in an autocratic political system and in a society dominated by a landed elite. The roadblocks were many. No one—not the bureaucracy, nobility, or, perhaps least of all, the intelligentsia—believed that the factory owners possessed such bourgeois virtues as self-reliance, thrift, and a capacity for work.[9] They were generally re-

[8] For a good summary before 1905, see [Osip] A[rkadevich] Ermanskii, "Krupnaia burzhuaziia do 1905 goda," in *Obshchestvennoe dvizhenie v Rossii v nachale XX-go veka*, ed. L. Martov, P. Maslov, and A. Potresov (St. Petersburg: Tipografiia "Obshchestvennaia pol'za," 1909–14), vol. 1, pt. 2, esp. 318–21.

[9] For a discussion of the image of the Russian businessman, see Jo Ann Ruckman, *The Moscow Business Elite: A Social and Cultural Portrait of Two Generations* (De Kalb: Northern Illinois University Press, 1984), 6–14.

garded as creatures of the regime, undeserving beneficiaries of government largess.

Even more, the bourgeois virtues themselves were highly suspect in the eyes of much of Russian society. What might have been thrift and initiative in England was petty materialism and dryness of soul to Russians. Similarly, industry did not always connote progress but often the degradation of native Russian patterns of life in the interest of an artificial Westernization. The industrialists' claims that they represented enlightenment and modernity, and thus were indispensable to Russia's future, which echoed throughout their publications in the last decades of the old regime, were as often as not greeted with skepticism or hostility. This profound sense of their own tenuous social acceptability and of the fragility of their social position haunted the Russian factory owners and helped shape their relations to other classes and the state.

These fundamental sources of weakness were compounded by the striking diversity of the Russian industrialists, partly a consequence of the rapidity of the country's economic growth. Excluding Poland and the western regions of the empire, Russian industry consisted of three key regions, each with a distinct modal type of industrialist.[10] Moscow, together with the surrounding "central industrial region," had historically formed the core zone of indigenous Russian industrialization. Centered on the textile industry, the city had witnessed dramatic economic growth during the early nineteenth century, largely without state subsidy, and Moscow, if anywhere, could claim to be the cradle of an independent entrepreneurial class. The Moscow industrialists' relative lack of dependence on government orders and loans, as well as their sheer distance from the Petersburg bureaucracy, encouraged a measure of self-reliance unusual in Russian industry. The Old Believer origins of a striking number of the Moscow business elite reinforced their sense of separation both from the regime and from other groups of industrialists. It is not surprising, therefore, that industrialist opposition to the regime in 1905 reached its pinnacle among a sector of the Moscow industrial elite, although it should also be noted that Moscow factory owners were also known for their traditionalism and that many opposed the initiatives of the more radical elements that would emerge in the city during the 1905 revolution.

The second major entrepreneurial group, centered on the newly industrialized regions of the Ukraine, differed dramatically from the Muscovites. The economic development of the Ukraine was the product of Witte's campaigns of the 1890s, with their encouragement of foreign investment and entrepreneurship in very modern branches of industry. Engineers and

[10] A fourth region, the old Urals mining and metallurgy industry still retained some significance, although its industry was eclipsed in the period of rapid industrialization.

foreigners combined to create what was for Russia a highly distinctive business culture, one very far removed from the social conservatism of the Muscovites but, like them, highly skeptical of the competence of the tsarist bureaucracy. Because of the heavy concentration of foreign enterprise and the apolitical professionalism of much of this group, the southern entrepreneurs could not claim to be the bulwark of a national industrial bourgeoisie, and political liberalism was not as marked as among some Moscow entrepreneurs.

The Petersburg industrialists were just as distinct from the Muscovites and the southerners as these latter were from each other. Like the southern region, Petersburg benefited from an enormous infusion of foreign capital, but it was also closely linked to the government bureaucracy and depended on government orders, particularly in military-related industries. As a consequence, the metalworking sector accounted for an impressive proportion of the capital's industry (roughly 40 percent of all employment, 35 percent of value of production in 1913)[11] and industry tended to be highly concentrated. Many of the most prominent industrialists circulated among the political elite—the head of the St. Petersburg Society of Factory Owners, for example, was a member of the State Council. Further, there was a long tradition of participation of Petersburg industrialists in government deliberations on matters concerning industry. Although less of a closed, conservative caste than their Moscow counterparts, the Petersburg entrepreneurs displayed less political independence and more rigidity on labor issues. The Muscovites regarded them with suspicion for their links with foreign capital and their intimate ties with the bureaucracy.

These profound differences in the economic and social traits of the key regions impeded the development of class unity among the Russian industrialists. Beginning in the late nineteenth-century, a plethora of industrialist organizations was formed. However, the organizations were specialized according to region and branch of industry, and as a result they tended to concentrate on local affairs and avoid the larger issues confronting the industrialists in Russian society. The 1905 revolution, and especially the threat of worker militancy, did much to galvanize them, but in general they could only act in a united way in the arena of class conflict. Unlike the early English entrepreneurs who could promote themselves as champions of modern technology and progress, the Russian industrialists had no positive unifying mission. The state had usurped much of the role played by the English entrepreneurs. As regards broader political issues, or even organizational unification, the Russian groups could never overcome their disunity. Efforts were made to establish all-national organizations, but the embryonic bodies that came into existence could never bridge the impor-

[11] Bater, *St. Petersburg*, 222.

tant divisions. The Petersburg industrialists, for example, continued to rely on their own very effective body. The historical legacy of this disunity was clearly visible in 1917, when the industrialists proved powerless to confront the increasingly militant labor movement.

These various sources of weakness were compounded by the industrialists' overall isolation from other groups and classes in Russian society. In their social segregation, the factory owners exemplified a more general pattern of social relations with long historical roots in Russia. For centuries the tsarist system had inhibited horizontal relations among social groups, preferring that all should look to the above-class state for protection and guidance. This logic found perfect expression in the *soslovie* system, according to which Russian society was officially divided into four main groups: the nobility, townsmen, peasantry, and clergy. The 1649 code which systematized these divisions was modified over time in practice, as new social groups emerged as a result of changes in Russian society. Thus, the townspeople were divided into three key categories, the artisans, small businessmen, and larger merchants and industrialists, and this last group was further divided into guilds. Rights and responsibilities were defined according to these soslovie divisions and the state did what it could to encourage a castelike mentality, whereby the different sosloviia were concerned only with their own affairs. By the late nineteenth century this system had in part broken down under the strains of social modernization, but the mentality behind it survived. The nobility, industrialists, and professionals, not to speak of the lower classes, largely lived apart from each other, shunning social contact and harboring prejudices that further inhibited joint action. The 1905 revolution demonstrated that this pattern of segmentation could be partially overcome at least in urban Russia, as students, industrialists, workers, and professionals came to participate, at least for a time, in an overall movement. As the later course of the revolution would demonstrate, however, this cooperation was fragile.

One important consequence of this politically imposed pattern was an almost insurmountable gap between workers and factory owners. The logic of the tsarist system inhibited the flowering of the kind of paternalistic labor relations found elsewhere, in Japan and Germany, for example. Instead, the state played an extremely active role in class relations, inserting itself between the workers and factory owners. In addition, and partly as a consequence of the lack of contact and reciprocity, factory owners frequently appeared as despots rather than protectors. The implications of this pattern of interrelations were clearly spelled out in a report by the southern industrialist V. Belov in March 1905.[12] Among many other inci-

[12] Central State Historical Archive, Leningrad, f. 150, g. 1905, op. 1, d. 484, ll. 69–80. All quotations come from this document.

sive insights, Belov recognized that the weight of the tsarist state had undermined the relationship between the factory owner and the worker by depriving the former of his independence of action. Complaining of the detailed government regulation of factory life and the controls imposed on the industrialists, Belov declared that "between the factory owners and the workers there grew up a wall," a situation that deprived the former of any moral influence over the workers. When disorders came, then, "we stand to the side, without any influence on the crowd; we don't have access to the stage."

The Russian industrialists could not transcend their own interests narrowly defined in order to assume a broader leadership role in Russian society because of their low legitimacy; weak and fragmented organizations; dependence on, yet fear of, the government; and isolation from other social groups, particularly the workers. As a speaker at the first congress of a new association of trade and industrial enterprises in January 1906 recognized, only if the status of the industrialist was raised would he "be in a position to understand what significance his activity has for the overall interests of the country." He will then come to understand that he must sometimes sacrifice his own personal interests for the overall good, a fact, said the speaker, that European industrialists well understood. Their new organization, he claimed, would be an important step in the right direction, helping them to understand their national patriotic duty.[13]

It would not be unfair to point out, however, that this transformation never took place. Certainly some industrialists recognized the need for reforms, both in the political sphere more generally and in industrial relations. The Association of Trade and Industry, for example, was a consistent advocate of a relatively free and open trade union movement, and it clearly understood the negative implications of government repression and control for class conflict in Russia. But a great many other industrialist organizations, including the powerful St. Petersburg Society of Factory Owners, distrusted the workers and fought against any greater independence for their organizations. In their private deliberations and in public forums, they frequently expressed their contempt for the workers, born of mistrust and fear. They were often unwilling to make concessions or take risks, opposing both the government's tutelary proposals and any efforts to grant the workers more independence. Ultimately, then, the industrialists threw in their lot with the tsarist regime, recognizing its deleterious effects on class relations but afraid to give up the apparent security it provided for an uncertain future. Groups of industrialists, particularly in Moscow, continued to sound an oppositional note until the fall of the regime, but the

[13] Central State Historical Archive, Leningrad, f. 65, op. 1, d. 156, l. 134.

majority of their peers continued to embrace the regime as their chief refuge from worker militancy.

The state's reliance on a private capitalist class thus compelled the government to betray its above-class principles and come to the aid of the capitalists it had itself done so much to weaken. Similarly, the industrialists, well aware of the tsarist state's infringements against their own interests, nevertheless were forced to turn to it out of a sense of their own weakness. This obscure and tangled liaison, so full of ironies and tensions, came to appear remarkably simple to many workers: the tsarist state was implicated in the class exploitation of the workers, and the industrialists were tarred with the sins of the regime. Contrary to its beliefs about itself and its promises, the tsarist state exacerbated, not relieved, urban class conflict.

It is only through an understanding of the implications of this overall pattern of autocratic capitalist modernization that one can explain the exceptional class consciousness and radicalism of the Russian proletariat, a group that was to play such a profound role in the 1917 revolution.[14] Class consciousness was particularly evident in the workers' unwillingness to contain their demands within the bounds of the moderate socialists' much vaunted bourgeois revolution. Instead, in 1905–1907 and again in 1917, Russian workers were less concerned with political rights and constitutions than with drastic changes in capitalist social relations, which they saw as inseparable from tsarist rule. They displayed extraordinary distrust and hostility toward both the capitalists and the tsarist regime, tending to group them together as exploiters of the working class. It is true that after the defeat of the 1905 revolution a stratum of moderate trade unionists appeared to be emerging, but the tsarist state never allowed them to lead the labor movement, which continued to revolve around two poles, militant mass action and a degree of guidance by socialist activists and organizations. Despite their frequent attempts to restrain the masses for fear that they were overreaching themselves, the socialists' leadership was generally only effective when it coordinated mass action; it was seldom able to subdue it in the name of strategy. This, then, is one clear-cut sense in which the Russian labor movement was radical: a great many workers participated in activities, whether strikes or mass demonstrations, aimed at threatening the foundations of the old regime. It was also effective to an unusual degree, for it proved able to threaten the regime's existence on a number of crucial occasions (late 1905, early 1914, 1917) and, when the regime was overthrown, to apply pressure for further radical change.

Aside from the objection that there was no organized social movement

[14] I recognize that the various elements in this statement are all highly controversial. I refer the reader to my book *Autocracy, Capitalism, and Revolution in Russia*, for fuller evidence and discussion than is possible here.

among Russian workers, which I have discussed and rejected elsewhere, this perspective on the roots of Russian worker radicalism differs from two well-known alternatives. The first view, whose most brilliant proponent is Trotsky, sees Russian worker radicalism as the product of leadership by a militant proletarian core of advanced workers employed in modern industry. Although, it is argued, capitalism could not completely transform Russian society and create the basis for an unalloyed modern labor movement, it did make possible the emergence of class conscious leaders with the authority to sway the backward masses. According to an opposing view, until recently more widespread in contemporary Western scholarship, Russian worker militancy can be traced largely to disoriented workers of peasant origin and to young recruits into industry. Proponents of the latter view tend to emphasize the "spontaneity" and unpredictability of worker militancy in Russia, denying to it the coherence and ultimate rationality ascribed by Trotsky.

From the present perspective, each of these interpretations captures part of the truth. Capitalism did indeed create a core of advanced workers with socialist ideas who helped orient and give coherence to worker militancy. In addition, the rapid development of Russian industry gave rise to typically proletarian forms of action and association—strikes, factory committees, and trade unions, even if none of these could develop to their full potential. Under the influence of the German labor movement, these organizations demanded democratization as the prelude to a more profound social transformation. But, on the other hand, the continuation of the autocratic system ensured that the Russian labor movement could develop few of the traits associated with the institutionalization of the labor movement in various European countries, including the emergence of moderate leadership and a significant degree of control over worker militants. Instead, in Russia the boldest and most daring, often those with least to lose, continued to shape collective action inordinately. Hot-headed young workers, often of peasant origin and with little political sophistication, made an undoubted contribution to overall labor militancy. Thus, in a political autocracy undergoing capitalist industrialization, both types of leaders, conscious workers and bold militants, supplemented each other in the context of a labor movement that embraced both proletarian "consciousness" and mass "spontaneity."

The links between autocratic modernization, capitalism, and labor radicalism must now be spelled out in more detail. The autocratic regime and its associated values did much on its own to generate worker anticapitalism and hostility to the industrialists. The weakness of legal consciousness and lack of respect for private property among Russian workers were often noted. Where, indeed, could they have imbibed these values when the state gave them so little priority? As a result, misperceptions about the capitalist economy and the government's role in it proliferated even in isolated areas untouched by socialist teachings. For example, the factory inspector Gvozdev observed that the provincial workers under his jurisdiction "completely unconsciously were preaching state socialism."[15] They thought that the factory owner had no right to close the factory and that if he managed his affairs poorly the state would requisition it. They were also mistakenly of the opinion that the employer was obliged to provide work and housing for the entire local population. Further, they assumed that the authorities could force the factory owner to raise their wages and use his profits to build more factories to increase employment. It is clear from this example that the workers took the state's above-class claims perfectly seriously, believing that the factory owner, too, was completely under the jurisdiction of the government. The myth of the welfare state was far more pervasive than the abstract rules of a private enterprise economy.

In addition, the castelike mentality of the industrialists was fully replicated among the workers. They, too, had few horizontal ties with other groups because of the strength of social barriers to interaction and the virtual nonexistence of representative bodies able to negotiate with their counterparts among other social groups. As a result, workers had little sense of the aspirations and perspectives of other social groups and less appreciation for their legitimacy. In these circumstances, mistrust and an unwillingness to compromise flourished just as much among workers as among the industrialists. Suspicion and the lack of established ties account for the extraordinary complications of interclass negotiations in 1917, as worker representatives frequently walked out rather than make concessions. In the context of their isolation and lack of rights under the old regime, it is completely comprehensible why so few workers could envision a society based on the mutual adjustments of contending social forces regulated by law. The alternatives were clear: either a worker or a bourgeois state.

Autocracy was thus strikingly effective in undermining the logic of capitalist social relations, but these latter exacted their price: the combination of autocracy and capitalism worked to undermine the state as well as the industrialists in the eyes of the workers. The state proved unable to fulfill its tutelary promises to the workers, despite its factory police and factory inspectors. It could not influence wages or define factory relations to any great extent in the context of the capitalist economy. Its impotence did not prevent the state from excoriating the industrialists and repeating its promises, but its exhortations increasingly rang hollow. Nor would it follow through on its commitments to give the workers the capacity to protect

[15] S. Gvozdev, *Zapiski fabrichnogo inspektora. Iz nabliudenii i praktiki v period 1894–1908 gg.* (Moscow: Gosudarstvennoe izdatel'stvo, 1925), 189.

themselves. After June 1907 the workers had virtually no electoral influence. Strikes and trade unions were formally legal but in fact repressed. In its proclamation of reforms that it could not fully enact, the regime created an enormous breach between word and deed and gave the workers a sense that its actions were unjust. This sense of the injustice of the regime fueled discontent and gave the workers belief in the morality of their opposition. It also strengthened the tendency to think in all-or-nothing, we-versus-they terms, that also emerged from their castelike isolation in the autocratic regime.

This belief in the righteousness of their cause was particularly marked among a group of self-defined "conscious" workers, often highly skilled and with a sense of their own worth and dignity. Most often found in the major cities and in advanced industry, such workers were especially receptive to socialist teachings based on Western ideas. Socialism, especially Marxist socialism, was not just a set of theoretical propositions but, as embodied in German Social Democracy, a blueprint for the future of their own movement. Marxism taught them that the worker would be at the forefront of social progress and that to fulfill this responsibility the working class must fight for political rights in an organized way. Society could not be reconstructed on the basis of individual heroic acts of terrorism, as many populists held, but only by means of coordinated and disciplined action in accord with a scientific understanding of society.[16] In embracing Western ideas, conscious workers did not oppose progress but rather blamed the regime for the terrible backwardness of Russian society. They had no sympathy for a romanticized past defined on the basis of premodern national traditions that had been undermined by modernization. Nor does religion seem to have held much appeal for them. Although one can find references in worker memoirs to biblical morality as a source of opposition to the regime, on the whole it appears that conscious workers identified religion with the irrational, with ignorance, with submission to authority, and with tsarist despotism. It violated their own growing sense of their ability to change the world on the basis of scientific ideas and modern mass organization.

Conscious workers insistently criticized the ignorance and "spontaneity" of the vast majority of Russian workers, who were deprived of the German workers' access to organization, proletarian culture, and education. These "mass workers," too, were the product of autocratic modernization, and precisely because of their lack of integration into Russian society their protest was less based on rational calculation and obedience to the appeals of worker organizations. Thus, when their many sources of discontent did

[16] For a good account of what Marxist socialism meant to such conscious workers, see A. V. Fisher, *V Rossii i v Anglii* (Moscow: Gosudarstvennoe izdatel'stvo, 1922), 15–16.

find an outlet, their action tended to be especially militant and dangerous to the regime. Time and again the "ignorant" mass of workers astounded the conscious workers and the intelligentsia by their uncompromising radicalism and, once unrest had erupted, by their receptivity to socialist ideas, even when they had been hostile to the socialists a short time before. It was this synthesis of the actions of a core of conscious workers, made radical by the combination of autocracy and capitalist development, and the broad mass of workers, more spontaneous in their militancy than their European counterparts, that accounts for the unusual radicalism of the Russian labor movement.

Particularly important in the equation was the weakness of organization among the workers. On the one hand, this deficiency meant that, to the dismay of the intelligentsia, the Russian workers could not struggle in a disciplined and coordinated way. But it also removed the many sources of conservatism and reformism that analysts from Robert Michels onward have identified with organization. Thus, there was no stratum of leaders with a stake in the status quo; no extensive calculation of the consequences of action based on a knowledge of the economic and political situation; little ability to direct the mass movement according to the leaders' prescriptions; and virtually no gap between an organized and privileged minority and the mass of the workers. In short, the very weakness of organization augmented the movement's radicalism and solidarity. The lack of associations also tied the workers to the socialist intelligentsia, no matter how little understanding the workers had of socialist ideas or how much hostility they felt toward the intelligentsia as domineering outsiders. Unable to generate their own leaders, ideas, and organizations, the workers had no choice but to rely on the intelligentsia in times of ferment.

The process of autocratic modernization thus generated a radical labor movement whose struggle against the industrialists and the tsarist regime dominated revolutionary politics in both 1905 and 1917. But the workers and factory owners were not the only actors in Russian urban politics.[17] Although, in comparison with their counterparts in Iran, Russian merchants remained politically marginal because of their social atomization and the paucity of large-scale enterprises,[18] students and professionals did on occasion play an important political role, most notably in 1905–1906. Although students had been relatively quiescent since the government's clampdown in 1884, unrest rooted in the government's heavy-handed controls reemerged around the turn of the century, as institutions of higher learning became influential centers of opposition to the regime. All of this

[17] For present purposes the revolutionary intelligentsia is excluded from consideration, since its role and significance is discussed at greater length in chapter seven.

[18] Ruckman, *Moscow Business Elite*, 51–52.

was dwarfed by student militancy in late 1905, when students succeeded in opening institutes and universities to the public as centers of public discussions and of mass meetings for opponents of the regime. The political space so provided facilitated ties among the different revolutionary organizations and groups, who in the atmosphere of the "meeting epidemic" fortified each others' resolve.[19] The government felt helpless to respond to this mass defiance of the laws on meetings and assemblies for fear of further intensifying the opposition. Yet despite the undoubted significance of these events, it would be hard to argue that the students played an independent and decisive role in the overall opposition to the regime, as evidenced by the overshadowing of student militancy by the worker strikes in the fall of 1905 that altered the pace of the revolution.

More significant in a sustained way was the liberal movement against the regime, involving an array of middle-class groups, particularly professionals. The origins of Russian liberalism as a significant movement can be traced to the era of the great reforms and the formation of the zemstvos and city dumas, which opened up the arena for political action for moderate opponents of the regime. The movement took on new life in the 1890s, with the infusion of significant numbers of the urban educated groups. These people—physicians, engineers, lawyers, teachers—soon began to exert a degree of influence incommensurate with their modest numbers, in large part due to the leadership of outstanding figures like P. N. Miliukov and Peter Struve. Liberalism was at the apogee of its prestige in the initial stages of episodes of widespread opposition to the regime, for in those moments, such as late 1904 and early 1917, it well expressed the generalized and not yet systematized opposition to the autocracy.

Yet as the general oppositional movement developed, liberalism lost much of its coherence and failed to gain influence over the masses. It was severely divided between more moderate reformers, who wanted to reach an accommodation with the regime and those like Miliukov who would settle for nothing less than a Western-style parliamentary system. In addition, the immense gap between the liberals, drawn almost exclusively from privileged Russia, and the masses of the urban population soon made itself felt, as the workers combined antiautocratic with anticapitalist demands and demonstrated little interest in political democracy per se. These considerations explain the declining political role of the liberals, who found themselves with little social base and slender capacity for sustained leadership.

In sum, in urban Russia, because of the contradictions endemic in the autocracy's sponsorship of capitalist industrialization, the cleavage between the lower classes, especially the workers, and privileged Russia was

[19] Ascher, *Revolution of 1905*, 196–206.

superimposed upon the cleavage between state and society. Modern social classes, the industrialists and the workers, were the predominant class antagonists, as the merchantry, even where numerous as in Moscow, had little political visibility, and crafts workers, though numerous and very significant in urban unrest, defined themselves in terms of modern class conflict, adhering to socialist parties and involving themselves in trade unions.[20] In this context of polarization, liberalism and the educated middle classes could not manage to establish a strong political role for themselves, although the liberals tried to claim leadership as an above-class party able to balance and accommodate competing interests.[21] Ultimately, in Russia the tendency was always toward division and polarization, not toward the synthesis of disparate groups in the pursuit of shared aims. Why the opposite was the case in Iran—why student revolutionaries cooperated with the clergy, bazaaris with the urban poor, and why class conflict was of so little note—is the key puzzle of Iranian urban politics.

Iranian Urban Relations and the Shah

Urban dominance in Iran, as in other Middle Eastern societies, had been expressed historically for centuries in the triad of court, mosque, and bazaar. The interplay of politics, religion, and economic life, especially commerce, that they embodied had found expression in a complex pattern of conflict and interdependence. Political authorities depended on the prosperity born of trade, but also sought to limit the bazaar's potential for political opposition. The rulers needed and pursued the legitimation of religion, but the ethical norms of Islam did not always coincide with the practices of secular rulers, and the political authorities were careful to limit the political role of the religious establishment. However these patterns of tension and symbiosis worked themselves out in different situations, it was this overall urban pattern that was the wellspring of political life in premodern Iran. Both domination and opposition were largely centered in the cities.

The Pahlavi modernization of Iran added complexity to the traditional pattern of urban dominance. The traditional craft and commercial activities centered in the bazaar were supplemented by modern financial, commercial, and industrial activities. The implications of economic modernization can be appreciated from the following statistics. The urban population increased its proportion of the total from roughly 28 percent in 1950 to

[20] See Victoria Bonnell, *Roots of Rebellion* (Berkeley: University of California Press, 1984).

[21] William Rosenberg, *Liberals in the Russian Revolution* (Princeton: Princeton University Press, 1974).

47 percent in 1976.[22] Peasant and agricultural wage workers declined from almost 60 percent of the labor force in 1956 to slightly over 30 percent in 1976, while wage earners in industry, construction, and related fields based in the cities increased from roughly 18 percent to 27 percent.[23] In a period of twenty years, Teheran almost doubled its share of the total population, from 7.9 percent to 13.3 percent.[24] In numerous dimensions the capital attained an overwhelming position in Iranian life. For example, 67 percent of university students were enrolled in institutions in Teheran; 29 percent of all, and 46 percent of large, industrial establishments were located there; it possessed 43 percent of hospital beds; and an amazing 61.5 percent of all newspapers and periodicals were published there.[25] The economic development of the cities, especially the capital, combined with the cultural and educational resources located there, encouraged an extraordinarily rapid rural to urban migration, which produced a proliferation of shantytowns in the large urban centers.

These quantitative indices give only the shadowiest image of the profundity of the changes in urban Iran. The cities continued their earlier domination, but they also lost much of their former coherence. Economically, the world of the bazaar coexisted and partly collided with modern industry and retail distribution. Iranian cultural and religious traditions, still especially strong in the bazaar and among the recent migrants from the countryside, confronted the Westernized culture adopted by many of the new privileged strata. The former mingling of classes in the traditional city was largely replaced by a new pattern of social segregation, the elites moving to their own precincts in the north of the city. According to a member of the privileged class, from the mid-1960s "living in 'our Teheran' was not very different from living in a European city; our homes, our offices, our clothes, our children's schools, our restaurants, and especially our mode of behavior, were pale carbon copies of the Western version. Henceforth, we rarely had the occasion or the desire to visit the southern part of the city."[26] Partly isolated from each other, partly in direct confrontation, these different social worlds coexisted to create a grand montage of often ill-fitting elements.[27] Despite its stubborn claims to be guiding the process by a higher wisdom, the regime was in no position to give deeper meaning to

[22] Farhad Kazemi, *Poverty and Revolution in Iran* (New York: New York University Press, 1980), 14.

[23] Behrang, *Le maillon faible*, 174.

[24] Ibid., 17.

[25] All figures from ibid., 25.

[26] Habib Ladjevardi, *Labor Unions and Autocracy in Iran* (Syracuse: Syracuse University Press, 1985), 236; see also X. de Planhol, "The Geographical Setting," in *The Cambridge History of Islam*, ed. P. M. Holt, Ann K. S. Lambton, and Bernard Lewis (Cambridge: Cambridge University Press, 1977), vol. 2B, 458–59, for the larger Middle Eastern context.

[27] Mottahedeh, *Mantle of the Prophet*, 270–72.

the changes and provide coherence to urban life. Much more than in Russia, with its older tradition of modernization and Western influence, the identity of the city was called into question. Two sets of social elites, virtually two social systems—the bazaar-clergy nexus with its mass base in the traditional economic sectors and the modern professional, financial, and industrial elites—embodied incompatible cultural, social, and economic models.

In this struggle to define Iranian urban life, the modern sectors suffered from disabilities that turned out to be insurmountable—a fact that goes far to explain the virtual non-existence of the democratic impulse in the Iranian revolution. The extraordinary concentration of industry, education, and culture in the capital facilitated central government control over the elites in each sphere. No equivalent to Moscow, with its embryonic organized industrialist opposition to the regime, could easily emerge in Iran. In addition, the regime's vast oil wealth and its ability to rely on foreign entrepreneurship and professional expertise lessened the regime's reliance on an independent industrialist class. Whereas the Russian factory owners had to make profits in the context of a certain amount of foreign competition, a feat that required a degree of entrepreneurial ability and independence, the enormous oil wealth in Iran reduced the imperatives of efficiency and profitability, at least for the heavily subsidized modern industrial sectors. The state, or often simply the court, could grant licenses, loans, and subsidies to its favored proteges with little regard for their entrepreneurial abilities. The industrial elite, then, tended to be made up of creatures of the regime, utterly dependent on political favors for their economic prosperity. The corollary of their unearned privileged status was naturally a striking vulnerability to the changing political winds. The Iranian regime dared to undertake populist measures against the economic elites and in favor of the workers that would have been unthinkable in Russia. The only formidable weapon in the industrialists' arsenal was capital flight, which did indeed lead the government to reverse many of its populist policies of 1975–1976. But recourse to flight also indicated their ultimate sense of helplessness in social and economic life.

The government's immense economic resources and its relative independence with respect to the industrialists also shaped the stance of the industrial working class, which could not easily define its position in terms of the traditional vocabulary of class conflict. Further hampering all modern urban groups—industrialists, workers, and professionals alike—were the political controls preventing independent corporate organizations. Political repression and the infiltration and penetration of social groups by government organizations, whether by SAVAK agents or state-controlled political parties, prevented even that development of civil society that existed before the revolution in Russia.

As a result of all these factors, modern social groups could not predominate in urban Iran, whose politics were not primarily centered on modern class conflict. In periods of disruption, it would not be factory owners or industrial workers who occupied center stage, but groups that to much of the rest of the world looked like museum pieces, and whose significance it was all too easy to overlook. In their opposition to the regime they could call on older loyalties and more resilient forms of organization than could the modern groups, and so could gain leadership of a broad and heterogeneous following that even included those who might logically have been their opponents.

Ironically, then, the regime proved much more effective in weakening the modern than the traditional urban sectors, although its intent was clearly to dominate all of society. But modern Iran it wanted merely to control and mobilize; traditional Iran it wanted to transform or destroy.

Yet it was unable to follow through on the kind of totalitarian measures necessary for this policy of statist "progress." In March 1975 the shah dissolved the two existing puppet parties and announced his intention of creating a one-party mobilizational state. The new party was given the name Rastakhiz, or the Resurgence party. Its formation was accompanied by grandiose claims and high-flown rhetoric bespeaking a burgeoning cult of personality. "The Shah-in-Shah of Iran," said one handbook, "is not just the political leader of Iran. He is also in the first instance teacher and spiritual leader, an individual who not only builds his nation [*sic*] roads, bridges, dams, and qanats [irrigation canals], but also guides the spirit and thought and hearts of his people."[28]

Designed by an odd mixture of Western-inspired political scientists cum bureaucrats and ex-members of the Tudeh party still spellbound by the idea of democratic centralism, the party was counted on to penetrate all of Iranian society, replacing other organizations and previous forms of association. The parallels with the practice of Leninist parties in power are striking: state-controlled media; the creation of pseudorepresentative female, worker, and peasant organizations; the enlistment of a huge mass membership; obligatory voting for the party ("those who do not register are answerable to the party");[29] and an aggressive policy toward independent groups or organizations, whether traditional or modern.

Yet within the context of a modernizing autocracy, the changes necessary to sustain such a policy proved unrealizable. A consistently statist policy would have required the elimination of private social elites, including the capitalist entrepreneurs that the regime was trying to create and woo. The clergy, champions of an alternative view of Iranian culture and society,

[28] Abrahamian, *Iran between Two Revolutions*, 442.

[29] Quoted in Ibid., 442.

would have to have been silenced. On a more positive note, the regime would have to have nurtured some kind of authentic social base—the equivalent of that core of energetic party workers and youthful enthusiasts in the Soviet 1930s—who identified their own happiness with the creation of a radiant future. Artists and cultural figures would have to have been mobilized in the service of a new ideology, which would have sought an irremediable break with the past.

Taken together these measures would have constituted the equivalent of the quasi-civil war strategy undertaken by successful one-party mobilizational regimes. They were close to unthinkable, and perhaps impossible, for an autocrat unwilling to break so radically with the past. The new party and associated organizations were formed, and they issued enough threats and embarked on enough ominous new policies to arouse the resentment and resistance of large sectors of the society, traditional and modern, urban and rural. Half-measures arising out of the contradictory process of autocratic modernization, they exacerbated rather than resolved the social and political dilemmas of the regime.

A less ambitious alternative to such a social, political, and cultural rupture was some form of statist capitalism. In particular, the Iranian government, like the Brazilian government in the 1970s, sought to "reinvent the bourgeoisie."[30] The dilemmas inherent in this project, evident from the Brazilian experience, manifested themselves even more clearly in Iran, where the state had more resources and the industrialists were less substantial as a class.

The failure to establish a real bourgeoisie was not the result of the government's lack of appreciation for its necessity, for the regime never advocated state capitalism, always emphasizing its adherence to the private enterprise model. A series of measures was announced in the 1960s to increase the share of the private capitalist sector at the expense of the public sector. In March 1970 a "new economic policy" was announced, key provisions of which included the prohibition of the creation of new enterprises wholly owned by the government; the requirement that, in mixed enterprises, the majority of stock must belong to private investors; and the transferal of metallurgical, petrochemical, and other state enterprises to private capital. In April 1970 Prime Minister Hoveida announced that the government's goal was to direct all industry to the private sector.

The appeal of such policies for the weakly bureaucratized Iranian state, hardly possessing the coherence necessary for efficient industrial administration, should come as no surprise. But, as the Soviet scholar Ivanov dryly

[30] See Peter Evans, "Reinventing the Bourgeoisie: State Entrepreneurship and Class Formation in Dependent Capitalist Development," *American Journal of Sociology* 88, suppl. (1982): S210–47.

noted, these plans and goals contradicted the objective conditions and requisites of the development of the country.[31] The supply of local entrepreneurs was limited, and government revenues and foreign capital were readily available. The outcome of these conflicting conditions was neither private capitalism nor state capitalism, but a kind of neopatrimonial economic system bringing together the court, the bureaucracy, and private enterprise. In this conjuncture, the court seemed to play the predominant role, as all significant commercial or industrial initiatives required its approval, which in turn usually required that the shah or his family participated in the enterprise. As one scholar concluded, "at least some member of the Pahlavi family has a direct and legitimate voice, by dint of ownership, in the operation of nearly all commerce and industry in Iran"[32]—a situation for which it would be hard to find a parallel in any major country in the world, or proper concepts in political or economic sociology.

The patrimonial nature of the regime also included government control over the industrialists and the announcement of numerous populist measures to win over the working class to the regime. The most famous of these were the various programs to benefit the workers presented as part of the White Revolution and the 1975 law on worker shareholding in industry. These measures have universally been judged as ineffective for the protection of the workers—they were applied arbitrarily and to a limited number of workers—but they did succeed in frightening a great many industrialists. The workers, meanwhile, were denied independent organization, as the government sought to use the pseudoparties and the SAVAK to develop a network of government-controlled labor organizations.

Even more than in Russia, it was this contradictory mix of government policies that determined the shape of modern urban class relations in Iran. The industrialists had less autonomy and a less audible public voice than their Russian peers. In general, their social origins were dual: civil servants benefiting from their political connections and bazaar traders who moved to take advantage of the incentives given to investors in industry.[33] This industrialist class was also remarkably recent. Even some of the old merchant families with deeper historical roots as a social elite were new qua industrialists. In addition, the industrialists' dependency on the government and its populist rhetoric irritated many factory owners, as did the competition from the public-sector industries.[34] Some also opposed the closed political system, which frustrated their desires to have more input

[31] Ivanov, *Iran v 60–70-kh godakh*, 99–100.

[32] Zonis, *Political Elite*, 30.

[33] See Halliday, *Iran: Dictatorship and Development*, 151; Behrang, *Le maillon faible*, 123. It has also been argued that many landowners deprived of their land became industrialists. The figures gathered in Najmabadi, *Land Reform*, 203–5, cast doubt upon this claim.

[34] Bashiriyeh, *State and Revolution in Iran*, 42.

into policy making.[35] Yet this deep ambivalence among many industrialists never took the form of organized political opposition. As a class they were politically invisible.

Little has been written about the implications of the industrialists' overall social position for their relationship to the workers. They certainly opposed the government's populist reforms, which they could not succeed in blocking, but could refuse to implement—one of the key reasons for the measures' general lack of efficacy. In addition, according to some observers, Iranian factory owners and managers tended to replicate the autocratic practices of the regime in their own enterprises, displaying "feudal" patterns of behavior.[36] How far this pattern is generalizable to modern foreign-owned or state enterprises is impossible to say given the absence of detailed studies, but it would be surprising if the overall traits of the regime and the workers' lack of rights were not reflected throughout all sectors of the economy to some degree. Further, whether by industrialist consent or not, SAVAK agents were very visible in the factories, monitoring the workers' attitudes and behavior, and owners and managers inevitably reaped part of the blame for government repression.

Mutual isolation and mistrust were the inevitable consequences of this pattern of industrial relations, once again duplicating more widespread traits of Iranian society. The gap between industrialists and workers seems to have become even wider during the economic boom of the late 1960s and 1970s. The oil boom "brought to the rich business empires unimagined by earlier entrepreneurs, palaces worthy of ancient kings, and scandals that far overshadowed those of the previous generation."[37] Efficiency was unnecessary; corruption flourished. The opulent displays of wealth, encouraged by the example of the royal family, seemed parasitic, not the earned reward of contributions to progress in Iran. The chances for a perceived community of interest between workers and industrialists grew even dimmer.

Autocratic repression, populist promises, massive oil wealth, foreign capital, a weak and divided industrialist class, rapid industrial growth: this complex of traits holds forth little hope of coherent working-class action, whether reformist or revolutionary. As compared with the activities of the tsarist regime, both repression and benefits were more pronounced. A comparison of SAVAK with the tsarist political police reveals some of the most important contrasts. The tsarist police were unable to institute police-controlled worker organizations because of the threat they posed to the

[35] Halliday, *Dictatorship and Development*, 42–43.

[36] Assef Bayat, *Workers and Revolution in Iran* (London: Zed Books, 1987), 55–56. This book, though inadequate, is one of the few sources of information on the contemporary Iranian working class in English.

[37] Abrahamian, *Iran between Two Revolutions*, 448.

vulnerable capitalists and because of opposition within the regime to any form of worker organization or mobilization, even progovernment. SAVAK ran a far-flung network of worker organizations in order to prevent independent unions and to be able to monitor the workers' political activities. In Russia, the police often attacked capitalist exploitation of the workers but, despite repeated threats, could do little to change wages or working conditions. In addition, the Ministry of Finance and factory owners worked together to reduce the presence of police in the factories, for fear of undermining the authority of the industrialists. In Iran, SAVAK officials often had offices in the factories, and not only attempted to root out subversion using agents and paid informers but also sought to mediate between the workers and the factory owners in order to mobilize worker support for the regime.[38]

Finally, there can be little doubt that SAVAK's efficiency and brutality far outstripped that of the comparatively old-fashioned and civilized tsarist secret police. The combination of greater repression and greater rewards had larger consequences as well. No stratum of conscious workers or embryonic trade union movement could develop in Iran. Similarly, virtually no political space was open to activist members of the intelligentsia, who were thus induced to instigate guerrilla-type activities in order to publicize their existence and persuade the workers that resistance to the regime was possible. For it was the general conviction among the revolutionaries that the workers believed the government to be omnipotent and themselves helpless.[39] Meanwhile, a significant sector of workers did benefit from the profit-sharing and share ownership programs and from government pressure to raise wages during the period of economic boom. The gap between the privileged workers of the modern sector and more small-scale traditional industry appears to have widened during the rapid industrialization, and many writers speak of the emergence of a workers' aristocracy in Iran. Others assert that the industrial workers as a whole were "bought off" and consequently played little role in the political opposition to the shah.[40]

In some respects the Iranian working class did resemble its Russian equivalent. Both were numerically small. No adequate figures exist for Iran, and problems of definition abound, so that the estimates vary widely. But even according to the most generous figures, modern industrial workers did not number much more than 2 million out of a total population of roughly 40 million, and some estimates were much smaller. According to Halliday, over 72 percent of "workers" were employed in shops of less than 10 employees; the "core" industrial labor force in enterprises larger than

[38] Halliday, *Dictatorship and Development*, 81.

[39] Bayat, *Workers and Revolution*, 64.

[40] Mottahedeh, *Mantle of the Prophet*, 308; Arjomand, *Turban for the Crown*, 107–8.

this numbered about 700,000, or about 7 percent of the economically active population.[41] In addition, both industrial labor forces were highly heterogeneous, characterized by large influxes of peasant migrants unacquainted with socialist ideas or traditions of worker struggle. In both, too, because of the rapid pace of industrialization, "industry" was very heterogeneous, ranging from traditional craft-type establishments to modern plants with advanced technology.

Obviously, these traits shared by the two industrial labor forces were not decisive in shaping labor protest, for they cannot explain the very great differences in militancy and class consciousness. Rather, of key significance is the contrast between a basically capitalist model of industrialization with pre–twentieth-century styles of political despotism and a neopatrimonial model with the most modern technology of repression.

Despite these differences, the Iranian like the Russian working class had numerous grounds for complaint. Even the most privileged sectors lacked freedom and were victimized by the threat of government repression. The discrepancy between the government's rhetoric of solicitude for the downtrodden, accompanied by ambitious policy initiatives, and its much more limited accomplishments could not but be evident, and many worker struggles aimed to force the government to honor its commitments.[42] Nor could the government sustain the pace of economic growth or guarantee ever-increasing standards of living, despite its assurances and the vast oil wealth. Consequently, both in periods of general political opposition, such as the early 1960s and 1978, and at times of economic distress, worker strikes did make their contribution to the overall ferment. But for the reasons already suggested, the modern industrial workers were not at the forefront of events and worker militancy did not tend to define itself so much in terms of class conflict as part of the all-national opposition to the shah.

In contrast to the very divergent political roles of the Russian and Iranian working classes, the modern middle classes's political trajectories were remarkably similar in both countries. In both cases, autocratic modernization opened new possibilities for the modern middle classes by vastly expanding their share in the labor force and thus providing the socioeconomic basis for a strong political presence. In Iran the new middle class first emerged as a significant social category in the 1930s under Reza Shah. It continued to grow and develop during the rule of his son, increasing from an estimated 852,000 in 1956 (14 percent of the labor force) to 1,907,000 in 1977 (18 percent of the labor force).[43] The autocratic re-

[41] Halliday, *Dictatorship and Development*, 182.

[42] Behrang, *Le maillon faible*, 264.

[43] See the table in Arjomand, *Turban for the Crown*, 218.

gimes also potentially augmented the political saliency of the middle classes by giving cogency and urgency to their most characteristic goals, constitutional government and, in addition to this in Iran, enhanced national sovereignty. Their demand for political participation and law emerged from the contradiction between their high level of professional attainments and their social and political emasculation. In Iran, for example, other than the bar association, there were no significant professional associations and, of course, no independent political parties. Yet this demand arising from their own experience had the potential of exercising broad appeal to social groups with highly discrepant class positions. In the abstract, then, autocratic modernization did create some preconditions for strong middle-class political leadership.

Equally significant, however, were the numerous ways in which the regimes undermined the middle class's political role. The middle class has much to lose and so is especially vulnerable to political repression. Its predominantly urban location and social visibility worked to increase the effectiveness of government controls. As a result, the middle class inevitably suffered from political atomization and an inability to act collectively. Its relatively privileged status and modern Western education effectively cut it off from the masses, who inhabited a different social world. Nor, even if it were possible sociologically, would the regime have permitted the middle class to organize a mass political base among the lower classes.

This complex blend of factors created the following pattern in Russia and Iran. In the early stages of opposition to the regimes, the new middle classes had a substantial political role. Their knowledge and skills combined with the appeal of their all-national demands for political freedom allowed them to exercise initial leadership in 1904–1905 Russia and the Mossadegh period in Iran. Yet this leadership was inherently fragile, as different groups came to interpret their shared political opposition to the regimes in very different ideological terms and as the leaders of the middle class proved unable to mobilize a mass base on their own.

Thus, by the end of the early period of antiautocratic mobilization they had already begun to lose their centrality. This process of political decay continued during the succeeding years of autocratic retrenchment and socioeconomic modernization in both countries. As the opposition became more differentiated, the limited political goals of the middle class seemed anemic beside the ambitious programs of social reconstruction offered by their rivals. In addition, with the economic dynamism there was the constant danger of reabsorption of the middle sectors into the status quo. In Iran, for example, the oil boom of the late 1960s and early 1970s created massive opportunities for professional employment, and many former radical opponents of the regime joined the state bureaucracy.[44] (In Russia, too, many professionals abandoned revolutionary politics after the defeat of the 1905 revolution in order to resume their careers in an expanding economy.) Despite the promising beginnings, after a number of years of autocratic modernization, the advantages of the middle class's position were far outweighed by the dilemmas, to the detriment of the middle class's potential for leadership in the oppositional movement.

Students in Iran experienced a similar set of contradictions. Often from privileged backgrounds and able to expect good jobs in an expanding economy with a shortage of skilled professionals, they nonetheless suffered directly from the regime's control over the universities and its muffling of public opinion. Like students elsewhere, many also appeared to feel the weight of their society's injustice more deeply and empathize with its victims. The impact of modernization on the country's culture pained them and stimulated many to search for more authentic sources of personal and collective identity. Not yet established in careers and family life, the costs of opposition were in some ways not so severe, though one should always remember the arbitrariness and ferocity of SAVAK. Ties to Iranian student organizations abroad, which were able to publicize the struggle against the shah, gave them a degree of political space unavailable to the more traditional groups. For all these reasons, Iranian students were among the most consistent groups in opposition to the shah. Their activities were all the more significant in the context of the relative absence of organized labor protest. They became the most visible source of opposition in the modern sector. However, because they did not participate qua students but as adherents of a number of competing ideological currents and political groups, their actions were fragmented and often isolated from the other main oppositional tendencies. Although they could keep alive the spirit of opposition and initiate major episodes of protest through courageous exemplary acts, they could not stir the masses and lead a revolution.

In the relative saliency of modern and traditional social groups in oppositional movements, the Iranian pattern was the reverse of the Russian. Whereas in Iran modern factory owners and industrial workers were of comparatively minor importance in politics, a number of traditional urban groups decisively shaped events. Of particular importance were the groups composing the bazaar, with its retail and wholesale shops, craftsmen, petty tradesmen, and substantial merchants. In addition, a plethora of urban associations—discussion groups, religious circles and brotherhoods, neighborhood organizations—helped define and channel discontent. Although the precise significance of this assortment of urban associations is difficult

[44] Richard Cottam, *Nationalism in Iran* (Pittsburgh: University of Pittsburgh Press, 1979), 344.

to assess, there can be no doubt that these loose networks generated and propagated sentiments and social ties vital to sustain social protest. The intimate ties of many of these groups with the ulama gave coherence to their ideas, resources for struggle, and a sense of broader purpose and solidarity. Although it was the ulama who consolidated power after the overthrow of the shah, their victory would have been inconceivable without the support of the bazaar—much of which became disillusioned with the policies of the new regime rather quickly.

An important clarification is in order. The concept of "traditional" social group should not be misinterpreted. The Iranian city and all of its constituent social classes and institutions underwent immense changes in the late nineteenth century and throughout the twentieth century. In the bazaar many old specialties declined or disappeared, and new ones emerged to take their place. The nature of the guilds and the social role of the bazaari elite likewise experienced major transformations. As noted in chapter seven, the role of the ulama in society and politics was also far from static. The concept *traditional*, therefore, does not imply immobility or stagnation. A great deal of flexibility and innovation was required for these groups to sustain their positions. The concept merely denotes that these groups were a survival from preindustrial Iran, from a time when their preeminence was not challenged by groups rooted in modern industry, politics, and culture; and that, although they adapted many of their practices to the modern age, much of their outlook and way of life derived ultimately from a preindustrial society with its different rhythms and values. The discrepancy between their cultural beliefs and customary social practices and many features of the Pahlavi modernization program inevitably set many of them against the regime, although neither the bazaar nor the ulama were united against modern society tout court.

The persistence and vitality of social protest by traditional urban groups have no parallel in any other twentieth-century revolution. Two preconditions merged to make possible this remarkable phenomenon. First, of great significance was the historical predominance of the city and its elites in Iranian and indeed in Middle Eastern history, closely linked to the significance of large-scale trade. Second, although the regime's modernization program threatened to undermine the traditional groups' roles in Iranian society, it had not yet left them defenseless. If the oil boom and rapid industrial growth had continued for another decade or two, the bazaar might well have been economically marginalized. But by the late 1970s it still had the wealth and power to finance and help organize, if not lead, the revolution.

The unique role of traditional urban social groups in Iranian revolutionary politics thus partly derives from the strength of historical survivals. Middle Eastern cities, and Iranian cities in particular, had historically lacked corporate organizations but, as noted in chapter one, they did possess other forms of association with a political role. These included strong neighborhood territorial divisions, whose internal solidarity provided a basis for collective action. The bazaar itself was not simply an economic unit, for its geographical location in the heart of the city, in close contact with mosques and government institutions, augmented its political role. In addition, its economic importance to the rulers and the symmetry between its economic practices and the religious injunctions of Islam facilitated close ties between the clergy and the bazaar merchants. The bazaar also had its own forms of guild associations, which engaged in religious and political activities as well. Other types of associations that could become important in urban life included various types of neighborhood and youth organizations, most notoriously the gangs of urban toughs called *lutis* in Iran. The lutis often had close connections with leading clergymen and bazaaris, who could deploy them for their own political purposes.[45] The lack of formal corporate organization allowed the different participants to negotiate shifting and ramified sets of relationships that did not have to be validated through fixed procedure, imparting great fluidity and unpredictability to urban political life.

Much of the old structure of urban Iranian politics was necessarily weakened or eliminated as a result of modernization. The rivalry of competing urban districts lost its saliency. The youth organizations, athletic groups, and lutis continued to exist, but their independence of action diminished in the face of a changing social structure and more effective government control. The shape of the cities changed, as the old centers with their richly textured associational patterns coexisted with highly stratified new districts. The north of Teheran, where the new elites settled, had little connection with the old patterns of urban life; nor did the bazaar and mosque dominate the urban experience of the new migrants in the shantytowns. The relative economic role of the bazaar declined with the industrialization of the country, and even retail trade was often conducted in shops in the avenues of the new districts.

Just as significantly, both Pahlavi monarchs were convinced that the bazaar was an emblem and symptom of Iran's backwardness and might oppose their modernization programs. In line with this belief, they initiated many measures to control or undermine the bazaars—urban renewal programs, which sometimes involved building modern roads through the heart of the honeycombed streets of the bazaar; encouragement of bazaar merchants to invest in industry; and the formation of state-controlled

[45] See Willem Floor, "The Political Role of the Lutis in Iran," in *Religion and Politics in Iran*, ed. Michael Bonine and Nikkie Keddie (New Haven: Yale University Press, 1983), 83–98.

guilds, merchant associations, and chambers of commerce to rival the older patterns of leadership. Most ominous of all was the campaign of 1975–1976 against profiteering, when the government sent thousands of agents to ensure that the merchants obeyed the government's rules. According to the minister of the interior, by the end of 1977 approximately ten thousand had been incarcerated; it was also determined that more than half of the Teherani shopkeepers had violated price controls and were under criminal investigation. Aside from the numerous bankruptcies caused by the price controls, many merchants who violated the rules lost their licenses and were forced to close.[46]

The merchants naturally resented the state's incursions into the life of the bazaars, although some did benefit from the economic boom and the opportunities to invest in industry.[47] They were also embittered by the growing prominence of the "petrobourgeoisie" and the need for merchants to prostrate themselves before the court to obtain the licenses, credits, and the like necessary for business. In addition, closely linked to traditional religious sectors, they also opposed the cultural Westernization of the country and the regime's attacks on the religious establishment. In autocratic Iran, they could not form oppositional parties and associations, as had their Iraqi counterparts under the monarchy,[48] nor, because of their lack of corporate organization and the effects of autocratic controls, could they act as a pressure group. Yet, though undermined, enough remained of the traditional economic and social patterns of urban Iran to permit explosions of urban unrest at times of crisis. Indeed, for this kind of protest the very lack of modern organizations was an advantage, for formal leadership and institutions would have been more vulnerable to repression.

The urban networks of which the bazaar merchants, craftsmen, and workers formed a part cannot be described precisely, for indefiniteness and subtly ramifying connections were of their very essence. A listing of some of the associations with which the bazaar was closely interconnected would include mosques, Sufi houses of worship, sports houses, coffee and tea houses, *dowrehs*, and *hayats*.[49] Dowrehs were informal groups that met irregularly at the homes of different participants or in local coffeehouses in order to discuss cultural, political, or religious affairs. Their participants were brought together by shared cultural interests and ties of emotional

[46] Misagh Parsa, "Economic Development and Political Transformation: A Comparative Analysis of the United States, Russia, Nicaragua and Iran," *Theory and Society* 14 (September 1985): 669–70.

[47] Balta and Rulleau, *L'Iran insurgé*, 170.

[48] Hanna Batatu, *The Old Social Classes and the Revolutionary Movements of Iraq* (Princeton: Princeton University Press, 1978), 293–94.

[49] See Majid Tehranian, "Communication and Revolution in Iran: The Passing of a Paradigm," *Iranian Studies* 13, nos. 1–4 (1980): 19.

sympathy, which allowed them to communicate with each other in ways discouraged in Iranian public life. In general their participants were relatively well-established bureaucrats or intellectuals. Hayats were similar associations formed within the bazaar or often in new parts of the cities populated by migrants. The bazaar hayats were sometimes confined to a single trade, but also could comprise members of diverse trades and social backgrounds. Religious issues were frequently discussed in these meetings, but they also branched out into broader social and political topics as well.[50] Neighborhood hayats had a somewhat different character: they were not so much functionally based as formed around local contact and shared village or regional origin. The religious element in the hayats in the shantytowns was particularly strong, as members of the clergy were invited to give lessons on the Koran or discuss other religious themes. The late 1960s witnessed the proliferation of cassette sermons, which also made their way into the neighborhood hayats in the urban shantytowns. This was one of the many ways in which religion became articulated with society at the grass roots, in marked contrast to the regime's efforts to impose organizations and values from above.

Observers are in accord on the importance of these almost invisible but infinitely reticulated patterns of urban association in Pahlavi Iran. They constituted "a resilient informal network of communication" (Tehranian) relatively immune to government repression, which could yet foster intense ties of collective belief and loyalty. To Bill, writing in the early 1970s, before the implications of these dense networks for communicating oppositional ideas had become fully apparent, "mechanisms like the dowrah encourage plotting and omnipresent interlaced antagonisms but discourage concentrated and shattering confrontations. Finally, a system of such informal politics thins and splinters opposition although it at the same time covers and hides the same."[51]

Bill does not draw out the full consequences of this pattern for political protest. In times of quiescence, their mutual isolation and lack of corporate organization appeared to make discontent and dissidence a private affair, invisible to the public at large and unable to challenge government policies. But once a certain threshold of protest had been reached, as occurred in the 1960–1963 period and in 1978–1979, these informal but strong personal associational ties could throb with life and serve as powerful conduits of protest. Emotions entered into collective action in ways difficult to imagine for more formal patterns of organizations, such as professional associations or trade unions, with their functional, rather than territorial bases and their hierarchies of authority and decision making. For the ter-

[50] See Thaiss, "Religious Symbolism and Social Change," 192–235.

[51] Bill, *Politics of Iran*, 48.

ritorial dimension of these various urban associations was also important: the tempo of protest could be heightened through the mutual influence of direct contact among people who knew each other. In all this, the diverse Iranian associations resembled the underground factory organizations in tsarist Russia, which also gained strength from informal ties and the lack of fixed organization. The factory organizations, too, had little visibility or impact during periods of tranquillity, but once protest had begun they became effective sources of mobilization, though not of control based on larger strategic considerations.

In both the Iranian urban associations and the Russian factory organizations, protest thus had a rhythm very different from that characteristic of societies with more developed civic and interest organizations. In most periods discontent simmered beneath the surface, contained in its expression by repression, the lack of a sphere of public debate, and a strong sense of isolation and impotence among the dissatisfied. Yet once a certain level of protest had been passed, these informal territorial associations proved to be more powerful channels of militant action than the legal and more institutionalized organizations found elsewhere. As a consequence, both in Russia and Iran, protest had a highly uneven character, marked by extreme oscillations of artificial calm interposed with intense militancy.

Not all of these associations were connected to the bazaar, nor can all be called "traditional" in the sense just discussed. But the bazaar was undeniably at the heart of much of the associational life in urban Iran. As noted, merchants and craftsmen themselves formed various types of groups. Men of property subsidized the ulama, whose activity increasingly extended to the new slum areas of the cities. They also endowed or built mosques, sometimes in these outlying areas; in fact, leaders of neighborhood hayats would sometimes attempt to locate wealthy patrons to construct a mosque for their districts. These activities presupposed a great deal of wealth and considerable social prestige, at least in more traditional circles. In this connection, it should be emphasized that, despite the bazaar's relative economic decline, it remained rich and powerful throughout the period of rapid modernization. According to one estimate, it controlled roughly half of Iran's handicraft production, two-thirds of its retail, and three-fourths of its wholesale trade. These economic activities sustained roughly half a million merchants, shopkeepers, traders, and workshop owners[52]—not many fewer than the total number of modern industrial workers. Indeed, as noted previously, it was precisely this contradiction between the traditional sector's continuing prosperity and the acute threat posed by the shah's political system and economic policy that explains its oppositional stance. On the lower levels, from among the craftsmen and employees, the

[52] Abrahamian, *Iran between Two Revolutions*, 433.

bazaar furnished recruits for radical Islamic movements, such as the Devotees of Islam.[53] These same organizations received financial support from wealthy Teheran merchants, whose class also, as we have seen, participated in, encouraged, and subsidized a wide variety of other religious and traditional organizations and activities. It is perhaps not too much of an exaggeration to say that the bazaaris funded the Islamic revolution.

The Islamic clergy were also indispensable in giving a degree of unity to the many-layered urban protest movements. Their organization and ideas will be examined in a later chapter, but here it will be appropriate to point out some of the sources of their influence in the urban milieu. With respect to the bazaar, there had been a high degree of interdependence with the ulama for centuries. The ties of shared interest and belief did not weaken in the period of rapid modernization, but were rather fortified by the state's hostile policy toward both groups. In these circumstances, the bazaar and the mosque were natural allies against the state, which had previously been part of the elite triad. More interesting was the ability of the ulama to extend their influence to the new urban lower class districts and prepare the ground for their participation in the revolution. Faced with the threat from the state, the clergy's motivation for developing new constituencies is obvious. As opposed to the revolutionary parties, the clergy also had greater scope for action, for no matter how hostile the regime may have been to the ulama, it could hardly use repression on a wide scale against the representatives of the religion it claimed to embrace. The hayats, with the frequent participation of the ulama, were generally the only possible independent associational life among the urban poor. Truly representative parties and trade unions were of course prohibited.

Yet there is surely more to the urban poor's receptivity to religious teachers and ideas than their greater accessibility. For not only in Iran, but throughout the Middle East, the urban masses have always been less drawn to modern nationalism or socialism than to religious fundamentalism of various kinds.[54] In most contexts, these religious beliefs centered on miracles, on magical powers, and on the world to come, serving as a refuge for people with little hope.[55] What is remarkable in Iran is that the more activist conception of Islam and increasingly militant opposition to the shah's regime among a large part of the ulama found a ready response among the urban poor, thus calling into question generalizations about the political

[53] Farhad Kazemi, "The Fada'iyan-e Islam: Fanaticism, Politics and Terror," in Arjomand, *From Nationalism to Revolutionary Islam*, 168.

[54] Enayat, *Modern Islamic Political Thought*, 116.

[55] See, for example, Michael Gilsenan, *Recognizing Islam* (New York: Pantheon, 1982), 90.

conservatism of urban migrants in Third World countries.[56] Clearly, as Eric Hobsbawm showed for peasant politics, oppressed classes can be receptive to different political teachings.[57] In Iran, as in Italy and Spain, their political orientation depended ultimately on the initiative of outsiders, who were able to shape how they interpreted their experiences and influenced what political implications they drew.

On the surface, the previous analysis of the textured social relations of traditional urban Iran, which partly extended to the shantytowns as well, contradicts the theoretical discussion of the atomization, lack of trust, incoherence, and frailty of society during autocratic modernization. Considered more deeply, however, it in fact confirms the earlier analysis, for it was precisely these traditional groups, survivals from the past, that were best able to avoid or resist the shah's policies. The regime attempted to impose new organizational and cultural patterns on the bazaar and the mosque, and in time it might well have succeeded. At least in the short run, however, these groups were able partly to adapt to, partly to oppose the new society in gestation. Their success was due to a significant degree to the enduring strength, perhaps even reinforcement, of traditional ties, which provided a measure of trust, predictability, and solidity to the society—traits visibly absent in modern Iran. The remnants of traditional society provided a refuge from, points of resistance to, and a foundation of opposition against the Iran of the shah and his planners. Ironically, the vitality of the traditional sector also stemmed from the regime's devastating mutilation of modern Iran in the cultural, economic, and political spheres. In this context, neither a capitalist class nor a modern proletariat nor a nationalist or socialist intelligentsia promised to provide leadership for a reconstructed Iran. Instead, the vast majority of Iranians looked to those groups least tainted by the distorted modernization sponsored by the regime.

In urban social and political life in Russia and Iran, the process of autocratic modernization reshaped social relationships and facilitated the emergence of powerful forces of social protest. Despite the very important differences between the two countries—in the relationship between the state and urban elites, the relative saliency of modern social classes, and the possibility for organized opposition—both countries exhibited the following characteristics: fundamental ambiguities and inconsistencies in the political model; political repression and arbitrariness; weak social elites with little independent authority over their social subordinates; social mistrust and

[56] For example, Samuel Huntington and Joan Nelson, *No Easy Choice: Political Participation in Developing Countries* (Cambridge: Harvard University Press, 1976), 109.

[57] *Primitive Rebels* (New York: Norton, 1959).

polarization; and mass discontent of various types that, finding no outlet in legitimate organizations, could express itself only in dangerous forms. Such a pattern made possible two polar alternatives to the everyday hurly-burly of mutual adjustment in more democratic modern societies: either eerie calm based on repression or else intransigent revolt against the system as a whole.

Six

Autocracy, Landlords, and Peasants

THE NATURE of agrarian classes and relations and the transformation of these during economic development shape the politics of modernization in fundamental, sometimes decisive, ways. Whether agrarian elites can provide an economic foundation for industrial growth through increasing agricultural productivity will influence a whole range of political and economic issues, from tariffs to taxation policy. Successful economic performance will also buttress the overall social and political position of the agrarian elites. Just as significant as whether the landowners transform agriculture is the question of how they themselves undergo metamorphosis as a result of economic development. Do they lose their precapitalist traits in order to become a modern economic elite employing wage labor and developing ties with urban capitalists and financial interests? Or do they isolate themselves from the cities and minimize as far as possible the spread of the market? Of equal political significance is the fate of the rural lower classes. Whether they remain a peasantry exploited by a landowning nobility, or become wage laborers in commercial estates or independent farmers will condition the potential for agricultural progress and the prospects for modern forms of political participation in the rural areas.

In insisting on the dominance of the cities in revolutionary politics in the pattern of autocratic modernization, one need not minimize the impact of rural affairs, either in giving shape to the overall process of development or in affecting the process and outcome of the revolutions. Indeed, the elites sponsoring autocratic modernization in Russia and Iran were unable to devise solutions to the challenge of rural modernization in their countries, a failure that was connected with urban crises in many ways. Economically, rural underdevelopment entailed higher food prices, poor living standards in rural areas, and a growing gap between cities and the countryside. Socially and politically, the deficiencies of agriculture, the inability to create elements of a modern rural social structure of prosperous agricultural entrepreneurs, large or small, deprived both regimes of potential elite and mass support from the countryside. In neither country could the rural areas serve as bastions of stability. And in Russia, of course, peasant militancy sapped the strength of the autocracy and threatened the survival of the nobility well before the 1917 revolution, when the peasants' dream of a "black repartition" was fully realized.

The fundamental weaknesses of rural modernization in both countries were parallel to those of industry, without the compensating provision of state sponsorship and benefits, which endowed industry with a certain dynamism. The rural elites, like their urban counterparts, could not rely on a stable system of property or a lawful and predictable pattern of government action. Although the Russian nobility as a class did display some entrepreneurial potential in the late eighteenth and early nineteenth centuries, they never recovered from the political shock of the emancipation of the serfs and underwent further decline as a result of the policy of rapid industrialization. In Iran, Reza Shah arbitrarily confiscated estates, which were often incorporated into his private domain. As we will see, landed property was even less secure during the rule of his son, even if the methods applied were less capricious. With their futures so uncertain, landowners in both countries generally lacked confidence and the expansive vision necessary for long-term risks. Nor, for reasons that will be spelled out later, did peasant agriculture in either country ever exhibit any significant dynamism. The difficulties were not purely social and political. The regimes' commitment to rapid industrial growth precluded, in their own eyes, the kind of attention to agriculture that might have ushered in dramatic changes. In the last decade of the shah's rule, his planners did begin to perceive the social and economic costs of a backward agriculture, and more resources were devoted to agricultural investment in the plans, but the results were not impressive. The deficiencies of Iranian agriculture were too deep to be solved simply by more investment or voluntarist decrees from above.

Beyond these core similarities, the social, political, and economic contexts of agriculture in the two countries varied considerably, with decisive implications for the role of the countryside in social change. In Russia the assertion of autocratic power and the commitment to industrialization undermined the economic position and legitimacy of the landowners, but they remained the political bedrock of the regime. Their dominance in provincial government and their immense influence in national politics remained indispensable for the autocracy and were even enhanced after the 1905 revolution. The tsar's laments about the hardships afflicting the landed gentry were certainly sincere, as was his assurance regarding them that, "the ancient stronghold of order and of the moral strength of Russia—it will be my constant concern to consolidate [them]."[1]

Ironically, too, the directing hand of the state had also "consolidated" the peasantry, especially in the form of the peasant commune, which had been granted the right to dispose of property collectively after the emancipation. The government unintentionally created a potential for collective

[1] Gurko, *Features and Figures of the Past*, 228.

action through the provision of collective rights and responsibilities. In Iran, neither the landowners nor the peasants were "consolidated" by the state to any significant degree. It is striking, in fact, how weak the reach of the autocratic power had historically been in the countryside. The immense oil wealth made possible an increased government presence in the villages, so that by the mid-1970s rural Iran had also experienced the weight of the modernizing state, which did not so much consolidate as atomize rural society. As compared with landowners in Russia, the Iranian landlords proved to be more politically dispensable, as the land reform demonstrated. Without the impetus to action provided by a landowning class regarded as parasitic, and with weaker communal traditions than in Russia, the Iranian peasantry was in no position to mount an independent challenge to the regime. But neither was there any landed elite to come to the regime's defense. Thus, although both countries suffered from low agricultural productivity and fundamental weaknesses in agrarian society, the Russian state was unable to alter social relations radically, whereas the Iranian state did manage to reform the land tenure system. And the Russian countryside, but not the Iranian, came to nurture powerful revolutionary peasant movements.

The Genesis of Peasant Radicalism in Russia

If 1917 was partly the outcome of the failure of the Russian government and industrialists to create an industrial order recognizing and imparting rights to a new stratum of industrial workers, it also stemmed from a long-term crisis in rural Russia, expressions of which were an increasingly threatened gentry and a peasantry unwilling to abide the prevailing distribution of land and power. To interpret the rural crisis, one must go beyond abstract theories of dependent development or general models of the impact of capitalism in the countryside by giving due weight to the specific role of the state in the countryside. For the autocratic regime shaped property relations, rural institutions, investment priorities, and modes of rural political expression, simultaneously seeking to sponsor changes but attempting to keep them within limits defined by the regime. Ultimately its faltering attempts at social engineering in the countryside did little either to shore up the old Russia, as was sometimes its goal, or to hasten the emergence of a dynamic and productive rural society. Peasant discontent with the remnants of the old regime was a constant in the last decades of imperial Russia; they rebelled when circumstances seemed propitious.

The most visible dimension of the weakness of rural Russia in the last decades of the old regime was its overall economic backwardness. Agriculture was poorly capitalized and innovation rare. The technological changes that had transformed rural economies in much of Europe and North America had barely made their appearance in Russia by the time of the revolution. In 1904, 40 percent of the land was owned by some twelve million peasant households; roughly 80 percent of this total was held communally. Meanwhile, approximately a hundred thousand noble estates had title to 16 percent of the land.[2] Peasant cultivation was highly inefficient, frequently based on the wasteful three-field system of tillage. Peasants had little access to credit or agricultural education, with the corresponding brakes on agricultural productivity.[3] Especially serious was the rapid rural population growth rate, which was largely responsible for a 45 percent reduction in size of holdings per male peasant from the 1860s to 1900.[4]

Scholars have recently questioned the traditionally bleak portraits of Russian agriculture and peasant living standards, arguing that acute poverty and land hunger were confined to certain regions, especially the sixteen black earth and Volga provinces, which accounted for less than 30 percent of European Russia's peasants; and that per capita grain production, agricultural productivity, and peasant purchasing power increased during the period of rapid industrialization.[5] Improvements were especially notable after 1905 as a result of new government policies supporting emigration to Siberia, cooperatives, and land reform. The Siberian peasantry stood out for its prosperity, partly traceable to a burgeoning dairy industry.

Although these findings call into question some of the central traditional postulates of late imperial economic history—that, for example, industrial growth was purchased at the price of increased peasant immiserization—many standard conclusions remain valid. Many Russian peasants were desperately poor; the villages were overpopulated, with large amounts of surplus labor; and the countryside was afflicted with hunger, and at times famine, as well as by ignorance and cultural marginalization. Whatever progress was recorded, rural society remained impoverished, and there was no guarantee that a threshold beyond which continuous improvements were highly probable had been crossed.

The social moorings of agrarian backwardness consisted of two largely premodern social classes, a landed nobility and a peasantry. The decline of the nobility from the time of the emancipation of the serfs to the 1917 revolution was a classic theme of the literature of the period; the withdrawn, listless, and fatalistic landowner became almost a stock figure.

[2] Rogger, *Russia in the Age*, 85. State-owned land accounts for virtually all the remainder.

[3] Nove, *Economic History*, 23–24.

[4] Rogger, *Russia in the Age*, 82.

[5] See the summary of these arguments in John Bushnell, "Peasant Economy and Peasant Revolution at the Turn of the Century: Neither Immiseration nor Autonomy," *The Russian Review* 47, no. 1 (January 1988): 75–88.

However much revisionist historians may have called into question other scholarly stereotypes of the period—the dark and uncomprehending masses, the impoverished peasant, the obscurantist bureaucrat, the all-controlling state—no serious scholarly work has challenged the overall pattern of continuing economic decline of the gentry under Nicholas II.

Their plight was most visible in landownership, the very foundation of their power in the countryside. At the time of the emancipation the nobility had received roughly half of all privately owned arable land, but by 1905 only about a quarter of it remained in their possession. The decline in their fortunes was even more pronounced after the 1905 revolution, as many terrorized landowners sold their land and fled the countryside. In some areas there was even a shortage of nobles meeting the land requirements to stand for election in the estate-based electoral system. The zemstvos also had trouble filling the available positions due to a lack of qualified nobles.[6] Thus, although according to the 1897 census landed gentry families numbered 120,000, after the 1905 revolution only about 30,000 adult male heads of household with enough land to qualify to represent their estate in the zemstvos, state council, and Duma remained.[7] The resulting absurdities are evident in the case of Tver guberniia, where the number of qualified nobles dropped from 853 in 1891 to 475 in 1912 and where many gentry seats, at times from one-quarter to one-third of the total, remained unoccupied.[8] Even among those nobles who managed to retain or expand their holdings, a great many preferred to rent the land to peasants rather than run their estates themselves.

There were, of course, a great many exceptions to the overall pattern, and also regions, such as the western Ukraine, where the nobility managed to modernize their farms and make a successful transition to commercial agriculture. Economic difficulties and the increasing recruitment of non-gentry to the government bureaucracy stimulated many noble landowners to return to their estates. Michael Ignatieff's grandfather Paul, a scion of the highest Petersburg nobility, discovered Tolstoy in his youth, returning to his estate to work together with his hired peasants in the fields until he was called to high government office.[9] Although the motives of many others were not so idealistic, enough estate owners returned to the land for various reasons to give rise to the most cohesive and active gentry provin-

[6] Ruth Delia MacNaughton and Roberta Thompson Manning, "The Crisis of the Third of June System and Political Trends in the Zemstvos, 1907–14," in Haimson, *Politics of Rural Russia*, 200.

[7] Rogger, *Russia in the Age*, 89; Leopold Haimson, "Introduction: The Russian Landed Nobility and the System of the Third of June," in Haimson, *Politics of Rural Russia*, 7.

[8] Rogger, *Russia in the Age*, 92.

[9] Michael Ignatieff, *The Russian Album* (New York: Viking, 1987), 62–63.

cial society in modern Russian history.[10] This new-found identity as members of independent local elites, united not just by class interest but by common political activities and frequent social contact, competed with and partially displaced their earlier sense of themselves as a service estate. In line with these changes, many noble landowners prepared themselves for a more autonomous political role in both local and national politics. In general terms, the political consequences of this return to their estates and the formation of a provincial society were more significant than the economic results, for relatively few of the gentry were able to adapt to the new economic conditions of industrialization, international competition, and commercial agriculture based on wage labor.

The government was not of a united mind in its response to the decline of the landed gentry. Even before 1905 some officials, including Count Witte, wrote them off as a lost and outmoded class, the inevitable sacrificial lamb of the country's modernization. Some even argued that the above-class government could not favor the nobility over the peasantry, who had an equal claim to state favor. Especially at the time of the 1905 revolution, many officials went so far as to advocate the distribution of gentry land to the peasants in order to quell the agrarian disorders. In general, however, the regime did try to protect the position of its main political base, through subsidized loans, highly favorable tax policies, and the like. But these measures could not compensate for the landowners' unwillingness to adopt more modern labor practices or for their overall psychological disposition, so foreign to the demands of modern capitalist enterprise. They exalted the ideal of the amateur, abhorring professional training and methodical work habits.[11]

The modernization of Russia posed political as well as economic challenges to the landed gentry, but in this arena they proved somewhat better able to protect their positions. Their relative success was not due to their continuing predominance in the key organs of government and the bureaucracy. Rather, numerous statistics indicate that the general process of decline of landowner control over these offices in the nineteenth century continued in the reign of Nicholas II. For example, in the early years of the twentieth century, just short of 60 percent of government ministers were

[10] Haimson, "Conclusion," in Haimson, *Politics of Rural Russia*, 263.

[11] Geoffrey Hosking and Roberta Thompson Manning, "What Was the United Nobility?" in Haimson, *Politics of Rural Russia*, 144; Ascher, *Revolution of 1905*, 29. According to Paul Miliukov in his memoirs, many of this stratum switched to commerce, tried their hand at speculation, or simply mortgaged their land. "They usually lacked sufficient business experience, and they were forced to compensate for this deficiency by the privileged position of their class. This explains their political and material dependence on the government." Paul Miliukov, *Political Memoirs 1905–1917*, ed. Arthur Mendel (Ann Arbor: University of Michigan Press, 1967), 341.

landowners, as compared with 94.3 percent in 1853. If we consider a somewhat broader section of the political elite, those occupying the top four ranks in the Table of Ranks, 61.8 percent were landless in 1878, 72.4 percent in 1902. The separation of landowning from high political office was even more evident in the military officer corps, where roughly 10 percent of lieutenant generals and 20 percent of full generals owned inherited estates in 1903. These representative figures clearly show that the hereditary landed nobility no longer dominated the state bureaucracy by the time of the 1905 revolution.[12]

This decline was not the result of a considered policy by the autocratic government but rather stemmed from a series of social, economic, and political changes largely outside the ruler's control, many of them with unforeseen consequences. Modernization demands an educated and experienced administration, a requirement that can be ignored only at great peril to the regime. In Russia the nineteenth century witnessed a notable professionalization of the bureaucracy, civil and military, with stricter educational requirements, more emphasis on merit, and the usual stress on seniority. Just as Weber would have predicted, these new criteria for service and advancement conflicted with the anti-utilitarian ideals of the landed gentry, which, favoring a kind of elite amateurism based on status honor, was suspicious of professionalism and discipline. Many nobles did not qualify and many others eschewed service in an administration so increasingly out of touch with their own values and sense of themselves.

The economic crisis of gentry agriculture also convinced many nobles to withdraw from Petersburg politics in order to set aright their estates. Such pressures were all the more compelling given the increasingly unsympathetic reception accorded the noble amateur in government service. Further, the decision to return to the land was made more attractive by the burgeoning of local political offices created by the government's attempts to modernize local administration. Noble landowners imbued with the service ethos encountered a wider arena for participation in public affairs in their localities than ever before. Upon return to the provinces they could also take advantage of a richer and more diverse social and cultural life. Partly because of their own greater numbers, and also due to the spread of education and the growth of the professions, provincial society had now acquired unprecedented appeal.[13] By the last decades of the old regime, numerous local gentry "societies" could partly substitute for court life and the capital's salons. Thus, the gentry's very marginalization from the central government set in motion a series of changes solidifying their role in

[12] The previous figures come from Roberta Thompson Manning, *The Crisis of the Old Order in Russia* (Princeton: Princeton University Press, 1982), 26–28. The figures she cites are generally based on the work of P. A. Zaionchkovskii.

[13] Haimson, "Conclusion," in *Politics of Rural Russia*, 262–63.

the provinces. From this more independent base they could once again assert themselves in national politics with enormous effect.

Many of the sources of the gentry's decline in national politics were thus largely unintended consequences of Russia's economic and political modernization. But there were also quite intentional government policies that undermined or limited the gentry's political role, as well as a number of proposals that were never enacted but aroused widespread anxiety. The first set of these can be classed under the general rubric of administrative modernization, involving the extension of the state machinery into the localities. One of the most notable policies along these lines was the creation, by an 1889 statute, of the office of "land captain." Bestowed with considerable formal independence and broad executive, judicial, and legislative powers over local peasants and craftsmen, the government-appointed land captains had the general function of maintaining order in the countryside and monitoring the activities of the peasant communes. Appearing at first in central Russia, the following decades witnessed the appointment of land captains and similar officials ("peasant captains," "peasant supervisors") throughout the empire.[14] These officials hardly exemplified the prototype of bureaucratic administration. In the words of one specialist, Tsar Alexander III envisioned them as "virtuous knight-servitors, each of whom would ride out alone to rule over the peasants in his district as a patriarchal chieftain."[15] In principle (though less and less in practice) chosen from among the gentry, they were to act above gentry interests in order to protect the interests of the state as a whole, embodying the disinterestedness of the above-class autocrat. A great many nobles, including the marshals of the nobility, resented the land captains' intrusion into the prerogatives of their estate and felt their own authority threatened. Many marshals withdrew from local affairs; the great majority would come to participate in the liberal opposition to the autocracy.[16]

Despite the romantic and patriarchal overtones of the office, it soon became integrated into the expanding state bureaucracy in the countryside. The most important new government agency established to oversee rural affairs was the Ministry of Agriculture, formed in 1894. Employing large numbers of technical specialists, including agronomists and economists, and headed at its inception by a well-known agricultural economist, Aleksei Ermolov, the ministry quickly took an activist approach to the problems of rural Russia, sponsoring a series of conferences and forming commissions to diagnose the problems and propose remedies. The ministry be-

[14] By 1908, there were about twenty-five hundred land captains. See Yaney, *Urge to Mobilize*, 50–51.

[15] Ibid., 52.

[16] Rogger, *Russia in the Age*, 93; Hosking and Manning, "What Was the United Nobility?" in Haimson, *Politics of Rural Russia*, 152.

came one of the most effective sponsors of the series of programs eventually known as the Stolypin reforms, which sought to release the initiative of the peasants through loosening or dismantling some of their communal institutions.

The landed nobility did not generally oppose proposals to weaken the commune, for many, especially after 1905, saw the commune as one of the sources of peasant rebelliousness. But they clearly perceived the challenge to their positions posed by reforming bureaucrats. They felt great hostility toward the world of the bureaucrat that had gradually excluded them—even more so now that these distrusted officials began to intrude themselves into what had previously been their uncontested terrain. Especially troublesome was the propeasant rhetoric of many officials, who sometimes identified the nobility as the cause of the peasants' poverty and of agricultural stagnation in general. The culmination of the reformers' threats to the gentry was the proposal, made after the 1905 peasant unrest by figures as important as Prime Minister Witte and Minister of Agriculture Kutler, to expropriate all gentry land currently rented out to and worked by the peasants. An explosion of landowner hostility and the opposition of the tsar doomed this proposal, but it gave eloquent testimony to the deep potential conflicts between the state administration and the landowning gentry. Less extreme but still threatening measures tendered by Prime Minister Stolypin in subsequent years to reform local government and grant more political rights to the peasantry aroused their anger once again. By that time, the landowners, though shrinking in numbers and wealth, were strongly enough entrenched in the political system to defeat all such proposals, creating irresolvable stalemates in Russian political life.

For the gentry were not passive in the face of their multifaceted decline. Many of the preconditions of gentry opposition to the autocracy had long been germinating in the post-1861 social order. The growing differentiation between gentry and the state bureaucracy had weakened the gentry's identification of itself as a service estate. Or sometimes service was reinterpreted as obligation to the people as a whole rather than to the regime. The increasing interference of the state in local affairs, as exemplified in its stricter regulation of the zemstvos, aroused further hostility to the government, even among the staunchest defenders of autocracy. The new-found vigor of provincial society fortified the sense of separation between the noble elite and the central authorities. And the gentry-dominated offices and institutions—the marshals of the nobility, the zemstvos, the assemblies of the nobility, originally created by the regime to further its own modernization blueprints—furnished ready forums for political activity. Finally, gentry activism already had a long history in postreform Russia by 1900, as gentry assemblies had made numerous appeals for the formation of estate-based representative bodies.

Before 1905 gentry activism was a rather tame affair. There were frequent calls for greater autonomy for the zemstvos; the marshals of the nobility began to convoke annual conferences to discuss the problems of their class and attempt to influence the government on their behalf; and a considerable percentage of the zemstvos (roughly half of the province-level organizations) had espoused the creation of representative institutions.[17] After 1900 discussions on the zemstvos became increasingly stormy, embracing a range of previously prohibited social and political topics. Especially noteworthy was the visibility of a group of liberal gentry, later to join the ranks of the Kadet party, who harbored more ambitious plans for change. Linked by social ties and by shared outlook to educated professionals and sectors of the intelligentsia, these men were soon to assume leadership positions in the liberal opposition.

The great events of 1905 and 1906 led to a radicalization and then disarticulation of the gentry opposition movement. Led by the gentry intelligentsia, much of the landowning nobility was initially sympathetic to the cry for a constitutional government because of the military fiasco with Japan, general hostility to the regime's arbitrariness and lawlessness, and sympathy with the ferment rife throughout the country. Thus, by late January 1905 two-thirds of the provincial zemstvos called for the creation of a legislature able to make laws and limit the authority of the tsar. Several, too, advocated universal, equal, secret, and direct suffrage.[18] In speeches, resolutions, and illegal meetings, a large proportion of the dominant social elite and key social support of the regime openly defied its authority and called for fundamental changes in its nature—surely a most unusual event with few parallels in other revolutions.

Yet the upsurge in gentry oppositionism, which culminated in late spring after the disastrous defeat of the Russian fleet by the Japanese at Tsushima, was not to last. Numerous factors were at work to divide the gentry and bring to the fore more moderate voices, including government concessions and impatience with the stridency of the most liberal advocates of reform. But towering over all other causes was the upsurge of peasant rebellion in the villages in the fall of 1905. An increase in disturbances had been recorded earlier, especially in the month of June, but largely as a result of the fall political strikes in the cities peasant rebellion took on new dimensions in the period following the publication of the October Manifesto. Encouraged by the preoccupation of the army and police with the urban disorders, peasants vented their rage against the landowners in full, burning and looting estates with terrifying fury. Fear and panic spread among the gentry, causing many of them to abandon the countryside and

[17] Manning, *Crisis of the Old Order*, 46.

[18] Ibid., 83.

take refuge in the cities or even flee abroad. Above all, the disorders worked a momentous political change in their midst, weakening the commitment to liberalism and giving primacy in their minds to a set of issues unrelated to constitutions and civil liberties. Gentry liberalism by no means disappeared, but its predominance in the zemstvos was eliminated, and right-wing groups took the lead in forming political organizations and parties among the gentry. The issue of most significance to them was of course the protection of their estates and personal safety. Since their property soon came to be threatened not just by direct peasant action, but also by reforming bureaucrats and the newly created state Duma, the protection of their land required political mobilization at the highest levels of government.

For despite the shared concern of gentry and the regime with peasant disorders, which dampened gentry opposition to the autocracy, the government with its independent program posed a threat in many ways as serious as that of the peasants. As mentioned earlier, some high officials believed that the landed elite had long outlived its economic usefulness, and that agricultural productivity would best be served by independent peasant farming. Others, most notably Witte, based their case for partial or full expropriation on more political grounds: it was the only way to appease the peasants and salvage the autocracy. After the defeat of the peasant insurgents, enthusiasm for expropriation of gentry estates began to wane in government circles, but prominent officials like Stolypin and Kutler continued to favor and prepare projects for expropriation of at least some types of gentry holdings. Stolypin's reformist program also envisioned a number of other measures that would have disturbed gentry economic and political dominance—most notable was greater involvement of peasants in local government.

The regime's commitment to economic and political modernization had been one of the root sources of gentry oppositionism in the prerevolutionary period. Clearly, once peasant radicalism had taught the majority of the gentry where antiautocratic activism would lead, the advocacy of a basic change in the form of government was no longer so attractive. Thus, in the changed situation after 1905, the critical mass of the landowning nobility altered its goals from political reform of the government to political influence and power within it. A plethora of political groups and parties emerged to aggregate and propagate the gentry's positions and to pressure for their adoption. Members of the gentry also continued to make use of their contacts with high government officials, some of whom, like V. I. Gurko, had played a critical part in opposing Stolypin's expropriation policy in favor of the reforms that ironically came to bear Stolypin's name. They also cultivated the tsar's sympathy and made use of his commitment to them as the historical foundation of autocracy.

Procedurally, the gentry's most important victory was the change in the electoral law after the dissolution of the Second Duma in June 1907, which ensured their predominance in forthcoming Dumas. It was a triumph in which the regime itself fully acquiesced, as it sought by this measure to quell the voices of the Social Democrats and Kadets and to ensure stable conservative parliamentary majorities. The dissolution of the Second Duma and the change in the electoral law proved beyond any question how little the autocracy was willing to allow itself to be reformed.

Substantively, the gentry succeeded in altering or defeating all major reform proposals threatening their interests. Despite his formidable skills, Stolypin, himself a member of the landowning class, suffered defeat after defeat, evidence of a political impasse that, had he not been assassinated, would most probably have ended in his resignation or dismissal. His regime, as we shall see, was not without its accomplishments. But on the outstanding political issues of the day, land distribution and the labor question, his government was captive, largely through its own actions, to the dominant agrarian elite, which was concerned above all with safeguarding its own narrow interest.

On the eve of World War I, the Russian state had a poor record indeed in dealing with the social and political imperatives of modernization. Hostage to a narrow and declining class, the regime was unable to act upon a broader vision of the preconditions for its own survival.

The other premodern rural social class was a peasantry whose economic and social life and institutions still bore the imprint of the Russian past much more than they expressed the traits of a modern agricultural system. The Russian past was most obvious in the comparative poverty of the Russian peasant. But numerous underlying historical traits of Russian rural society were even more significant in the genesis of rural unrest. These traits, rooted in the peasantry's relation to the state and the landed gentry, gave rise to patterns of attitude and action much more consistent than those of their gentry opponents, who were caught in the cross fire of conflicting forces—including their historical loyalty to and dependence on the state, their economic decline, the rise of modern political administration and government reformism, the influence of new ideological currents, and the peasant threat. Whereas gentry politics was characterized by major shifts and reversals, the Russian peasantry doggedly espoused a rather simple socioeconomic vision with striking unanimity.

Russian agrarian institutions from the time of the consolidation of Muscovy to the 1861 emancipation were founded largely on the interests of the state and the gentry, which were seen to be mutually consistent. The key institution, serfdom, developed gradually in the sixteenth and seventeenth centuries, not as the result of a Western-style feudalism but concomitantly with the rise of the centralized state. The state fixed the peasant population to the land and delivered both into the hands of the service gentry in order to enable the latter to discharge its financial and military functions. The imposition of serfdom checked the peasants' proclivity to escape from gentry control through flight and guaranteed the gentry a stable labor force. The logic of the institution emerged within the context of a sociopolitical system based on a service ethos, according to which all groups, each in its own way, existed to serve the state.

This same statist logic lay behind the development of the peasant commune (*mir* or *obshchina*), which was favored as an effective way of ensuring that the peasants performed their obligations to both the lord and the state. Already by the sixteenth century the mir had become the lord's agent in regulating peasant affairs. The practice of periodic land partitions emerged in the following century as a way of ensuring that the peasants paid the taxes due the government. The state, in sponsoring redistribution, sought to make certain that all serfs would be supplied with the resources to pay the soul tax.[19] Finally, the predominance of state interests and the ideology of the service state shaped the development of a strikingly powerful and enduring monarchist peasant political culture. Throughout the tsarist period a great many peasants continued to express deep reverence for the person of the tsar, their benefactor by the will of God. Their ills they blamed upon his corrupt officials or the landlords, who subverted his will and oppressed the peasantry without his knowledge.

This social logic was undermined by a powerful blow during the reign of Catherine the Great. It will be recalled that Catherine attempted to transplant elements of the European estate system into Russia, with its very different political traditions. The nobility received corporate autonomy and was legally relieved of its service obligations. The peasants did not understand why they should continue to serve a nobility no longer serving the state but acting in their own private interests. Disappointed in their expectations that they too would be freed from their bonds, large numbers of peasants rebelled in the famous Pugachev Revolt. The revolt was brutally suppressed, but the contradiction that was largely responsible for it remained. In the eyes of a great many peasants, both serfdom and gentry property were now illegitimate. They had lost their warrant with the partial dismantling of the service state. Members of the gentry, who, unlike their medieval European counterparts, did not oversee a manorial economy—the land was worked by peasant households associated in the village commune—were regarded as little more than parasites.

Serfdom was also slowly undermined in the early nineteenth century by the incipient industrialization of the country, which brought many serfs to

[19] Francis Watters, "The Peasant and the Village Commune," in *The Peasant in Nineteenth-Century Russia*, ed. Wayne Vucinich (Stanford, Calif.: Stanford University Press, 1968), 138.

the cities even while they continued to pay their dues to the gentry who owned them. In these cases the legal framework of serfdom remained, but the bonds of subjugation were clearly loosened. In the same period many high officials in the government, including Nicholas I, came to believe that serfdom was inconsistent with the further progress of the country and should be abolished. Russia's defeat in the Crimean War gave a powerful impetus to this conviction, for it was widely felt that one cause of the defeat was the inherent weakness of a serf army in the age of modern warfare. With these considerations in mind, Tsar Alexander II led the campaign to emancipate the serfs, which was finally enacted in 1861. But, as is well known, the gentry was allowed to keep a significant part of its holdings (roughly one-seventh), very often the most valuable portions. In addition, the peasants were saddled with heavy redemption payments for land that they regarded as by right theirs. The peasants' first reaction was literal disbelief in the terms of the emancipation announced to them. Surely these must be false emissaries of the little father tsar. Peasant communities were known to seek out and pay speakers who would read out to them what they knew in their hearts to be the true terms of the emancipation.[20] Considerable unrest followed the promulgation of the emancipation decree. As with the peasant insurgency under Catherine, the return to normalcy did not mean that the peasants had accepted the terms forced upon them.

The second truly momentous policy decision in the emancipation settlement was the strengthening of the commune. Replicating the logic of centuries earlier, the government determined that taxation and redemption arrears could be more easily collected under a system of collective responsibility. The land and the repayment responsibilities were thus assigned not to the individual peasant but to the village commune, which was correspondingly given a great deal of power over its members. Indeed, the commune became responsible not just for taxes, but also for much of local administration and the safeguarding of public order. In addition, legal provisions made it difficult for peasants to separate themselves from the commune without its permission, a logical consequence of the principle of collective fiscal responsibility.

This communal settlement, intended to last only until repayment for the land had been completed but in fact enduring in much of the Russian countryside until the revolution,[21] was much criticized at the time for its effects on the economy. Through the practice of periodic partitions, the system of three field rotations, and the restrictions on mobility, small and inefficient peasant agriculture was artificially preserved. Although capital-

[20] See Terence Emmons, "The Peasant and the Emancipation," in Vucinich, *The Peasant in Nineteenth-Century Russia*, 59–61.

[21] Around the turn of the century the commune controlled roughly half of all arable land in European Russia. Rogger, *Russia in the Age*, 80.

ism certainly made many inroads into the rural economy, and a stratum of more prosperous peasants emerged, these communal practices continued to shape peasant culture, economic practice, and politics. Although communal administration involved much control and oppression of peasant by peasant and the commune did not prevent the emergence of class differentiation in the countryside, nonetheless for many peasants communal tenure and periodic redistribution provided a welcome safety net in the face of the insecurities of peasant life.[22]

Another feature of government policy in the period from the emancipation to the 1905 revolution was the special legal status of the commune, which exemplified the more general practice of treating the peasant as part of a separate class of subjects. They, and not other groups, could receive corporal punishment. Their tax burden, which included the head tax, was proportionately much higher. They alone suffered from restrictions on physical mobility. They were even subject to customary law, and not the legal code applicable to the rest of the population. In part these measures expressed a paternal view of the peasant as ward of the state; in part they stemmed from the fact that the fiscal power of the regime continued to rest upon the exploitation of the peasantry. Whatever the intentions, these measures eloquently communicated to the peasants that they stood apart from the rest of society, their lives regulated according to a different set of norms. The political significance of this castelike segregation proved to be enormous, because the peasants, when they became involved, acted without any regard to other social groups and had no conception of any possible larger interests of society as a whole. Such rigid divisions between social groups, fostered by the autocratic system, inhibited trust and cooperation, ultimately increasing the society's vulnerability to revolution during the process of modernization.

The economic, social, and political implications of the pattern of rural society that emerged after the emancipation all pointed in the same direction, to seething discontent that would break into the open under the right circumstances. Sometimes, as in the peasant unrest of 1902, the cause was primarily crop failure and the fear of famine. But it would be misleading to trace peasant rebellion mainly to the poverty and land hunger of the

[22] From Lenin and the populists onward, the debate on the origins, nature, and implications of the Russian peasant commune has been intense. Was the commune the harbinger of socialism, or an impediment to economic development? Was it the embodiment of social justice or a particularly oppressive mode of social control designed by the government for its own purposes? Did peasants welcome it as the truest expression of their social ideals, or did they seek to escape whenever it became possible? Such questions have inspired an immense literature and cannot be investigated here. For present purposes the key point is that the commune *did* continue to play a key role in Russian peasant politics in the last decades of the regime whatever its ultimate viability in a modern society.

peasants, although this always played a role. More broadly, the peasants interpreted their plight and sought remedies for it in the context created by the autocratic regime's insertion of itself into rural life. Only this larger context can explain such crucial traits as the absolute illegitimacy of the landlords in the eyes of the peasantry. The following parable, told by a member of a peasant delegation to a zemstvo board in 1905, communicates the essence of the situation eloquently: "When food is abundant in the summer, the worker bees are satisfied to feed the queen bee and the drones, but when autumn comes and food gets scarce, what happens to the drones? . . . Out they go."[23]

The major episodes of peasant unrest occurred at the time of the 1905–1907 revolution, especially in the fall of 1905 and the summer of 1906. The intensity of the turmoil varied greatly, but it tended to center in areas where the commune was widespread, where agriculture was impoverished, and where peasants were forced to work on the landowners' estates—traits characteristic of the central black-earth zone and the middle Volga.[24] At first violence took the form mainly of burning and looting; by mid-1906 economic and agricultural strikes became the predominant form of disturbance, testifying to the greater organization of the movement. It was during this period, too, that for the first time outright land seizures became widespread.[25]

Generalizations about peasant disturbances are difficult to hazard because of the great diversity of peasant customs and peasant tenure patterns throughout the empire. Vinogradoff makes a useful distinction between two major types of peasant political attitudes and action, *estate* and *class*, which varied systematically by region and were rooted in different types of agrarian systems. *Estate* peasants, by far the major type in Russia proper, were concerned only with the land question, to which they had a universally shared radical solution regardless of class differences. *Class* peasants, who could typically be found along the Baltic coast and in parts of Siberia, were more interested in general political issues, had more affiliation with nonpeasant parties and groups, and were more ideologically diverse.[26]

Several important generalizations appear to hold with respect to the estate peasants. First, their militancy was directed overwhelmingly against the landowners, not representatives of the state. Indeed, it is clear that peasants often believed, or chose to believe, that the tsar had authorized, or at least had implicitly approved, their activities.[27] As they had in the

[23] Ignatieff, *The Russian Album*, 80.

[24] Rogger, *Russia in the Age*, 87.

[25] Manning, *The Crisis of the Old Order*, 241–42.

[26] Eugene Vinogradoff, "Peasantry and Elections to the Fourth State Duma," in Haimson, *Politics of Rural Russia*.

[27] Ascher, *Revolution of 1905*, 163.

past, peasants put the monarchist myth to work for them: "mysterious generals rode about distributing mysterious proclamations, the tsar's will was concealed by nobles and officials, and so forth."[28] It is for this reason, and also because of the universally low regard in which the landowners as a class were held, that the peasants acted out of an absolute sense of moral justification. They were setting right an order based on usurpation and injustice according to a logic rooted in autocratic political traditions. If "revolutionary" implies a principled rejection of the social and political order, then the Russian peasantry was strikingly nonrevolutionary.

Second, the antecedents of the major episodes of peasant unrest were not so much economic as political.[29] They had less to do with bad harvests or seasonal rhythms than with political events outside the countryside that gave the peasants hope that their unchanging aspirations would be satisfied. Thus, the two major periods of peasant insurgency were late October–November 1905, following the massive strikes in the cities and the proclamation of the October Manifesto, which promised the convocation of a representative assembly and the rule of law; and the early summer of 1906, when the First Duma was debating the agrarian question and peasant hopes were aroused. In late 1905 the peasants were once again convinced that the tsar intended to transfer the land to them; in the summer of 1906 they were aware that the state Duma was on the point of advocating the expropriation of land. Aside from the contagion and hope generated by urban politics in these periods—ferment that also inspired the peasants—the urban unrest weakened the government's repressive capacity, thereby emboldening the peasants.

A third point is the peasants' unity on a narrow set of demands and their apathy toward political issues seemingly unconnected to their welfare. The peasants wanted the gentry's land and the right to run their affairs without bothersome outside influence.[30] They opposed wage labor and the sale of land, preferring land allocation according to households on a roughly egalitarian basis. Although it has been noted that peasants in 1905 adhered to many demands made by the liberal political opposition, favored some form of parliamentary government,[31] and took an avid interest in the debates of the First Duma, their interest in political reform was probably largely instrumental. Thus, when it had become clear that the government had no intention of expropriating gentry land, peasant interest in Duma politics declined—a disaffection also comprehensible in terms of the electoral system's discrimination against them. Isolated from the rest of the society so-

[28] Bushnell, "Peasant Economy," 85.

[29] This is a point made in John Bushnell, *Mutiny amid Repression*, 222–23.

[30] The "peasant dream" is well discussed by Teodor Shanin, *Russia, 1905–07: Revolution as a Moment of Truth* (New Haven: Yale University Press, 1986), 122–29.

[31] Ascher, *Revolution of 1905*, 165.

cially and culturally, for centuries subject to special legal disabilities, the Russian peasants had never formed part of a larger political community and in their own minds had no reason to transcend their particularism.

Equally crucial in the shaping of Russian peasant unrest was the "continuous training in collective action"[32] provided by the village communes. As noted, regions where communal organization was widespread tended to manifest the highest degrees of militancy. There is also ample evidence linking indigenous peasant leadership, whether official representatives or militant younger peasants who often had experience in the cities, with peasant disorders. The influence of the revolutionary parties, especially the Socialist Revolutionaries, was inevitably seized upon by the government as an easy explanation for the unrest, and there were clearly peasant organizations led or inspired by outside revolutionaries, but these were of considerably less weight than the traditional village assemblies and the peasants' own elected leaders. The work of planning and organization—decisions about what kinds of actions were to be taken and who was to take them—was effortlessly assumed by these representative bodies. Sometimes the elected peasant elders, previously responsible to the authorities for order in the villages and often acting with a heavy hand, themselves took the lead in the disorders.[33]

The response of the government to these peasant disorders after it had sufficiently regrouped its forces was a policy of ferocious repression. Military detachments spread throughout the countryside, rooting out activists, castigating whole villages when they would not deliver up the guilty. The punishments—the beatings, burning of peasant property, and executions by hanging—were cruel and arbitrary, in retaliation for what was rightly regarded as peasant defiance on a communal basis.

At the same time that soldiers were liquidating the disorders by force, debates raged within the government and among the nobility about more long-term solutions to the peasant question. As noted earlier, some in the government sought to purchase peace in the countryside by the expropriation of gentry land. By contrast, the gentry and its defenders in the government, most notably V. I. Gurko, identified the problem as the peasant commune and the solution as more freedom for peasants to leave the commune and establish independent peasant households. This position, widely supported among leading gentry figures, marked a major break with tradition. Previously members of the gentry had tended to favor the commune as a guarantee of rural stability—it promoted equality, they thought, and brought to the fore conservative peasant leaders. It also had come to

[32] Geroid Tanqueray Robinson, *Rural Russia under the Old Regime* (Berkeley: University of California Press, 1969), 35.

[33] Manning, *The Crisis of the Old Order*, 150–51.

embody Russia's distinctive identity. But the role of village institutions in 1905–1906 chastened them and gave rise to a more pessimistic view of the commune's political implications. They also came to accept the idea that the commune was at the root of rural economic stagnation. For these reasons the gentry espoused the reforms named after Prime Minister Stolypin, even though they did not enact Stolypin's own agrarian program, which was more radical.

The details of the Stolypin reforms need not detain us here. The main objectives were two: to allow peasant households to consolidate the scattered strips they worked into more efficient holdings; and to permit, even encourage, individual peasant households to leave the commune and transform their land into private property. The reform had both economic and political motives. It was hoped that independent proprietors would have more incentive to improve their productivity and that the most efficient farmers would be able to accumulate land and wealth and, so, in the aggregate, push out the inefficient producer and use their profits to modernize agriculture. This same "strong and sturdy" peasantry was also to provide a mass political base for the regime in the countryside.

Historians continue to debate the achievements and potential of the Stolypin reforms. Some have argued that they ran counter to the egalitarian and anticapitalist mentality of the Russian peasants, more concerned with security than with expanded opportunities for enrichment. Others contend that many peasants embraced the measures with enthusiasm and that, had the reforms been given more time, a prosperous capitalist agriculture would have emerged. Whatever the peasants' individual attitudes, the acceptance of the reform was surely diminished by the fact that, in autocratic style, it was imposed upon the peasantry without consultation. Just as the workers had almost no input into the reforms being discussed to enhance their rights, so the peasants were not deemed fit participants in the debate over their own fate. Similarly, the implementation of the reform suffered from the same weaknesses as autocratic administration in other spheres: the local authorities, primarily the land captains, were isolated from peasant society and so had limited political leverage.[34]

Whatever the merits of these rival views, it is certain that by the outbreak of the revolution Stolypin's program had not succeeded in alleviating the poverty or land hunger of the great majority of Russian peasants.[35] Fur-

[34] Yaney, *Urge to Mobilize*, 306, sums up their power in the following way: "Ineffective as they may have been in *promoting* land settlement, their presence in the countryside gave comfort to any peasant . . . who dared to rebel against the traditional power of his neighbors." He later argues (358–59) that the authorities gradually became more effective by adapting themselves to the aspirations of the peasantry, coming to place less emphasis on the creation of individual household plots in favor of more limited rearrangements of village land.

[35] Rogger, *Russia in the Age*, 245.

ther, the gentry remained in the countryside as a continuing irritant, dominating local politics and occupying land that the peasants, whether rich or poor, believed was rightfully theirs. The major ingredients of agrarian revolt remained, ready to be ignited by events with origins distant from the countryside.

What, then, can be concluded about the roots of peasant militancy in rural Russia? Many general theories have been offered to explain the potential for peasant mobilization in a variety of settings in the twentieth century. Most of these have been applied to Russia, or even developed primarily with the Russian experience in mind. According to one widely held perspective, peasant society everywhere is centered around a set of expectations and practices that provide stability and security to what would otherwise be an unpredictable and threatening way of life. In order to minimize insecurity and ensure at least subsistence, peasant societies develop egalitarian and welfare practices that share the risks according to what James Scott calls a "safety-first" principle.[36] In Russia, the repartitional commune might be seen as a prime example of this general tendency. In explaining the increased potential for peasant revolt in many modern societies, scholars such as Eric Wolf and James Scott point to the corrosive effects of expanding rural capitalism and the extension of the modern state into previously rather independent "little traditions," frequently as a result of colonialism. These processes undercut the "moral economy of the peasant" and destabilized peasant society, creating "social dynamite" ready to be exploded by unexpected shocks imperiling subsistence.[37]

The previous discussion of rural Russia casts doubt on the applicability of this model for the Russian peasantry. We recall that an economic interpretation of peasant militancy fails to account for the major episodes of peasant activism, which were linked to political events centered in the city. Russian peasants were prepared to lay claim to the gentry's land whenever the opportunity presented itself. The direct antecedents of its rebellion were political, not economic, although land hunger was always an underlying factor.

A review of the arguments presented earlier shows that the political roots of Russian peasant militancy must be traced to the role of the autocratic state in shaping social relations in a modernizing Russia. The peasants' monarchist political culture and the decay of the gentry's source of legitimation as a service elite after the time of Catherine the Great deprived the latter of its rights to land and political power in the eyes of the peas-

[36] James Scott, *The Moral Economy of the Peasant* (New Haven: Yale University Press, 1976).

[37] Scott's discussion is much more complex than can be indicated here, including, for example, an account of the many stabilizing forces at work in peasant society, including mystification and repression. These valuable distinctions can be passed over for present purposes.

antry. The autocratic political system did not permit the gentry to reclaim its legitimacy on a more modern basis, such as the ability to lead the nation or modernize agriculture. The gentry's weakness was further augmented by its precipitous economic decline, in part the consequence of the regime's modernization policy.

Rural society was made even more fragile, social relations between peasants and the gentry more polarized, by the mutual isolation imposed on both parties by the political system. The gentry and the peasant class were divided into isolated political compartments, each with its own rights, institutions, and laws defined by the state. Opportunities for common participation in social and political affairs were rare, and little trust, understanding, or sympathy could develop between the two groups. Romantic images of a hierarchical community based on reciprocity and mutual sympathy have little relevance to rural Russia. Historians have rather emphasized the lack of trust and mutual incomprehension characteristic of rural class relations, the "rigid particularism" of both peasants and gentry.[38] These cleavages were partly inevitable in a premodern rural social structure, but they were exacerbated by the impediments to a functioning rural civil society imposed by the autocratic state.

Ironically, the potential for conflict was increased rather than softened by the state's efforts to regiment rural society. Sustained efforts to penetrate the countryside and collect taxes from the peasantry had given rise to gentry and peasant institutions, such as the zemstvos, noble assemblies, and village communes, designed in large part to increase government control over the countryside. Inevitably the autocratic state was unable to prevent gentry and peasants alike from making use of these bodies for their own purposes as much as they could. (As we will see, no parallel developments occurred in Iran.) Unwittingly, then, the state gave structure to the countryside, and this structure facilitated collective action. Gentry organizations periodically opposed the state, particularly in its industrialization policies and its proposals for agrarian reform at their expense. They also sought to ensure the continuation of their economic and political advantages over the peasants. Peasant institutions, in turn, functioned in part as agents of the state and landowners, but they also expressed the peasants' "moral economy" and, when conditions permitted, helped initiate and lead disturbances. The state's attempt to control the countryside through organizing society and enlisting its assistance, a policy necessary for modernization, thus unintentionally exacerbated class conflict.

It was partly for this same reason that the autocratic state, with all its power and despite the proclamations of important officials, had such little

[38] For example, Haimson, "Conclusion," in Haimson, *Politics of Rural Russia*, 276–77; Manning, *The Crisis of the Old Order*, 147.

capacity to enact agrarian reform. Members of the gentry could not be directly threatened, not just because of the sympathy of the ruler for their estate, but because the regime had allowed them to develop the capacity to resist. Nor was peasant society so malleable, as the mixed success and uncertain fate of the Stolypin reforms demonstrate. Reform was also hindered by the more general deficiencies of autocratic policy making discussed earlier—lack of information, insufficient links to social groups, policy making divorced from social input. All of these traits limited the ability of the state to reshape rural society, defeating its plans for reform of local government and also the proposals for land expropriation.

A rural elite without legitimacy; a polarized rural society composed of mutually antagonistic and mistrustful social groups; and a state promising reform but unable to bring about far-reaching transformations, arousing the hostility of both sides: all these, in the context of a backward agriculture and an immense peasant poverty, generated a potential for social explosion whenever the government was weakened. Although the challenges to the tsarist regime first emerged in the cities, they inevitably ignited the countryside as well.

Reform and Marginality in Rural Iran

The Iranian Revolution must be unique in the annals of twentieth-century revolutions in the relative insignificance of peasant movements before and during the revolutionary crisis. Long-term historical causes that have little relevance to the pattern of modernization clearly have considerable bearing on this outcome. For example, scholars have long pointed to the weakness of rural society in Iran—the vulnerability to nomadic invasions, paucity of communal organizations, geographical dispersion in small isolated villages, and the tendency for peasants to flee as individuals, not struggle collectively, in hard times. These basic traits of rural life, all of them of undoubted pertinence, serve as a useful reminder of the limitations of an approach focused only on the period of rapid modernization. Clearly, just as in Russia peasant militancy long predated the rule of Nicholas II and thus stemmed partly from factors exogenous to the pattern of development, so in Iran the collective torpor of the peasants was not a recent phenomenon. Nonetheless, it is also true that the shah's rural reform program significantly reduced the potential for collective peasant political expression. In one sense, his regime's rural program partially belies the general argument that autocratic regimes are less able to transform society than their claim to omnipotence would suggest. But if one considers other elements of the reform—the government's inability to modernize agriculture and its own lack of connection to peasant life, the weakness of organization and coordination in the villages, the fanciful nature of the regime's plans—our hypotheses about autocratic modernization are strikingly confirmed.

In many respects, the agrarian reform, enacted in the early 1960s but with some antecedents in earlier programs and proposals,[39] accomplished far more than was possible for the Russian government. Whereas after 1905 the gentry's land remained politically inviolable and the gentry strengthened its hold on local political life (from where it shaped national politics as well), in Iran large landowners were forced to liquidate a significant portion of their holdings. Although critics have ceaselessly pointed out that large estates and absentee landownership were not eliminated, it remains true that the economic and political predominance of the landed elite in the villages was drastically reduced. Correlatively, a large number of peasant sharecroppers were transformed into independent proprietors. The arguments of skeptics—that many rural laborers were left out of the reform and that the plots allotted to the peasant beneficiaries of the reform were generally far too small—are certainly valid. Yet the importance of the changes in peasant status introduced also cannot be gainsaid. The long-term contradiction so fundamental in rural France and Russia, the persistence of noble economic and political power despite their overall decline as a class, was hardly to be found in the Iranian countryside.

The regime's motives for sponsoring land reform were complex and admit of multiple interpretations. Some scholars have stressed domestic economic imperatives: the need to modernize agriculture in order to provide a foundation for industrial growth by ensuring adequate food and making available a labor supply for the cities.[40] Such interpretations are strengthened by the latter course of the reforms, which witnessed a turn away from the encouragement of peasant agriculture toward an emphasis on large-scale, capital-intensive units. Without doubt the economic drawbacks of an agriculture based on highly concentrated absentee ownership and a sharecropping peasantry weighed heavily in favor of reform in the minds of the shah and his advisors.

Others, probably with equal justice, have emphasized the potential political benefits of agrarian reform for the shah. At a stroke he could weaken the landed nobility, who had always disdained the upstart Pahlavis and posed a potentially serious threat to his autocratic rule,[41] and also establish

[39] These are discussed in Najmabadi, *Land Reform*, 59–92.

[40] A good discussion of how agrarian reform fit in with the needs of capitalist industrialization can be found in Behrang, *Le maillon faible*, 123–24. Economic motives—the creation of a wage-labor force, capital accumulation, and commercialization of consumption and production—are also emphasized in Najmabadi, *Land Reform*, 33–42.

[41] Well before Kennedy administration pressure, in 1954, the shah had initiated an attack against the landed elites, which provoked strong resistance and had little impact. Cottam, *Nationalism in Iran*, 290. In *Iran and the United States* (Pittsburgh: University of Pittsburgh

a mass base in the countryside. In so doing, he could lessen the likelihood of the kind of peasant rebellions afflicting so many Third World countries in the twentieth century. Even if peasant revolutionism never posed an overt challenge to his rule or that of his father, historical circumspection suggested the wisdom of timely reform.

The reform also corresponded to the political logic of autocracy: as the shah's prime minister Ali Amini expressed it, the regime sought "to bring together the people and the government, to unite all layers and classes of the population."[42] The reform's domestic political appeal was enhanced by the possibility that the shah might succeed in seizing the political initiative in the early 1960s, a time of widespread ferment and challenges to his rule from diverse quarters. To champion "modernization" and the "peasant" was potentially to undermine the landowners and clergy and to outmaneuver the secular national reformists. Finally, the international political context favored reform, a result not just of the prestige of socialism and the Soviet Union in many Third World countries, which pushed many regimes to consider otherwise unthinkable concessions, but also of the direct pressure of the Kennedy administration in the United States, which unambiguously espoused agrarian reform in much of the Third World.[43] To please Washington and mollify American pressure, the shah appointed Amini, a former ambassador to the United States viewed as a champion of reform, as prime minister despite his deep suspicion of Amini's ambitions.

The Iranian land reform was not a single coherent program, but a series of measures stretching over a number of years. The provisions established in the various stages, officially three in number, were not always consistent with each other and promoted very different land settlement and tenure patterns. They also corresponded to quite different political situations, as landlord opposition, concern over peasant mobilization, and the desire for increased governmental control over the countryside all contributed to shifts in policy. The regulations enacted over the years were thus quite complex, and the complications were only augmented by the fact that enforcement and administration did not always follow the letter of the law. The reform policy thus illustrates the unpredictability and contradictions inherent in autocratic regimes sponsoring modernization. For present pur-

---

Press, 1988), 128, Cottam emphasizes primarily political motivations—the desire to create a peasant social base as a counter to elite opposition.

[42] Quoted in A. I. Demin, "Agrarnye preobrazovaniia v sovremennom Irane," in *Iran: Sbornik statei*, ed. D. S. Komissarov and N. A. Kuznetsova (Moscow: Izdatel'stvo vostochnoi literatury, 1963), 80.

[43] American pressure for agrarian reform actually began much earlier, at the end of World War II. However, domestic conditions in Iran at the time were not favorable and nothing was done. Behrang, *Le maillon faible*, 121.

poses it will suffice to outline the major goals of the reform as they evolved over the decade, leaving aside the many complicating details.[44]

The major land reform law was enacted by decree in January 1962. In this, the "first stage," landlords were allowed to retain one village (or its equivalent) from among their holdings, selling the rest according to the values previously declared for tax purposes.[45] The peasant recipients of the land assumed the obligation to repay the government (including an additional 10 percent) over a fifteen-year period. Eligibility was restricted to those peasants who already had traditional cultivation rights over the land. The very large number of peasants without such rights (roughly one million) were undoubtedly worse off after the reform than before. Many had no choice but to work for wages on capitalist estates in the countryside or migrate to the cities. The peasants who did receive land under the first stage were sensibly obliged to join government-sponsored rural cooperatives, which were to provide credit and otherwise help the new owners make the transition to independent proprietorship. Critics of this first stage justly point to the slow pace of the land settlements, frequent landlord evasions and deceptions, the law's incomplete coverage, and the small average size of the plots,[46] yet it is also true that a large number of peasant sharecroppers, roughly 90 percent of those who held cultivation rights,[47] eventually gained title over their own land, freeing them from the burdensome payments to the landowners.

The 1962 law was amended by additional articles and regulations, finally enacted in July 1964, which ushered in the second, more equivocal stage of land reform. As a result of landlord opposition and the shah's fears that peasant expectations might quickly get out of hand, the effect of the previous law was considerably weakened. Landowners whose holdings had not been affected by the first stage were now given a choice of five different paths to land settlement. The two options most commonly chosen (together embracing over 90 percent of the peasants involved) were land rentals on the basis of thirty-year leases and division of the land according to the previous cropsharing distribution. This second stage, which actually affected more peasant families than the first, was clearly less advantageous from the peasants' point of view and gave rise to considerable disillusionment. It also failed to stimulate agricultural productivity, and in 1968 a third phase of reform, whose aim was to convert the tenancy arrangements of phase two into actual peasant ownership, was announced. Taken to-

[44] For detailed studies, see Eric Hooglund, *Land and Revolution in Iran 1960–1980* (Austin: University of Texas Press, 1982); Lambton, *Persian Land Reform*; and Najmabadi, *Land Reform*.

[45] Some lands, including orchards, tea plantations, and mechanized estates, were excluded.

[46] See Halliday, *Dictatorship and Development*, 110–11.

[47] Hooglund, *Land and Revolution*, xv.

gether, the three stages of the reform granted land to roughly half of peasant households.

That these reforms could be enacted at all—regardless of their ultimate fairness or effectiveness—requires consideration of the relationship between the state and the rural elites in modernizing Iran. In their general reflections on land reform, Huntington and Nelson suggest the advantages of an autocratic system and the consequent limitations on participation for the ratification of reform.[48] But we have seen that the Russian autocracy was unable to produce reforms that would openly displace the landed nobility. Autocracy alone, then, cannot be the decisive factor. Several crucial contrasts between the two cases suggest additional requirements.

First, we recall that in Russia the crisis of noble landowning encouraged many of the gentry to return to their estates and attempt to revive their economic fortunes. In so doing they created social networks that came to comprise local provincial elites with a strong sense of cohesiveness and separation from the state. In Iran nothing similar happened. Indeed, Iranian landowners were almost always absentee, seldom residing in their villages or managing the estates. Production was largely carried on by sharecropping peasants. There was little to bind the landlord to the local community and relations between owners and peasants were based on suspicion and mutual fear, the landlord living in dread of being cheated or despoiled by a discontented peasantry. "Distrust, insecurity, faction, and intrigue prevailed on all sides."[49] In that minority of cases in which the landed elite did spend considerable time on their estates, relations tended to be better.[50] The generally low commitment to agriculture on the part of the landed gentry was reinforced by the modest profitability of most holdings. Both climate and the weak technological base of Iranian agriculture reduced the possibilities for the accumulation of great wealth. Many landlords relied more on government appointments, commercial activities, or professional abilities for income.[51]

The weak ties of the gentry to the land and the peasantry had several major consequences. First, landlords evinced much less hostility to the idea of selling their land to the government.[52] Many skeptics were further en-

[48] Samuel Huntington and Joan Nelson, *No Easy Choice: Political Participation in Developing Countries* (Cambridge: Harvard University Press, 1976), 76.

[49] Lambton, *Persian Land Reform*, 30. "All sides" included the government in its relations to the landowners. Also see Lambton, *Landlord and Peasant*, 393, 395.

[50] Lambton, *Landlord and Peasant*, 271–72.

[51] Goodell, *Elementary Structures*, 325; Demin, "Agrarnye," 123.

[52] Demin, "Agrarnye," 123. In Russia this phenomenon also existed. Many landlords simply gave up and sold their estates. But in general, Russian landlords, operating in a more competitive professional environment that required credentials, had fewer options. Further, as has been pointed out, many nobles did refuse simply to abandon agriculture, partly, no doubt, because of a stronger agrarian mystique in Russian culture.

ticed by the lucrative opportunities offered by the regime for investment of the funds they received for their land in industry. Second, the landlords' low level of commitment to agriculture gave both public opinion and the government ample chance to excoriate them for their parasitism. Thus, Minister of Agriculture Arsanjani was echoing a widely felt sentiment in the following declaration: "These people live abroad and from night to morning play in the casinos, and so it is repeated every day. . . . From where do they receive the money that they lose? . . . This money is the result of the labor of workers, of old men and women, minors."[53] Finally, and just as significantly, their lack of rootedness in the countryside deprived them of the capacity to form the local social and political connections necessary for solidary action. No institutions comparable with the zemstvos or noble assemblies existed in rural Iran.

Landlord resistance to the reforms certainly made itself felt, particularly in the period of the enactment of the 1962 law.[54] Leading newspapers published the landlords' cries of outrage, seeking to influence public opinion. Some landowners apparently attempted to organize disorders in the countryside; others refused to abide by the provisions of the new law and even reneged on their old obligations to the peasantry.

Most serious of all were attempts to involve the clergy, who themselves often owned agricultural properties. The landowners' appeals found a response among many mullahs, who made reference to the Islamic justification of private property and the consequent illegality of appropriation. In the fall of 1962 large meetings of the clergy and their adherents took place in Teheran, Qom, and Mashhad inveighing against the government's anticonstitutional practices and rule by decree. One Teheran professor of theology claimed that the agrarian reform law was incompatible with Moslem theology, for "Moslems cannot pray on land acquired by force."[55] Opposition to the land reform did much to inflame the religious community against the shah's government, a process that culminated in the violently suppressed demonstrations of 1963. In all this the ulama had to act gingerly, for the reform program had given rise to high expectations and great enthusiasm in the villages. In addition, some clergy—it is impossible to know the percentage—approved of agrarian reform in principle, if not of the shah's actual program. For these reasons the religious leaders, among whom Khomeini displayed notable activism, tended to emphasize the unconstitutional enactment of the reforms rather than their content, although the latter was at least as much a source of their ire.[56]

[53] Quoted in Sh. M. Badi, "Zemel'naia reforma v Irane," in Komissarov and Kuznetsova, *Iran*, 20.

[54] This is described in Demin, "Agrarnye," 117–18. The question has not been well studied and any estimates of landlord resistance can only be provisional.

[55] Quoted in Demin, "Agrarnye," 124.

[56] For a brief description of the conflict between the clergy and the government over the

The anger of the landlords did have its effect. As noted previously, the reform program was significantly watered down in the following years. The shah also channeled large amounts of oil money to them, turning them into "his earliest and most privileged social clientele."[57] But these concessions should not blur the significance of the underlying political vulnerability of the landed elite, the sources of which have already been described. In comparison with the situation in Russia, the crux of the difference lies in the contrasting historical roles of the state in the modernization of their societies. Since Peter, Russian rulers had organized and mobilized the rural elites for state service both in the central bureaucracy and the localities. The same institutions created to benefit the state could become a fulcrum for noble initiatives in the interests of their own estate, as occurred particularly under Nicholas II. The more limited modernization of Iranian society, expressed in the central state's weak penetration of rural Iran until the last decade of Pahlavi rule, simultaneously deprived the nobility of a strong political voice within the central state apparatus and in local politics. Their protests against land reform, though occasionally vociferous and at times accompanied by violence, expressed the anguish and impotence of outsiders, who required unnatural allies in the shape of the mullahs to acquire a deep social resonance. When religious protest was defeated, the hopes of landlord opponents of the reforms were also dashed. In this sense, Huntington and Nelson's proposition that land reform requires limited political participation turns out to be valid after all.

However truncated the reforms turned out to be, they clearly did have a major impact on the village economy and social structure. In undermining the position of the landlords, the regime clearly responded to widely held aspirations of the Iranian peasantry, even though they, like the Russian peasants after emancipation, resented the payments they had to make to the government for land they regarded as rightfully theirs.[58] At the same time, however, the old system had generated its interdependencies and institutions that now needed substitutes. For example, previously the landowners had often supplied credit to their tenants; even if the rates were exorbitant, the vacuum would now have to be filled by other means. Similarly, the tenant sharecroppers had evolved cooperative practices of labor and land distribution somewhat similar to, though much weaker than,

land reform, see Shaul Bakhash, *The Reign of the Ayatollahs* (New York: Basic Books, 1984), 27–33.

[57] Katouzian, *Political Economy*, 359.

[58] The similarity to Russian peasant attitudes is striking. According to Lambton, many peasants felt that, in the words of some Arasbaran peasants, "the shah says that the land is ours and that we should not pay the landowners' share." Lambton, *Persian Land Reform*, 263. Although not as well developed, peasant monarchism cum populist ideology clearly existed in Iran as well.

those of the Russian commune. The right to tenancy under the old system had not generally applied to specific plots or amounts of land, and many of the most crucial decisions had been made by work teams (*bunehs*) which allocated the available land and farmed it cooperatively. Although primarily economic in origin, the bunehs became significant institutions in village life, and membership and position in them affected the villagers' overall influence and status.[59] As with the mir, the egalitarian aspects of the bunehs should not be exaggerated. The head of the team—the *sarbuneh*—was appointed by the landlord and clearly benefited from his position. In addition, the distribution of the portion of the harvest that remained after payments to landlords and other creditors had been deducted was often unequal, with the sarbuneh and his assistants receiving a disproportionate share.

Whatever the merits of these traditional village practices, they clearly served a function in organizing village agriculture. Although government officials hardly seemed to be aware of the bunehs and their importance in the villages—they had, after all, no intimate knowledge of village life—they certainly did perceive the need to develop institutions appropriate for small independent peasant proprietors. In the minds of the most committed reformers, especially Arsanjani, the ideal solution was the creation of local peasant cooperatives endowed with the right to form extralocal federations. Recall that the original agrarian reform had even made membership in cooperative societies mandatory for the recipients of land. As originally envisioned, these cooperatives would have the primary role in the provision of credit, so crucial to an agriculture on the borders of subsistence. Peasant contributions were to be supplemented by government resources. The cooperatives were also to be responsible for the general supervision and management of agricultural affairs.[60] The societies themselves were given an organizational structure: an assembly composed of all members, which had the ultimate power of decision; and an executive committee to run day-to-day affairs, which in turn appointed a chairman, secretary, and manager.

The cooperative societies suffered from the predictable shortcomings of new organizations after their creation. Skilled peasant administrators were often difficult to locate and all of the peasants lacked experience in formal organizations of this type. Yet according to the most seasoned foreign analyst of the Iranian countryside, in their early period the societies also aroused a great deal of enthusiasm and were surprisingly effective. They gave to the peasants a sense of independence and also pride in the cooper-

[59] For a discussion of the bunehs, see Hooglund, *Land and Revolution in Iran*, 23–28, and also his "Rural Socioeconomic Organization in Transition: The Case of Iran's Bonehs," in Bonine and Keddie, *Modern Iran*, 191–210.

[60] For a discussion of these cooperatives, see Lambton, *Persian Land Reform*, 291–366.

atives as their own organizations, the embodiment of their promised new role in Iranian life.[61] Many of the societies also functioned reasonably well, despite numerous deficiencies and the hostility of local merchants and middlemen. At first, too, there was considerable idealism among the government officials, usually young, appointed to oversee and organize the cooperative societies.[62]

Taken together, these promising beginnings seemed to justify the guarded optimism expressed by Lambton in her book, based on direct observation in the period until 1966. However, it was Lambton's fears more than her hopes that were realized in the ensuing years. In a postscript written in the autumn of 1968, she already expressed skepticism about the new programs to create large-scale agrarian corporations in the countryside, expressing her continuing faith in the cooperatives, which had made "astonishing progress."[63]

But this was not to be the direction of the future. In retrospect it is clear that small-scale peasant agriculture based on cooperative organization—in many ways a model not so different from what Shanin called "the peasant dream"—was completely at odds with the fundamental outlook and basic economic and political goals of the regime. The modernizing autocracy favored gigantism—demonstrations of achievements that would impress world public opinion, the symbolism rather than the reality of "development"—which, in a country like Iran would have involved not large-scale, capital-intensive agriculture but precisely the kind of agrarian structures envisioned in the reforms.[64] The shah and his technocrats also favored management, control, input-output ratios—a mentality hardly compatible with small-scale peasant agriculture.

Nor did the agrarian model advocated by Arsanjani and his fellow reformers have much economic appeal to the regime after the mid-1960s. The new technocrats, trained abroad, looked with envy at capital intensive American large-scale farming and, since some of them had backgrounds in the Tudeh party, occasionally at the Soviet *sovkhozes* as well.[65] Neither of the two great modern economic powers, despite their very different patterns of economic organization, depended on small-scale peasant agriculture, which, it was assumed, could never produce a surplus for the really vital arena of economic expansion, modern industry. It was thinking of this

[61] Ibid., 317, 322.

[62] Ibid., 123, 328.

[63] Ibid., 366.

[64] See the United Nations study emphasizing this latter strategy of agricultural development, which would have absorbed excess labor: International Labor Office, *Towards Full Employment* (Lausanne: Imprimerie Vaudoise, 1970).

[65] Halliday, *Dictatorship and Development*, 113, also states that Iranian officials studied and were influenced by the Israeli moshavim.

kind that lay behind the regime's shift in policy in favor of large-scale commercial operations in the late 1960s.

The law permitting the creation of farm corporations was enacted in 1967.[66] Peasants were persuaded, often against their will, to join a corporation, to which they would give over title to their land in exchange for shares. The new, larger units were administered by government officials sent by Teheran. The machinery and infrastructure expenditures (housing, schools, roads) of the government were high, contributing to the corporations' doubtful economic viability. In addition, the widespread use of machinery decreased the demand for labor, so that many of the shareholding peasants, not to speak of the landless laborers left out of the reforms altogether, could not obtain work.

Despite unimpressive economic performance and the evident lack of enthusiasm of the peasants, the government did not retreat from its plans to create a large-scale modern agricultural sector. In 1975, drunk with oil wealth and unable to perceive the fantastic hubris of its vision, the government passed its "poles of development" law.[67] According to this measure, 1.5 to 1.8 million hectares of the richest irrigated land in the country would be regrouped into zones, which would be cultivated in sections of at least 20 hectares. Peasants who refused to cooperate in this scheme would have their land expropriated. By 1976 twenty poles had been defined, and the following year five of these were inaugurated. Due to the need for immense study and planning, progress in forming the poles of development was slow. Officials thought the peasants were too stupid to know what was good for them, finding them to be "hesitant to cooperate with the government," but resolved that "such resistance must be overcome."[68]

In addition to the agricultural corporations, the state also encouraged the creation of private agribusiness along the lines of American corporate agriculture. Sometimes of huge scale—Keddie mentions farms of up to 25,000 hectares[69]—these enterprises were often owned by multinational corporations. One farm was even named "Iran—California." In the entire Dez Project, a massive program of dam construction and irrigated commercial farming begun in Khuzistan with the advice of David Lilienthal of TVA fame, there was only one significant private Iranian investor—a retired army general living on the Georgia estate of his American wife.[70] Although these massive projects were planned for newly developed land,

[66] The following information is based on Halliday, *Dictatorship and Development*, 113–15, and Nikki Keddie, *Roots of Revolution* (New Haven: Yale University Press, 1981), 164–66.

[67] Behrang, *Le maillon faible*, 161–62.

[68] Quoted in ibid., 162.

[69] Keddie, *Roots of Revolution*, 165.

[70] Goodell, *Elementary Structures*, 183.

this was not always the case, and numerous peasant farmers were displaced. Nor, as with the farm corporations, did all this effort and the resulting dislocations appear to be accompanied by improved economic performance. On the contrary, the results seem to have been inferior to the accomplishments of the peasant farmers.[71] Some of the large units were even expropriated by the government because of the disappointing level of production.

The political implications of a cooperatively organized peasant agriculture were just as alien to the modernizing autocracy as were its economic traits. Even if the cooperative movement had remained primarily economic in orientation, the richness of horizontal ties it required and embodied would have violated the autocracy's insistence on social atomization and government overlordship. But in the early years the cooperatives displayed a degree of incipient political independence disquieting to the shah. In a congress of "The movement of free men and women of Persia" convoked in August 1963 by the government to gather support for the reforms, the peasant delegates demonstrated gratitude and enthusiasm for Arsanjani, who naturally became a potential political menace to the shah and had to be dismissed. It was this nascent political threat as much as opposition to the economic implications of peasant agriculture that occasioned the government's overall change of policy in the late 1960s. The shift in economic strategy has already been noted; it was accompanied by much more comprehensive government control over peasant institutions and rural life than ever before in Iranian history.

Increased government penetration of rural institutions was evident in all spheres. Most significant, perhaps, was the fate of the cooperatives. Consolidated into larger units often spanning a number of villages, they quickly fell prey to bureaucratization. These large units also facilitated government control, the main objective of the reorganization. This same purpose was furthered by parallel administrative changes in Teheran, which resulted in a significant loss of independence for the Central Organization for Rural Cooperation and the creation of a hierarchy of officials to regulate the societies' activities. The nominally elected cooperative representatives were in fact subject to the dictates of these government agents, who in turn merely followed the orders of the central ministry in Teheran.[72] With the formation of the Rastakhiz party, the role assigned to the cooperative societies became even clearer: they became officially incorporated into this feeble attempt to mobilize all Iranians behind the regime's modernization policy. In enforcing collective and obligatory membership on the peasant members of the cooperative societies, the regime found itself in the familiar

[71] Keddie, *Roots of Revolution*, 166.

[72] See Hooglund, *Land and Revolution*, 107.

trap of attempting to stimulate initiative and enthusiasm through coercion, one of the central dilemmas of autocratic modernization.

Many other government agencies and officials, of diverse kinds, arrived in the villages during the period of rapid modernization. Some of these, such as the Literacy Corps, the Health Corps, and the Extension and Development Corps, were specifically concerned with rural development. Composed of young men and women drafted into national service, these tens of thousands of urban emissaries surely contributed to health and education in the villages. But many of them also resented their terms in the rural backwaters and transmitted the customary urban superciliousness toward the peasantry. If the portrait given by Goodell is typical, and it has the ring of truth, these young bearers of modernization were afflicted by formalism and proved unable to integrate themselves into village life.[73] Little else could be expected from a program that none of the participants had freely chosen to join.

The government also imposed its will on the villages more directly. Under the new system, the village head, previously chosen by the landlord with the tacit approval of the villagers, was formally elected, but in fact no longer depended upon grass-roots support so much as on a network of political ties extending beyond the village.[74] Local administration was also tightened up and rationalized. Key decisions about village affairs originated in the relevant ministries and were transmitted to the local level passing through provincial, county, and district bureaucracies. The shah's regime was thus able to promote the kind of bureaucratic organization in the countryside proposed by Stolypin but effectively blocked by the nobility.

The increasing intervention of the state in Iranian rural life brought with it important changes in peasant perspective. For the first time the peasantry was incorporated into national life, even if as objects more than subjects of politics. The age-old political isolation of the villages was broken, a change facilitated by parallel economic and cultural changes. The government had now made promises to the peasantry; it had sought their support, if only temporarily; and it had tried to organize them. On the other hand, it was the peculiar genius of the modernizing autocracy to transform potential gains such as these into liabilities. Local government officials were high-handed and corrupt. Teheran was distant and unresponsive to peasant needs. Its policy shifts were unpredictable and contradictory in their most essential features. The regime simultaneously raised the expectations of the peasantry and disappointed them. The resulting change of consciousness is eloquently expressed in the following statement by a young Kurdish

[73] See Goodell, *Elementary Structures*, esp. 95–97, 102–5, 148–52.

[74] Mary Hooglund, "Religious Ritual and Political Struggle in an Iranian Village," *MERIP Reports* 102 (January 1982): 12.

farmer: "Before, the elders said that if a child died, it was the will of God . . . , but now, I think that it's the will of the government."[75] Much the same might have been said by a Russian worker, who also confronted a modernizing government unable and unwilling truly to modernize social and political relations.

From the regime's point of view the overall balance of its efforts to transform rural Iran must have been equivocal. Unquestionably the old system had lost whatever vitality it had formerly possessed. The landlord lost his political control over the villages and ceased to pose any threat to the shah's power. Traditional peasant institutions lost their authority with remarkable speed. Private ownership, albeit on a scale hardly offering subsistence, deprived the bunehs of many of their functions and they registered a notable decline.[76] The solidarity upon which they were based and which they in turn further augmented also deteriorated, as economic differentiation proceeded apace in the villages. There were no longer any cooperative measures to redistribute land or in other ways ensure security. In addition, there was now a major division between peasants who did and those who did not receive land. The village was quite incapable of acting as a cohesive unit, especially since it had been deprived of a clearly dominant landowning class as a focus for shared discontent.

New social relations had thus begun to take form in the countryside. Large-scale capitalist agriculture appeared in completely unaccustomed forms. A middle peasantry, heretofore virtually absent in Iranian agriculture,[77] had also made its debut. At the same time, a great many small peasant landowners had insufficient land and access to credit, and were at great pains to survive. By the time of the revolution the implications of these changes for the future were unclear. What can be stated with certainty is that all the oil wealth and planning did little to alleviate the economic backwardness of the countryside. Shortfalls in food production were made up by massive import programs, but this was only a short-term solution. Whether there was in fact a long-term solution in the context of a regime given to fanciful plans that systematically stifled initiative is highly doubtful.

The Russian and Iranian experiments in rural change demonstrate, in their different ways, the difficulties of reform in autocratic modernizing regimes. In Russia the autocratic regime could not cut its ties with its traditional political base. The class that it had traditionally used to govern the country used its privileged position in government to counteract any pol-

[75] Quoted in Hooglund, *Land and Revolution*, 137.

[76] Hooglund, "Rural Socioeconomic Organization," in Bonine and Keddie, *Modern Iran*, 203–5.

[77] Farhad Kazemi and Ervand Abrahamian, "The Nonrevolutionary Peasantry of Modern Iran," *Iranian Studies* 11 (1978): 259–304.

icies that might have reduced its political dominance in the countryside or threatened its property. It is impossible to know what might have come out of the Stolypin reforms, but the process they set in motion was gradual, at a time when only dramatic changes might have provided the regime with a social base among the peasantry. The Iranian state, despite its illusions about itself, was equally unable to generate a modern, productive rural society. For reasons discussed earlier, the Iranian autocracy had more leeway in its relationship to the landed nobility and proved capable of enacting a significant reform in the face of considerable landlord opposition. This reform eliminated potential political threats from both landowners and the peasantry, but the regime's policies in the countryside were consistent only in their inability to encourage initiative and generate trust. They also opened the regime up to charges from leftist intellectuals and the religious establishment alike that it was destroying the country's traditional culture and betraying its interests to foreigners in the name of imported models.[78] Perhaps one of the shah's ministers, writing in retrospect, offered the correct judgment. The shah should have supported and developed peasant agriculture instead of undermining it, he claimed. The insecurity produced by his policies left the peasantry increasingly frustrated and uncertain of the future. "It was promised much, but given little. No longer cut off from the rest of society, and traditionally religious, it will lend a favorable ear to the revolution."[79]

The implications of autocratic modernization for revolutionary change in the countryside are thus highly complicated. In one sense, no generalizations seem possible, for peasant militancy was a marked feature of the end of the tsar's but not the shah's regime. We have seen that the Russian government's inability to reform land tenure in order to eliminate a declining, but highly visible and politically potent, gentry elite provoked peasant discontent. In addition, government modernization of social relations and the intrusion of the bureaucracy in Russia never destroyed the peasants' capacity for solidary collective action, particularly through their communal institutions. In Iran the peasantry had neither a clearly definable class opponent nor authoritative indigenous institutions. The landed elite maintained some of their property but as largely invisible absentee owners. The old forms of peasant association, the bunehs, declined, while the new cooperatives were crippled by state control. In addition, the spread of small proprietorship increased economic differences among the peasantry and removed the sense of shared interests and grievances. For all these reasons,

[78] See Mottahedeh's discussion of the leftist writer Al-e Ahmad's attacks on the cultural effects of the land reform in *Mantle of the Prophet*, 309.

[79] Nahavandi, *Anatomie d'une revolution*, 67.

peasant rebellion did not play a significant part in the opposition against the shah.

Despite these differences, autocratic modernization did have some common effects. With their internal divisions rooted in the contradictory project itself, neither regime could act effectively and consistently to reshape rural society. A multitude of proposals were entertained and government officials were sent in increasing numbers to regulate and oversee change. Ambitious promises and commitments were made to the peasantry. But the lack of connection between the government and rural society in both countries and the inherent limitations of autocratic administration, with its overlapping jurisdictions and inconsistencies, reduced the efficacy of state action. Peasant tenure patterns and agrarian class relations in Russia proved resistant to change from above, at least in the short run. In Iran the regime could destroy the old social forms but not create new ones of any vitality.

In addition, rural society continued to lack the kind of social cohesion that might have offered resistance to the threat of revolutionary change coming from the cities. Class egoism and particularism remained strong in both countries. Mutual suspicions and distrust flourished, both among classes and between classes and the governments. No stable, conservative elements attached to their property and committed to the political system emerged in either rural Russia or Iran. When combined with the continuing impoverishment of rural life, partly the consequence of the high priority given to industry in both countries, the lack of social cohesion and the absence of conservative forces made the rural areas in both countries at the very least receptive to social revolution. And in Russia, if the peasants were in no position to spearhead or channel revolutionary mobilization, they nonetheless played an indispensable role in the ultimate victory of the radicals.

Seven

Cultures of Rebellion

THE ECONOMIC, political, and social changes of nineteenth-century Europe—the development of capitalist factory industry, the challenge of democratization, the development of the modern nation-state, the decline of old social hierarchies, and the movement toward egalitarianism—inevitably gave rise to uncertainty, debates, and innovations in the realm of culture. The cultural changes were not simply adaptations to the more potent transformations in other areas of society, for much of the cultural response to the emerging society challenged its very foundations, whether from a conservative or radical standpoint. At the same time, there did emerge a body of elaborated cultural models that gave meaning to the new institutions and practices. Classical economics, utilitarianism, political liberalism—for many, all these explained and validated the new kind of society in gestation.

In countries like Russia and Iran, in which modern institutions and ideas came from outside, frequently as a result of state initiative, no such new cultural synthesis could become dominant: first, because the changes themselves were much more incomplete, and so their benefits even more questionable than in the West; second, because they tended to clash much more starkly with indigenous patterns; and finally, because the debates and ideologies developed in Europe at different periods could find expression simultaneously in countries making the transition later. Thus, Adam Smith, Marx, Trotsky, and Spengler could all find their adherents in the shah's Iran.

In both countries, then, there was great cultural uncertainty and conflict among cultural elites as well as the masses. For the former, exposure to contemporary Western culture and politics, as well as the changes in their own societies, had dissolved whatever sense of certainty and coherence of perspective that may once have existed. Dostoevsky, a representative figure in this respect in Russia even because of his idiosyncracies, which highlighted widespread perplexities, is reported to have remarked: "Everything is abnormal in our society; that is how these things happen, and, when they do, nobody knows how to act—not only in the most difficult situations, but even in the simplest."[1] Similarly, in Iran the writer Baraheni expresses the plight of many of his profession in both countries: they were,

[1] Quoted in Isaiah Berlin, *Russian Thinkers* (New York: Pelican, 1979), 305.

he noted, twice aliens—strangers both to their own traditions and to those of the West.[2] This sense of alienation gave rise to a quest for authenticity on both the social and individual levels—in Ali Shariati's phrase, for a "return to one's [original and authentic] self."[3] This sense of cultural impoverishment and estrangement led groups of secular intellectuals in both countries to reinvestigate the religious roots of their own and their countries' identities.[4]

In the case of the masses, more characteristic was an erosion of traditional beliefs, more rapid in the cities than in the countryside, with less explicit and systematic awareness of the implications of the changes. The effects on elites and masses were equally deleterious, as elite culture became disconnected from the larger society and mass culture became stagnant and petrified, turning in upon itself in attempted defense.[5] For the elites, their own identity was called into question, even devalued; for the masses, their own anti-Western identities became schematized, defined not positively but negatively and thus resistant to inner development.

In both Russia and Iran there emerged a stratum of modern intelligentsia who sought to reorient the countries' culture. Making allowance for considerable differences rooted in history and also for important internal variations within each country, striking similarities in the secular intelligentsias in the two countries are apparent. First, due to rapid modernization combined with autocratic restrictions on the development of more open communication and participation, both intelligentsias were unusually cut off and alienated from the great majority of their societies. Alienation from the "people" and lack of sustained contact with them are standard themes of any history or sociology of the Russian intelligentsia. In Iran this isolation, much of it the product of the intelligentsia's adoption of Western ideas, became part of the intelligentsia's self-critique. For example, Al-e Ahmad and Ali Shariati, two of the most influential intellectuals in the period under consideration, both took great pains to analyze

[2] Baraheni, *Crowned Cannibals*, 82.

[3] Quoted in Ali Gheissari, "The Ideological Formation of the Iranian Intelligentsia" (Ph.D. diss., Oxford University, 1990), 293.

[4] The most famous source for this revived interest in religion among the Russian intelligentsia is the collection entitled *Vekhi* or *Landmarks*, first published in 1909. The furious attacks to which it gave rise demonstrate that the renewed interest in religious issues was far from universal. See *Landmarks*, ed. Boris Shragin and Albert Todd (New York: Karz Howard, 1977). For Iran, both Ali Shariati and Al-e Ahmad exemplify this tendency. For Al-e Ahmad, see Mottahedeh, *Mantle of the Prophet*, 299–305, and Jalal Al-e Ahmad, *Iranian Society* (Lexington, Ky.: Mazda, 1982), 41.

[5] For Russia, see Raeff, *Understanding Imperial Russia*, 75; for Iran, see Nikkie Keddie, *An Islamic Response to Imperialism* (Berkeley: University of California Press, 1968), xvii, xix; also Al-i Ahmad, *Occidentosis*, 73.

the intelligentsia's estrangement from Iranian society and its adverse consequences for cultural and social life.[6] This isolation from the mass of the people also conditioned a fundamental ambivalence toward them: they were ignorant and passive, yet at the same time the bearers of the country's authentic identity; and, in the case of leftists, they were both the innocent downtrodden and the bearers of a historical mission.

The assertion of autocratic power cut the intelligentsia off from the government at least as much as from the people. In Russia to be a "thinking person" virtually necessitated a critical stance toward the regime, which betrayed indigenous beliefs and traditions through its pursuit of modernization but which also did not live up to Western standards of justice. In Iran, the constitutionalist intelligentsia of the early years of the century and the opposition to Reza Shah tended to favor the rule of law, the separation of powers, and individual rights. The generation growing up and maturing in the shadow of the shah's modernization campaigns were inclined to advocate more profound changes in the fabric of society.[7] Nonetheless, uncompromising rejection of the autocratic state and refusal to cooperate with it were widespread throughout the period. The consequences of this intransigence were also similar in the two countries: as in Alexis de Tocqueville's classic analysis of Old Regime France, the intelligentsia's lack of experience with the world of affairs gave rise to an abstract cast of mind characterized by dogmatism and rigidity.[8] The goal of political action was not gradual improvement, or even the elimination of the autocracies, but "the happiness of the people."[9]

From everything mentioned already, it also follows that both intelligentsias were highly sectarian and polarized.[10] But the resulting tendency toward fissure into small, mutually hostile groups also has other sources. First, government repression in both countries undercut generalized trust and the development of impersonal ties of loyalty. Intellectual life and political movements thus tended to be highly personalized, centered around particularistic ties to a leader. A not insignificant proportion of the infighting and schisms in the cultural and political life of both countries had its

[6] Al-e Ahmad's critique is entitled *On the Vices and Virtues of Intellectuals*. Shariati developed his viewpoints on Iranian intellectuals in several lectures and essays. See Gheissari, "The Ideological Formation," 302.

[7] Ervand Abrahamian, *The Iranian Mojahedin* (New Haven: Yale University Press, 1989), 84.

[8] For Russia this theme is too well known to require further elaboration. For Iran, see Gheissari, "Ideological Formation," 260–61, 324–25.

[9] The phrase comes from R. V. Ivanov-Razumnik, *Istoriia russkoi obshchestvennoi mysli* (St. Petersburg: M. M. Stasiulevich, 1911), 2:3, where it is applied to Russian populism; it is also applicable to Russian Marxism and to the Iranian intelligentsia.

[10] For Iran, see Mottahedeh, *Mantle of the Prophet*, 282–83, 307–8.

source in personal conflicts. This personalism was in turn reinforced by the lack of formal procedures for selecting leadership—the development of such mechanisms was of course ruled out by the nature of the political system. Leaders were thus free to act with little regard for grass-roots sentiments.

Thus isolated from the population at large and unable even to cooperate among themselves, the modern intelligentsia seemed to be doomed to political impotence. Their audacious dreams appeared to clash ridiculously with their real capacity for social leadership. For Iran this judgment corresponds to the secular intelligentsia's actual role in the revolution: not only did they not lead it, but they supported a movement bent on their own marginalization.[11] In Russia, of course, the Bolsheviks, a branch of the revolutionary intelligentsia, were able to come to power after a stormy nine months of turmoil; and the party of Lenin, led by members of the intelligentsia, could heap scorn on the stratum of their own origin as one composed of impotent Hamlets.

The contrasting outcomes of the struggles for power in Russia and Iran inescapably raise a number of difficult comparative questions. Given the shared contexts of autocratic modernization, how do we explain the Marxist victory in Russia and the relative impotence of the left in Iran? Why was Khomeini's version of Shiʿism so compelling to large sectors of the Iranian population? What insights into the global patterns of social change in the two countries can be gained from a consideration of these discrepant outcomes? Paradoxical as it may seem, part of the answer to these questions lies in traits shared by Russian Marxism and Shiʿism, which, though doctrinally poles apart, both displayed unusual advantages for revolutionary mobilization. Just as crucial will be a reexamination of many of the contrasts between the two countries—in their historical backgrounds, modernization processes, politics, and culture—adumbrated in previous chapters. Throughout this interweaving of cultural themes and social, political, and economic contexts, it should become clear that this is neither a cultural nor a structural argument. Ideas become effective only when they interpret social realities in a persuasive way and so provide guides for action; in this sense, they are not "autonomous." Similarly, as Lenin's and Khomeini's daring demonstrates, structural possibilities for change require actors driven on by ideas. To insist on the primacy of ideology against structural preconditions, or the reverse, is to separate what in actual revolutions are always found together; each is a necessary complement to the other. Finally, it bears emphasis that not everything can be explained: neither outcome was inevitable, and so should not be treated as such in an exercise of retrospective determinism.

[11] For critical remarks, see Arjomand, *Turban for the Crown*, 137–38.

Russian Marxism and Shiʿism as Revolutionary Cultural Frameworks

In the following pages a number of shared cultural traits of Russian Marxism and Shiʿism, all with an elective affinity for revolutionary politics, will be discussed. Not only did they have the potential to encourage political opposition, but they pointed the way to deeper social changes whose totalism could justify the necessary sacrifices—sacrifices that would sanctify the victims as martyrs for the cause. They held forth standards of justice inconsistent with existing social and political conditions and sought to convince people to judge their societies in terms of these alternatives. All of this they claimed on the basis of a deeper knowledge that left them no doubt of the ultimate triumph of their visions.

Despite these shared postulates, there were also deep divisions within both schools of thought about the timing of change and the role of human agency. Many Shiʿites believed that the fulfillment of divine promises must await the return of the Hidden Imam to earth; until this blessed event all human institutions, and especially politics, will suffer from profound and inevitable imperfections. Similarly, some currents of Russian Marxism taught that socialism could only be the end product of a long and gradual historical evolution, which could be shortened but not avoided. Thus, the revolutionary potential in each school could only be fulfilled with the emergence of more activist interpretations urging the efficacy of immediate action. It was the singular contribution of Lenin and Khomeini to elaborate such activist frames of interpretation, thus promising that profound improvements could be achieved without delay. Only on the basis of these visions of immediate change could the values implicit in both doctrines justify, and even compel, revolutionary action. This combination of utopian vision and practical politics in the ideas and strategies of the two leaders empowered their followers to act even against the threat of savage repression.

If Russian Marxism and Shiʿism were alike in providing the cultural matrix for totalistic mobilizational ideologies, the parallels between them should not be exaggerated. Indeed, stark contrasts between Marxism as a modernizing ideology and Shiʿism as the long-established official religion of the great majority of society are immediately apparent. Marxism was the chosen belief of a small minority subject to persecution if they acted on their convictions; most Iranians were born into Shiʿism and those not part of the tradition might suffer discrimination or persecution. Marxism preaches the need for an irrevocable break with the past in the name of secular progress, whereas Shiʿites waited in expectation of a future that would consummate the prophetic tradition and transcend earthly happiness. In addition, the respective doctrinal traditions appealed to different groups and for different reasons: Russian Marxism had its social roots in the secular intelligentsia and the labor movement, whereas Shiʿite activism tended to flourish among more traditional groups in Iranian society. Finally, largely as a result of these contrasts, the significance of each in the respective revolutions was quite different: militant Shiʿism succeeded in mobilizing huge numbers of Iranians for a long campaign of protest before the shah was actually overthrown; Russian Marxism only became influential on a large scale after the February revolution, and then its appeal was much more based on class divisions. As will be discussed later in the chapter, these differences corresponded not only to variations in the ideological context but also to contrasting relations between the revolutionary elites and masses.

Two additional caveats are in order. First, the traits to be discussed are not as clear-cut as the kind of condensed discussion necessary here might imply. Indeed, all major intellectual traditions are defined more by the debates and points of contention than by the precise answers they give. Global characterizations inevitably hide the tensions and nuances at the heart of traditions, tensions that may be vital for understanding social action. For example, the death of Husain has been variously interpreted in Shiʿism as an example of patient suffering and endurance, and as uncompromising revolt against oppression and injustice. The implications for social action are in direct conflict with each other.[12] Every general statement is in part a distortion. Russian Marxism tended to exalt the knowing elite of party leaders; but both Menshevism and Bolshevism also included elements of self-denigration and glorification of the masses. Shiʿism held temporal political power to be in an ultimate sense illegitimate but, over the centuries, made many accommodations to it. Some qualifications to the generalizations offered here will be mentioned, but more often a high degree of schematicism will be necessary.

Second, nothing to be said is meant to imply that either cultural tradition can be understood apart from the larger society. Both emerged out of complex historical conditions from which they are in a fundamental sense inseparable. Russian Marxism, for example, is incomprehensible outside the context of Russian political culture and institutions. Iranian Shiʿism developed as a minority current, often persecuted, within Islam; it also had to establish stable relations with the Iranian autocracy, which was not entirely compatible with its fundamental teachings. As a consequence, although the stress here will be on similarities, the contrasts rooted in the different historical contexts do not thereby lose their significance. They are

[12] See Moojan Momen, *An Introduction to Shiʿi Islam* (New Haven: Yale University Press, 1985), 236.

simply underplayed for the sake of analysis. For example, I do not quarrel with the objection that the symbolism of martyrdom differs appreciably in its deeper implications in Russian Marxism and Iranian Shiʿism, and that in some ways they are quite distinct. The inevitable shortcomings flowing from these observations may be forgiven if the discussion casts light on some unexpected similarities vital to the understanding of revolutionary change in the two societies.

Elitism

Russian Marxism and Shiʿism claim to possess a store of knowledge largely unknown to ordinary men and women yet vital to the comprehension and ordering of human affairs. By this knowledge they justify the authority of a small elite, whose task it is to act on the basis of their superior understanding and also to propagate it in the society at large. This is not to deny the populist elements in each tradition, for both promise deliverance for the oppressed; but it is the elite who define what oppression means and show the way to the great reversal.

The elitism of Russian Marxism stems partly from the intellectual difficulty of the doctrine but more importantly from its lack of fit with Russian conditions. It was not immediately apparent how this Western analysis of the contradictions of capitalist industrial society applied to Russia, and the converts to Marxism had to perform impressive intellectual acrobatics to make the adaptation. Even if there is some truth to the postulate that European workers would come to accept Marxist ideas on the basis of their own experience and would learn, largely on their own, to develop a mass labor movement, these assumptions could not be transferred to Russia. The party, guided by the intelligentsia, must bring knowledge to the workers from outside. This well-known fundamental of Leninism was only slightly modified in theory by most Menshevik leaders, and in practice hardly at all. It was reinforced by the scarcely bridgeable cultural gap between social elites and the masses opened up from the time of Peter the Great onward.

Shiʿism has an equally high regard for the potential of human reason and low appreciation of the capacity of the masses to utilize it. All schools of Islam exalt the book and those who transmit its teachings, and even in Sunni Islam this involves a degree of esotericism.[13] Shiʿite Islam, however, carries esotericism to much greater lengths, developing a set of binary oppositions expressing the polarity of the seen and the unseen worlds.[14] Dis-

[13] See Gilsenan, *Recognizing Islam*, 30–36.

[14] Enayat, *Modern Islamic Political Thought*, 21–22.

cussion of the true meaning of the words of the Koran and the central doctrines of the faith is only appropriate for initiates; the ignorant many must be content to live in the world of appearances. The consensus of the community, so fundamental to Sunni Islam, is relativized. Instead, the knowing minority have the right to make binding decisions, even to make doctrinal innovations, on the basis of their superior learning and religious experience.[15] The clearest indication of the special role of the minority in Shiʿism is the key myth of the tradition, the revolt of Husain against the corrupt worldly powers. His defeat proved that the embattled minority, though temporarily vanquished, might still have superior moral right.

Dualism

Russian Marxism and Shiʿism oppose the truth and value of their own positions to the corruption and falsity of all other doctrines. Both also explicitly identify an enemy upon which this dichotomized world view can be focused. For Marxism, of course, the key opposition is between the bourgeoisie as exploiters and the proletariat as exploited. But this sense of polarization is heightened by the concept of bourgeois society as system, according to which all the major institutions protect the interests of the bourgeoisie. Russian Marxism witnessed the further complication of separation from its own theoretically defined mass base, further heightening its sense of itself as an isolated but righteous minority.

Shiʿism, from its very emergence as a separate tendency within Islam, defined itself in opposition to the corrupted status quo. It stood for the authentic suppressed values of Islam, counterposing its idealism to the compromises made by the established authorities. In many places and periods Shiʿites have been more hostile to the majority Sunnis than to members of other religions. Their sense of otherness has been graphically expressed in ritual avoidance of contact with polluted unbelievers.

These various doctrinal and ideological sources of polarization have in both cases been fortified by repression. The Russian state's persecution of Marxists further sealed their identity as an outcast sect, in part, ironically enough, through furnishing shared experiences in jail and exile. The persecution of Shiʿism has waxed and waned over the centuries, but even in Iran, the only official Shiʿite state, the culture of persecution has also flourished. The shah's attacks against the religious authorities and the threat posed to the religion by modernization have evoked historic Shiʿite images

[15] Not all schools of Shiʿism accepted the authority of the highest clergy to issue innovative judgments. The Akbari school, eclipsed in the nineteenth century, held positions closer to the Sunnis on this issue, relying more on tradition.

of unjust persecution. The shah becomes Yazid, the murderer of Husain. The Shiʿite community closes in upon itself for protection against the demonic secular forces in the name of betrayed ideals. When it is in a position to attack, it does so under the assumption that "all those who are not for us are against us."[16] Russian Marxism, especially its Leninist variant, also honored and acted upon this principle, which embodied a completely dualistic and polarized view of the world.

Emphasis on Knowledge

The opposition between the world of the believer and the corruption of outside forces found its justification in the claim to superior knowledge. This claim, in turn, can be broken down into two cardinal assumptions: first, that the truth about human nature, history, and society is knowable; and second, that the intellectual hierarchy of the movement possesses this truth. Russian Marxism and Shiʿism located these truths, respectively, in the Marxist theory of history and in Shiʿite religious doctrine and law. The theorists and scholars in the two traditions possessed exclusive claim to elucidate and interpret these truths on the basis of their knowledge. Mastery of the sacred texts that embodied this knowledge became a prerequisite for leadership within the movement and sometimes a justification for the movement's right to rule over the rest of society. For example, to an extraordinary degree intellectual virtuosity defined the elite of the Russian Marxist movement. Young converts such as Lenin and Martov made pilgrimages to Europe to visit virtuosi such as Plekhanov and Axelrod, whose prestige was based not on their political skills but on their theoretical works. Krzhizanovsky, a leading Marxist of the 1890s, declared in his memoirs that he was "firmly convinced that no good would ever come of anyone who had not gone through Marx's *Capital* two or three times."[17] The special knowledge of an elite also occupied a special place in the Shiʿite tradition. According to the doctrine of *ilm*, Ali's descendants inherited from Muhammad "the unique capacity of perceiving the 'branches' or subsidiary rules [*furu*] of religion,"[18] a claim naturally offensive to Sunnis. The knowing elite were bid to withhold knowledge from the uninitiated and to disseminate it gradually when appropriate. Similarly, as with the Russian Marxists, position in the status hierarchy of Iranian Shiʿite

[16] This was the principle behind Khomeini's politics. It was not shared by the more moderate Shariatmadari, who sought to build bridges to different social groups. See Shahrough Akhavi, *Religion and Politics in Contemporary Iran* (Albany: State University of New York Press, 1980), 167–71.

[17] Quoted in Neil Harding, *Lenin's Political Thought* (London: Macmillan, 1983), 1:72.

[18] Enayat, *Modern Islamic Political Thought*, 36.

Islam also required scholarly achievement. Young theological students flocked to the seminaries that could boast of the most accomplished scholars. Like the Marxist leadership, the Shiʿite hierarchy was extraordinarily bookish. Knowledge of the texts and intellectual virtuosity as demonstrated in published works were the *sine qua non* of status within the hierarchy. In the 1960s Khomeini was a rather junior figure among the religious scholars, despite his fame, because of an undistinguished publishing record.[19]

The political implications of this stress on elite knowledge are equivocal. Some Marxists assigned a minor role to human agency, believing that history unfolded according to an objective set of causal laws relatively immune to manipulation. Knowledge thus implied patience until the objective conditions for change ripened. Various strands of Shiʿism also inhibited political activism. Belief sometimes took the form of inner illumination, to which adepts opposed the necessary corruption of the world of appearances.[20] Another possibility was to distinguish between secular and religious spheres, each with its own standards and laws. According to religious law, the monarchy might be of doubtful legitimacy, but in the secular world it was politically necessary.[21] Or, the idea of a constitution based on legal innovation by a legislature might be incompatible with norms applicable to religion, but in modern conditions it was necessary in the political realm.

Yet in both Russian Marxism and Shiʿism the opposing tendency to translate superior knowledge into concrete political life always remained at least latent and had a degree of doctrinal validation. When leaders sought to make good the claims of their beliefs, the inevitable consequence was to undercut the very rationale of politics as compromise based on human diversity and the value of opposing perspectives.

Transhistorical Mission

This suspicion of politics was also rooted in suprahistorical expectations of the fulfillment of history. Despite their differences, both cultural tendencies incorporated a chiliastic world view, according to which a momentous

[19] Akhavi, *Religion and Politics*, 101.

[20] Arjomand, *Shadow of God*, 163, quotes Henri Corbin: "the idea of the occultation of the Imam forbids all socialization of the spiritual, all materialization of the spiritual hierarchies and forms which would identify these with the constituted bodies of the external, visible history."

[21] Enayat, *Modern Islamic Political Thought*, 171. This was one important argument made by clergy who supported the Constitutional Revolution against their clerical opponents, who saw the idea of a constitution as dangerously secular.

event would introduce a radical break in human history. Whereas all human history had been dominated by class exploitation, socialism would actualize the values of freedom and community. In Shiʿism the coming Imam of the Age would reappear to redeem humanity. This redemption had both terrestrial and eschatological dimensions. The hidden Imam will return from occultation and a just government free from oppression and tyranny, the embodiment of the ideal Moslem society, will be created. The reappearance of the Twelfth Imam was also interpreted eschatologically as the beginning of the "End of Time" and the subsequent resurrection of the dead.[22]

Again, discrepant political implications could be drawn from these beliefs. Belief in the coming fulfillment of history could entail passive expectancy or an active drive to bring about the millennium. It was compatible with withdrawal from worldly corruption as well as with a belief that, however transitory, secular affairs were not without present significance. Or, as the vast majority of Iranians thought, according to Al-e Ahmad, the state could be regarded as "the agent of oppression and the usurper of the rightful rule of the Imam of the Age."[23]

In some senses, these different political interpretations are of considerable significance. It matters a great deal whether a suprahistorical vision induces passivity or revolutionary activism in any given historical context. But regardless of which possibility is dominant at a particular time, they all imply a certain devaluation of institutions, law, and politics in the here and now. This is not to say that all individual Russian Marxists or Iranian Shiʿites lived and thought on the basis of these suprahistorical standards. But these transcendent judgments constituted a vital part of both traditions and thus had the potential to inspire radical actions and beliefs. A key belief shared by all who accepted the central doctrines was that present-day institutions had only contingent, if any, value.[24]

Universality

From all that has been said so far flows another cardinal trait of both Russian Marxism and Shiʿism: their claim to universality. Socialism is the best form of social organization for all human communities and will eventually

[22] The relations between these two aspects of Shiʿite doctrine on the return of the hidden Imam are exceedingly intricate and need not be discussed here. For clarification, see Abdulaziz Sachedina's interpretation as excerpted in Nasr, Dabashi, and Nasr, *Expectation of the Millennium*, 24–43.

[23] Al-i Ahmad, *Occidentosis*, 71.

[24] For example, the Marxist critique of bourgeois law is well known. Shiʿism had parallel suspicions, based on the imperfection of legal norms before the coming of the Imam.

triumph everywhere. All beliefs other than Shiʿism are flawed, their adherents impure; their disappearance is assured. There is no room in either doctrine for moral relativism. There is only one ethic, the ethic of the proletariat, alongside which all others lose their significance. Traditionally, non-Shiʿite law was no law at all, although it is true that modernist tendencies in Shiʿism (as well as in Sunnism) have reduced the force of this exclusivity.

Both systems of belief are also universal in the sense that they ultimately touch upon all aspects of individual and social life. Under socialism individual morality, work, the family, culture, and politics will all be transformed. It follows that prior to this historical fulfillment all practices and institutions are flawed. At most it can be said that bourgeois institutions contain the germs of further development and so must be viewed dialectically. In Russian Marxism, in common with other Russian socialist tendencies and much more than in European Marxism, socialists despised the bourgeois world as a whole, seldom granting it those advantages accorded by Marx.[25] Lenin, of whom Plekhanov said that "those things which bourgeois liberalism must bring to a country and everywhere in Europe has already brought, never occurred to [him],"[26] is only the clearest example of a general tendency.

Shiʿism also embraces all spheres of life, even if, before the reappearance of the Imam, perfection cannot be demanded in any of them. Nonetheless, even in this world people must strive to live according to the laws given by God through his Prophet. A large number of ritual and ethical practices involving many spheres of life are incumbent on the believer even before the Imam returns to fulfill history.[27] These obligations were given particularly broad scope by Shiʿite modernists, who interpreted the traditional injunction to enjoin the good and prohibit evil as a call for the reform of society.[28] Because of God's revelation, which teaches moral standards relevant for all times, the discontinuity to be brought about by the coming of the Imam will be less dramatic in Shiʿite Islam than in Marxism.[29] Nor will a revolutionary government seeking to implement religious norms in this

[25] See Ivanov-Razumnik, *Istoriia russkoi obshchestvennoi mysli*, 1:516, 520.

[26] Quoted in Nikolai Valentinov, *The Early Years of Lenin* (Ann Arbor: University of Michigan Press, 1969), 245.

[27] See Momen, *An Introduction to Shiʿi Islam*, 178–83. Many of the prescribed practices are shared with Sunnism.

[28] Akhavi, *Religion and Politics*, 120.

[29] Max Weber's general statement is relevant to cite here: "The concept of a religious revolution was consistent most with a rationalism oriented to an ascetic mastery of mundane affairs which taught that sacred institutions and institutions pleasing to God exist within this world." *Economy and Society*, ed. Guenther Roth and Claus Wittich (New York: Bedminster Press, 1968), 2:595–96. An Augustinian split between the two cities of God and of man is incompatible with such revolutionary commitments.

world be forced to make such a radical break with past practices as have revolutionary Marxist governments.[30]

The Significance of Consciousness

Important aspects of both Marxism and Shiʿism might impede any great estimate of the creative role of human consciousness in society or history. Marxism has often been interpreted by its adherents as a deterministic, evolutionary doctrine explaining the course of history quite apart from the input of creative individuals or movements. Shiʿism, like other theistic religions, stresses the overwhelming significance of God's will, to the point that some Shiʿite divines in the early period taught that God wills every act of sin.[31] Although later teachings reversed this view, emphasizing man's freedom of will, the idea of a powerful God guiding human action and history, culminating in the return of the Imam, remained a fundamental postulate. Further, the Koran and the traditions put certain limits on doctrinal creativity and innovation in social life—how strict these were to be aroused major debates among different schools. In any case, one can well imagine a Shiʿism focused on past traditions in passive expectation of the millennium to come.

These deterministic elements that might have instilled a sense of impotence among followers were in fact overshadowed in both traditions by an emphasis on the independent role of human consciousness. Russian Marxism, in part influenced by the legacies of populism, placed great stress on the independent role of the "conscious" elite and their responsibility to instill this consciousness into the masses, who would remain largely benighted without their help.[32] Indeed, consciousness was the *deus ex machina* that could compensate for the huge gap between the social conditions described as necessary for socialism by Marx and Russian realities. Even Plekhanov, that model of orthodoxy, declared that the revolutionary party in Russia could shorten the stage of the bourgeois revolution and thus partly modify the historical process. More deterministic ideas continued to have a strong pull among many Russian Marxists, who, for example, opposed the Bolshevik program in 1917 for its audacious attempt to skip

[30] This explains the Islamic government's approval and preservation of private property, which is regarded as sanctioned by religious law. There is little that a truly Marxist government could accept from the past.

[31] Momen, *An Introduction to Shiʿi Islam*, 74, 77.

[32] The necessary allowances must be made for doctrinal differences between the Mensheviks and the Bolsheviks. However, it is not clear how greatly their concrete action differed in this respect.

stages, but the Russian movement always, and most especially at times of ferment, contained this more voluntaristic tendency.

The question of the religious scholars' right of independent interpretation of the texts and traditions was at the core of the great dispute in the seventeenth and eighteenth centuries between the Akhbari and Usuli schools of jurisprudence. The Akhbaris' views more closely approximated those of the Sunni majority in their emphasis on the traditions, their distrust of human reason, and the restricted scope of interpretation that they wanted to permit the *mujtahids*, the authoritative legal scholars. Their viewpoint was effectively defeated in the early eighteenth-century, however, and it was the Usuli doctrine that became the basis for Shiʿite orthodoxy, achieving great intellectual subtlety. The chief assumption of the Usulis was the competence of human reason to make judgments about the religious law. Interpretation, or *ijtihad*, was regarded as both valid and necessary for the faith. The mujtahids possessed the knowledge and the authority to innovate in their interpretation of the teachings on the basis of reason and knowledge. Since Shiʿite leaders in the past century have often found social and political institutions wanting, this sanction for the exercise of free opinion has potentially revolutionary implications.[33] For example, based on their confidence in human reason and their acceptance of innovation, the majority of Shiʿite scholars accepted the desirability of constitutionalism at the time of the Constitutional Revolution.[34] Creative interpretations of doctrines have been facilitated by acceptance of the principle of "argumentation through hypothetical construction," which permitted the extension of religious values into new areas of concern.[35] The theological innovations of the Ayatollah Khomeini, his argument for the legitimacy of government by the jurisconsults, are incomprehensible apart from these developments.

Martyrdom

Suffering and martyrdom are potent themes of Russian culture, with roots in ascetic religious traditions and the history of schismatic opposition to the state. Redemption through suffering is a central motif in Russian literature, especially, of course, in the work of Dostoevsky. A culture of heroic martyrdom also finds powerful expression in the populist movement,

[33] See Enayat, *Modern Islamic Political Thought*, 160–61.

[34] Later, a great many religious authorities became disaffected from the constitutional movement, but their opposition was practical and political more than theoretical.

[35] Akhavi, *Religion and Politics*, 121–22.

with its celebration of the valiant few willing to give their lives for the people's good, even when reviled by the people themselves.[36]

Nurtured in similar conditions of harsh governmental repression, Russian Marxism was the legatee of all these cultural currents.[37] The example of the self-sacrifice of populists inspired imprisoned Marxist revolutionaries. They read many of the same texts, sang many of the same songs. For example, in his youth Martov, one of the most European of Russian Marxists, pored through old newspaper accounts of the trials of the populists, learning their names and sentences by heart. Their daring and sacrifice impressed him to such an extent that he still remembered the details when writing his memoirs decades later.[38] The commemoration of workers martyred by government repression became key events in the Russian labor movement—for example, the commemoration of Bloody Sunday or the Lena Massacre. The words of famous martyrs, such as the weaver Alekseev, were invoked on suitable occasions to inspire self-sacrifice and heroic action. At the All-Russian Congress of Soviets after the Bolshevik assumption of power, the delegates intoned the words of the famous funeral march, "You Fell Victims," which begins:

> You fell victim in the fated struggle
> For your boundless love for the people.
> You sacrificed all that you could for them.
> For their lives, their honor, their freedom.

To appreciate fully the significance of this heroic tradition of martyrdom, one must take note of the absence of the kinds of traditions characteristic of movements in more open societies, such as commemorations of the founding of organizations or the birthdays of important figures, events that give continuity to a publicly recognized organizational life. The tradition of Russian Marxism was that of the underground. The movement never enjoyed a normal political existence. The myths of martyrdom and self-sacrifice largely substituted for traditions based on routine organizational life, providing an alternative model of action and a source of hope for committed activists.

[36] Examples can be found throughout Franco Venturi's *Roots of Revolution* (New York: Grosset and Dunlop, 1966). One example (568–69) of the religious symbolism often involved is the claim by the marchers in an 1876 funeral procession for the student Chernyshev who had died in prison—that they were burying a boy "who had been martyred in prison, and who had borne witness for truth and the people." This same incident inspired a famous revolutionary song, "Tortured to Death in Prison," which became a traditional song of mourning among Russian revolutionaries of all persuasions.

[37] This large topic, which in my view has been insufficiently studied and appreciated, can only be touched upon here.

[38] L. Martov, *Zapiski sotsial-demokrata* (Berlin, 1922; reprint, Cambridge, Mass.: Oriental Research Partners, 1975), 61.

The strength of the ideal of martyrdom in Shiʿite Islam can hardly be overestimated: it is the central myth of the religion. The drama of the martyrdom of Husain at the hands of usurpers, an act that determined the course of subsequent Islamic history in the eyes of the Shiʿa, provides the cognitive and emotional core of belief. Yet the meaning of the events and its significance for the believer are far from self-evident. Does the event teach the impotence of goodness in the face of temporal power and thus suggest an attitude of inner suffering and atonement? Or was Husain's hopeless defiance a call to militancy in the name of the eventual triumph of the Shiʿite cause? Both interpretations are possible and have been dominant at different times. The shahs favored the passive interpretation, encouraging the passion plays and tales of martyrdom as forms of emotional release and inner lamentation devoid of political implications. "Weeping, and not edification or political indoctrination, came to be recognized as the sole aim of *all* reminiscence of Husayn. . . . The dominant trend is an elegiac account of the episodes in the drama, a concern which seems to stem from the conviction that submissive endurance of pain and suffering is the hallmark of all worthy souls."[39]

Yet the alternative view, of Husain's martyrdom as a call to revolt, can also come to the fore. This conception corresponds to the historical nature of Shiʿism as "the persistent custodian of the revolutionary challenge of Islam."[40] A number of Shiʿite modernists have interpreted Husain's rebellion as a call to reform the world and his martyrdom as a symbol of the sacrifices that must be made in the service of justice. Reminiscent of Russian populists, Khomeini urged students to go to the people and create contemporary versions of Husain's tragedy.[41] The same imagery of activist martyrdom continued to be used to animate young Iranians in the war against Iraq. Such beliefs in the holiness and efficacy of martyrdom can be potent tools in the hands of leaders organizing resistance to violently repressive governments. And, because of its historical centrality in Iranian culture, it pervaded secular as well as religious movements in Iran. The culture of the leftist guerrilla movement in Iran, for example, promoted the mystique of martyrdom in quasi-religious ways.[42] But a significant difference between religious and leftist images of martyrdom remains. Whereas the tradition of martyrdom in Russian and Iranian Marxism taught the need for self-sacrifice and reconciliation with one's cruel fate for the sake of the people and a better world, and so reconciled revolutionaries

39 Enayat, *Modern Islamic Political Thought*, 183.

40 Hodgson, *Venture of Islam*, 2:39.

41 Akhavi, *Religion and Politics*, 166.

42 See Suroosh Irfani, *Revolutionary Islam in Iran* (London: Zed Press, 1983), 233–60, for many examples of speeches and poems of martyred revolutionaries expressing these themes.

to their destiny, the Shi'ite tradition taught them to welcome martyrdom for the spiritual rewards it would give, especially in the afterlife.

As suggested earlier, the import and meaning of the parallels that have been described should not be pressed too far. Russian Marxism was a strand of a secular Western doctrine of progress. It proposed a model for the complete transformation of society through human agency. Its suspicion of mundane law was not based on belief in an even higher universal moral standard but in a deep hostility to formalism and the very idea of fixed moral laws transcending the class struggle. Shi'ism, by contrast, had many conservative elements incompatible with the idea of progress, including a deep sense of the fallibility of mankind, a roadblock to any overly optimistic view of human history. The model society, that envisioned in the revelation given to Muhammad, had already been partly realized in the past in the early Moslem community. It did not represent such a radical break with present institutions, entailing neither the elimination of private property nor the transcendence of traditional social institutions, such as the family or the state. Above all, the Shi'ite good society would be a community based on law, for no degree of social harmony could obviate the need for fixed norms of justice. Consequently, there was no justification in Shi'ism for the use of violence to bring about a perfect society; and indeed, in the Islamic republic repression has served to extirpate many enemies—religious opponents, Westernized groups, leftists—but it has not been called forth by a utopian commitment to total change.[43]

Yet the many striking similarities cannot simply be dismissed as superficial coincidences. They had many deep roots in the shared history of autocracy in both countries. Elitism and dualism partly emerged as responses to the alienation of the respective elites from power[44] and, especially in the case of Russia, from their weak ties to a mass base. As Tocqueville teaches us, an emphasis on knowledge as a foundation for power is more likely to emerge in repressive political systems that limit debate and public opinion.[45] The myth of a suprahistorical mission takes shape naturally in a society felt to be wholly corrupt and unjust.

In another sense, these traits are as much mirror images of the autocratic regimes as they are caused by them. The elites' celebration of consciousness, interpretation, the will—does this not have its counterpart in the autocrat's arbitrariness, at times even voluntarism? The elitism of the ruler

[43] This is not to deny certain utopian elements in Khomeini's policy—the attempt to purge the earth of corruption, for example. But full redemption of sinful man must await the return of the Imam.

[44] Thus, Sunni Islam, in which the ulama were generally more integrated into the state, did not accept the independent role of the mujtahid.

[45] Alexis De Tocqueville, *The Old Regime and the French Revolution* (Garden City, N.Y.: Doubleday Anchor Books, 1955), 138–48.

also finds its mirror image in the culture of his opponents—are they not both convinced of the ignorance and unreliability of the masses? At heart the autocrat, the religious scholar, and the revolutionary intellectual are alike in their independence from a developed civil society that might subject them to its norms. Thus, they all relate to society as in some sense outsiders bent on reform, manipulation, and purification. Indeed, one of the autocracy's fundamental contributions to social change was unwittingly to nurture rival elites with many of its own traits. The revolutionaries' paradoxical willingness to make use of the tools of autocracy after their victory—the jails, the secret police—stems partly from this paradox.

This brings us to our final point. Just as these shared characteristics were in large part caused by and parallel to the regimes themselves, so they constituted unusually dangerous challenges to the regimes. A small elite dogmatically convinced of its superior wisdom and righteousness is a formidable opponent. Belief in the inevitability of a suprahistorical transformation of social life clearly inspires dedication and fearlessness. Acceptance of man's capacity to intervene in historical processes encourages an activist orientation to politics. Finally, the high value put on martyrdom, its richness of symbolic associations, and the overall emphasis on self-sacrifice all increase the ranks of intransigent opponents of the regime, whose heroism can inspire the masses. When committed revolutionary elites leading movements based on these cultural traits could establish inroads in the larger society, the regimes, no matter how repressive, came face to face with formidable rivals.

Elite and Mass Revolutionary Cultures

The process of autocratic modernization gave birth, as we have seen, to unusual social and political vulnerabilities. It also provided the soil for the rise of cultural elites proposing totalistic and uncompromising ideologies of change. Two crucial issues about the significance of the cultures of rebellion for the respective revolutions remain to be addressed. First, apart from the underlying similarities between the two doctrines, why did an ideology based on class conflict have significant appeal in Russia, whereas in Iran the most potent revolutionary ideology was one or another version of Shiʿite belief? Second, how could these elitist and totalistic revolutionary doctrines serve to mobilize a mass base?

The answers to these questions go to the heart of the contrasts between the two modernization processes, as they also involve fundamental differences in the historical backgrounds of the two modernizing societies. As opposed to Iran, the long history of state-induced modernization in Russia had curtailed the independence of the religious establishment and marginalized many traditional social groups. It had also given rise to the embryo of civil society, with nascent modern elites and social movements increasingly chafing under autocratic restrictions. The regime sought to stimulate capitalist development, and thus nurture an entrepreneurial elite, even while it struggled to protect the nobility from its long-term decline.

In advocating class conflict, the Bolshevik party played upon a theme already sweet to the ears of Russian workers and peasants—not, indeed, because they understood the dialectic of finance capitalism in the age of imperialism but because of their own experiences during the process of autocratic modernization. The tsarist regime undermined both industrial and agrarian elites, curtailing their independence and making threats toward them based on an above-class model of politics with populist overtones. As we have seen, however, both elites were indispensable to the efficacy and even survival of the regime. The state's support of these elites whom the majority of workers and peasants regarded as illegitimate parasites only exacerbated class antagonism, which in turn damaged the credibility of the regime. For their own reasons, then, workers and peasants were receptive to a relentlessly class interpretation of politics and society. The Bolsheviks were not just playing upon the instincts of the masses, as is often averred, but touching themes of deep relevance to them on the basis of their own experience.

In Iran a modern civil society had hardly begun to develop by the time of the revolution. The industrialists and workers possessed almost none of the traits of modern social classes; social movements in the modern sector were insignificant. Class conflict existed only in embryo, overshadowed by the predominance of the state. Meanwhile, the religious establishment had maintained and in some ways even strengthened its independence. Traditional social groups, particularly the bazaaris and miscellaneous sectors of the petit bourgeoisie, remained vital in modern Iranian economic and social life. The ties between the religious leadership and these groups were strengthened by the regime's attacks upon both of them. And the cultural traditions they shared found increasing acceptance in the country at large, even in unexpected quarters, in the face of the onslaughts of Western influence.

Thus, despite the elitist and totalistic character of Russian Marxism and activist Shiʿism, there existed a significant potential mass base for both models of change based partly on shared cultural assumptions. The Russian Marxist intelligentsia, operating through underground ties to connect themselves in subtle ways to a repressed labor movement, and Islamic activists, extending their influence throughout networks of traditional urban ties, took advantage of these possibilities and won the sympathy of huge numbers of future adherents to their revolutions.

The Socialist Parties and the Workers in Russia

The many scholars who have questioned the strength of the ties between the socialist parties, always at their apex composed of revolutionary intellectuals, and the workers in prerevolutionary Russia have offered many telling objections. The social and cultural gaps between the intelligentsia and the workers were immense and sometimes only fortified through heightened contact. Very few workers had much knowledge or understanding of socialist doctrines. Only a few workers before the 1917 revolution affiliated themselves with the socialist parties. And organizations like trade unions or legal political parties that elsewhere did so much to propagate socialism among the workers were weak.

Yet it would be misleading to conclude, as so many have, that the revolution was made by the socialist intelligentsia. Too many other significant features of the socialist-worker relationship would thereby be missed. First, it is important to remember that a cadre of worker socialists had long existed in Russia, making its first appearance around 1870, and growing in significance after the turn of the century. These "conscious" workers were never more than a small minority, but their impact far outweighed their numerical weakness. It was partly through these worker activists that the intelligentsia exercised significant influence over the labor movement. The intelligentsia formed study circles in the factories and composed and distributed literature in order to remake the worker recruits into knowledgeable and disciplined activists.

Further, in many—though not all—decisive moments of struggle, socialist intelligentsia directly participated in events, risking their safety to guide and organize demonstrations, strikes, or even uprisings. Thus, although the mass of workers may not have understood the key ideas of Marxist socialism, the collective movement in which they participated was shaped in critical ways by Marxist activists. Whether the goals of the two groups corresponded is in some senses irrelevant. By suppressing independent worker organizations and moderate tendencies as much as the radicals, the tsarist regime gave the advantage to the more militant groups. As Martov recognized in 1906, "with a complete absence of 'freedom' the Bolsheviks must win, for the 'spontaneity' of revolution is for them; for them is the slight consciousness of the 'conscious' workers and the cursed, lifeless psychology of the circles and conspiracy developing in the underground."[46] In this sense, as the same thinker recognized, a strong tie between workers and socialists was forged by the tsarist state despite all mutual isolation and differences:

[46] Martov's thoughts appear in a letter to Axelrod, 17 February 1906, quoted in P. B. Axelrod, *Pis'ma P. B. Aksel'roda i Iu. O. Martova* (The Hague: Europe Printing, 1967), 150.

> Russian Social Democrats did what in free countries is accomplished by the mass organizations of the workers themselves—the trade unions, which direct the economic struggle. With the absence in Russia of any labor unions, the Social Democratic organization, secret and protected from police raids, was the only means of tying together the uncoordinated masses, of uniting them by means of general slogans and leading them in struggle.[47]

There were also inner connections between socialism and the culture of the workers deeper than this interdependence forged by the tsarist state.[48] Over the centuries the autocracy had shaped popular political culture as well as the culture of the intelligentsia, and the emergence of parallel assumptions cannot surprise us. The workers had as little experience with and commitment to fixed procedures, laws, and formal institutions as did the intelligentsia. They were interested in ends, not bothersome means. These ends they defined in terms of their experience as rightless outcasts deserving of special state solicitude. The aspirations and perspectives of their opponents were largely unknown to them, and in any case had no legitimacy. Bourgeois society—the society of calculation, of inequality based on the market, of private property—had no appeal for them. Far from holding anarchist ideals, workers appear to have had a statist vision of society deeply influenced by autocratic traditions. The state, they felt, should protect them from low wages and unemployment; it should even force factories to stay open despite the owners' claims that they were unprofitable. For factories existed not for private profit but for the common good, which the state had the duty to protect. Although the tsarist state claimed to have the interests of the workers at heart, it could not make good on its promises and so was in league with their enemies. For a state could not be neutral. It was either for or against the workers, since the idea of complementary class interests made no sense to them.

The patterns of political action flowing from these assumptions were visible during periods of militancy: an uncompromising insistence on the justice of their own demands; a refusal to consider the merits of the other side, as expressed in hostility to proposals for conciliation; an impatience with set procedures and laws, which might not result in the right substantive decisions; a rejection of political pluralism and its institutional expression; and a commitment, partly born of a lack of political experience, to goals that could not be satisfied without major social change. Although these assumptions and practices were largely rooted in the workers' experience of political autocracy, they accorded well with Marxist ideas on bourgeois democracy and on the proletariat as the favored class in society.

[47] Iu. Martov, *Proletarskaia bor'ba v Rossii* (St. Petersburg: N. Glagolev, n.d.), 93.

[48] This theme is developed at greater length in McDaniel, *Autocracy, Capitalism, and Revolution in Russia*, 43–45, 278–81, 322–26.

Workers untutored in Marxism could thus be sympathetic to Marxist agitation and strategies, particularly with respect to those tendencies most hostile to liberalism.

The organizational framework of Russian Marxism also facilitated the intensification of ties with the workers in times of ferment. This outcome, too, has a strong element of irony. Russian Social Democracy had two rival models of organization, that of the hierarchically controlled, disciplined proletarian army and that of the Western-style mass labor movement—ideals generally identified with, respectively, the Bolsheviks and the Mensheviks. In fact, tsarist repression prevented the realization of either model. In conditions of clandestine leadership and communication, both horizontal and vertical organizational ties were weak, so that the central party committees seldom knew, let alone controlled, the work of formally subordinated organizations. In addition, the flood of new members into the organizations in periods of ferment escaped the quality controls favored by Lenin. Many new recruits lacked even the most basic understanding of doctrine or party procedures. This was not a proletarian army. Neither was it a broad mass labor movement. Representative institutions were sadly lacking; the ties between leaders and members were tenuous; and few authoritative worker leaders had emerged to make the higher rungs of the party authentically proletarian.

In place of these ideal models, a quite different pattern of organization characterized the Russian labor movement in periods of militancy. There came into being quite unintentionally a relationship between the leadership of the socialist parties and the workers that was remarkably close to Rosa Luxemburg's prescriptions. On the one hand, socialist activists, mainly of the intelligentsia party leadership, formed broad coordinating organizations such as city and national soviets and trade union centrals. On the other hand, grass-roots workers created dense networks of overlapping local soviets, trade unions, and factory committees. The central organs gave political direction to the movement, defining goals and imbuing mass militancy with a degree of coordination. As agents of control and discipline they tended to be ineffective. In this they approximated Luxemburg's ideal of the role of leadership in the mass strike; it was to give direction to the struggle, to regulate tactics and guide action, but not to "command over its origins" or to reckon costs.[49] Local organizations thus had considerable autonomy of action, partly due to the difficulties of communication during rapidly changing episodes of militancy and partly because fixed hierarchies among organizations had never developed under the tsarist system. Thus, although the watchwords were control, discipline,

[49] Rosa Luxemburg, *Rosa Luxemburg Speaks*, ed. Mary-Alice Waters (New York: Pathfinder Press, 1970), 189.

and organization, the reality more often approximated spontaneity and local initiative. Local leaders, too, were seldom able to stem the tide of militancy even when they were so inclined. In an important sense, then, the organizational traits of the Russian labor movement synthesized the advantages of centralism and localism. Local initiative and enthusiasm were never sacrificed to the imperatives of larger strategies, yet they became incorporated into more inclusive struggles that reduced their isolation and imparted more generalized meanings to their activities.

Although effective in periods of struggle, this model of organization could not resolve the tensions between spontaneity and consciousness, between localism and centralism, between radical mass action and party discipline, at least not to the satisfaction of the party leadership. The Bolsheviks, unlike the Mensheviks, were temporarily willing to fan spontaneity, but no more than their opponents were they willing to renounce their claims to leadership. They were merely willing to extend the day of reckoning into the future.

One final point of crucial significance about the socialist-worker relationship requires emphasis. The two wings of Russian Marxism became increasingly polarized in their stance toward the "bourgeois revolution." The Mensheviks generally argued that the revolution would consist of a two-stage process: a bourgeois revolution to establish democracy, raise the level of culture, and develop industry, and only thereafter a proletarian revolution against capitalism. The first stage demanded temporary class collaboration. The Bolsheviks rejected this framework, arguing that the Russian bourgeoisie was incapable of leading a bourgeois revolution and that in the age of international capitalism and imperialism the stage was already set for a worldwide socialist revolution, for which Russia would strike the first blow. The establishment of a dictatorship of the proletariat in Russia was therefore not premature, and class conflict against the bourgeoisie was theoretically sound. Lenin and his party's incitements to radical action in 1917 were not simply opportunistic, but flowed directly from these principles. They also corresponded much more closely to the workers' own militant aspirations for immediate change than did the Mensheviks' more cautious approach.

In all these ways, Russian Marxists had succeeded in establishing ties with the labor movement on the basis of a certain coincidence of ideas and goals. These connections did not permit them to initiate great public demonstrations of protest, as could the Islamic leadership in Iran, much less to bring down the government. But multiple grounds for discontent and opportunities for its expression existed in Russia, particularly late in the war, and these links did play a most significant role in shaping the workers' perspectives and actions during times of ferment. They were crucial preconditions for the Bolsheviks' rise to power in October.

The Ulama and Urban Groups in Iran

In a number of respects the Iranian ulama were in an advantageous position to secure a mass base both in comparison with the Russian socialists and with their Sunni counterparts in other Islamic countries. They were neither a hunted sect advocating ideas of foreign origin nor a state-controlled religious establishment, as was the Ottoman hierarchy.[50] (In this regard, the Ottoman religious elite resembled that of the Russian Orthodox church, which had undergone reorganization by the state both to reduce its potential independence and to harness it to the state's own purposes.) Even under the Safavids, with their caesaropapist model, the Shiʿite elite had kept its distance from the regime, preferring, unlike the Sunni religious leaders, to be classed as part of the taxable subject population.[51] Later, in the course of the nineteenth-century there was a certain consolidation of an independent Shiʿite elite hierocracy, modifying the former amorphous organizational structure. An important indication of the greater degree of centralization was the creation of the institution of the *marja-i-taqlid* (source of emulation) in the mid-nineteenth century, a consensually recognized superior status granted to very few, and perhaps only one, religious scholar in a generation. When we recall the independent financial base of the ulama, particularly from the religious endowments, and their pervasive influence in law and education, the reverse side of the Qajar state's weakness, the potential threat to the regime posed by this consolidation can readily be imagined.

The ulama's influence was augmented by an almost monopolistic control over popular religion after the state's repression, at the ulama's behest, of Sufism and Babism. Again, this virtual monopoly had no parallel in the other major countries of the Islamic Middle East, where Sufism and other forms of popular religion maintained stronger holds on the population. By the turn of the century, the religious establishment had the organizational and financial resources and the popular legitimacy to oppose the regime. It did so during all the critical episodes of challenge to the autocracy from the Tobacco Rebellion to the Constitutional Revolution, presenting itself as the defender of the Iranian nation against government arbitrariness and excessive foreign influence and control. Through their ties to the bazaar and integration into urban networks, the ulama helped energize and coordinate popular protest.

Yet the limits to their political influence and activism should not escape

[50] See the statement on Turkey of Serif Mardin, as quoted by Ernest Gellner, *Muslim Society* (Cambridge: Cambridge University Press, 1981), 58: "Shackled to the state, official Islam could produce no original solution to the problems raised by the impact of the West."

[51] Hodgson, *Venture of Islam*, 3:35.

our notice. Unity of political perspective and stance always eluded them. During the Tobacco Rebellion, many privileged sectors of the clergy supported the shah.[52] Later, although the majority of the religious leaders seemed to be proconstitutionalist, important figures like Nuri adopted a more traditionalist position and defended the religious legitimacy of monarchism. Always, too, there were religious leaders who favored apoliticism, strictly demarcating the spheres of religion and politics. They often held that politics was inevitably corrupt until the reappearance of the Imam; that the state was nonetheless necessary for fallen man; and that the believer should take refuge in inner piety and avoid politics unless the rulers violated the norms of the shariʿa.

Further, even antiautocratic ulama active before the regime of Muhammad Reza Shah operated on the basis of essentially premodern political models. They made use of traditional social ties, traditional arguments, traditional modes of protest. Effective political action in contemporary Iran would require greater unity, appeals to modern social groups such as the new urban middle class and migrant workers, and the development of mobilizational ideologies. While in earlier periods the clergy could take advantage of traditional religious mentalities to promote protest against weak regimes, against the shah they would need more focused and vigorous ideas to inspire more daring and dangerous forms of protest.[53] The challenge, then, was not to establish connections with a social base, as it was for the Russian Marxists, but to reshape existing ties in accord with the demands of modern politics.

The impetus for the changes that would allow the Shiʿite clergy to participate in mass politics and play the key organizing role in the revolution was the campaign against them waged by the shah. Prior to Muhammad Reza Shah, the ulama had always been politically divided because of the variety of doctrines and different class positions.[54] Even the assault on their positions and functions in society by Reza Shah had not created unity against the regime.

Muhammad Reza Shah's modernization was different in two respects. First, social change was much more profound, displacing the ulama in the law courts, in education, and in the ownership of land much more deeply.

[52] See Mansoor Moaddel, "The Shiʿi Ulama and the State in Iran," *Theory and Society* 15 (1986): 527–31.

[53] On the advantages of ideologies as opposed to mentalities, see Juan Linz, "Totalitarian and Authoritarian Regimes," in *Handbook of Political Science: Macropolitical Theory*, ed. Fred Greenstein and Nelson Polsby (Reading, Mass.: Addison-Wesley, 1975), 166–68. Of particular importance are Linz's observations that the contradictions between ideology and actual conditions are more readily perceived than for mentalities, and that for this reason the former have more power to legitimate and delegitimate actions.

[54] On the latter, see Moaddel, "The Shiʿi Ulama," who probably goes too far in his class interpretation of the ulama's role in politics.

Harmful as they were, these measures were all indirect consequences of the general policy of modernization along Western lines. Even by themselves they inspired much fear for the future and antagonism. The old traditions were being cast aside and the time-honored hierarchies displaced. The shah even had the audacity to educate women and free them at least partially from the confines of traditional practices. All of this was enough to convince the ulama that the shah openly flouted religious law.

But second, and perhaps even more threatening, the ruler took numerous steps to control and undermine the position of the ulama directly, leading many to believe that he was bent on nothing less than their destruction. There were, for example, the ominous public statements:

> It is not improbable that we may create a religious corps in the future so that if some of the students of the religious sciences have to perform their service, they can do it [within the framework of this corps]. Just as we say religion must be separated from politics (and a few years ago we saw the results of mixing the two), and just as we are insistent in that respect . . . so, too, we encourage the people to piety and religion. No society is truly stable without religion.[55]

The statement is self-contradictory. One does not separate religion from politics by establishing a state-run religious corps. Nor was the shah willing to renounce a religious basis for his own authority. What he really had in mind was not a differentiation of spheres but state control over religion and the elimination of the religious establishment's independence. His ideal would probably have been an arrangement along the lines of church-state relations in prerevolutionary Russia.

This conclusion is fully in accord both with the overall logic of the regime and the shah's actual policies in the last decade of his rule. Measure after measure infringed on the most important functions, resources, and prerogatives of the clergy. Land reform aside, which had a more general rationale, among the most important of these offensives were:[56]

1. Increased government financial and administrative control over the religious schools.
2. The appropriation, often unofficial, of property belonging to the religious endowments by the state's Endowments Organization.
3. The formation of the state-run Religious Corps in 1971 as part of the White Revolution (its members were recruited from state institutions, not from the religious schools).
4. The creation within the Endowments Organization of a Department of

[55] Quoted in Akhavi, *Religion and Politics*, 23.

[56] See Ibid., 129–43, and James Bill, "Power and Religion in Revolutionary Iran," *Middle East Journal* 36, no. 1 (Winter 1982): 22–47.

Religious Propaganda, whose activists, together with the members of the religious corps, were to constitute "mullas of modernization."

5. The imposition of strict censorship over religious publications.

It would be misleading to say that the ulama were simply opposed to modernization. More to the point is the fact that the modernization against which they reacted came in the form of direct attacks against their beliefs and institutions. Many concluded that the regime, acting in the interests of the imperialists, was committed to the destruction of Islam, the last bulwark of defense against foreign domination. As Khomeini said of the regime in February 1971: "Invoking Islam and pretending to be Muslims, they strive to annihilate Islam, and they abolish and obliterate the sacred commands of the Qur'an one after the other. The religious scholars and students writhe beneath the pressure of the agents of imperialism."[57]

Before Muhammad Reza Shah's regime, Iranian Shiʿism had not produced a movement of Islamic reform comparable with the Salafiyah in Egypt. But, united as never before by the shah's policies in the 1960s and 1970s,[58] a series of innovations in interpretation and political practice transformed the religious establishment dramatically.

There are many strands in the doctrinal reinterpretation of Shiʿism during the shah's reign. Distinctions must be made between reformism arising from within the religious establishment itself and lay innovations generally more willing to import ideas from other traditions such as Marxism or liberalism. Similarly, the new ideas exhibit various degrees of social radicalism, from varieties of Islamic socialism to defenses of traditional property rights.

Beyond these fundamental discriminations, however, a few general observations may be pertinent. In toto the changes introduced implied a dilution of the distinguishing ethos of Shiʿism. It became less elitist, esoteric, and passive in its appeals to the masses for an Islamic activism.[59] The meaning of traditional concepts like *taqiyyah* (concealment of beliefs in order to survive persecution) and martyrdom were construed in ways to encourage resistance to evil. These changes have brought contemporary Shiʿism closer to Sunnism, and especially to Sunni modernism, facilitating, at least before the revolution, greater dialogue between the two great branches.

[57] Speech on 6 February 1971. In *Islam and Revolution: Writings and Declarations of Imam Khomeini*, ed. and trans. Hamid Algar (Berkeley, Calif.: Mizan Press, 1981), 197.

[58] Of course, this unity was never absolute. A conservative wing, heirs to the tradition of the Ayatollah Burujirdi, persisted. Perhaps its leading representative was the Ayatollah Milani of Mashhad, who spoke out in favor of a return to order at the time of the 1963 demonstrations. Akhavi, *Religion and Politics*, 102.

[59] Enayat, *Modern Islamic Political Thought*, 163.

Even Khomeini, in many ways so quintessential a Shiʿite mujtahid, has advocated ideas close to many Sunni doctrines.[60]

Brought to life by the shah's modernization program and his persecution of them, many Shiʿite divines embarked on the arduous task of revitalizing their beliefs. At the core of what were in many ways innovations was the vigorous reassertion of the cornerstone of traditional Shiʿi political theory, the idea of justice as a condition and requirement for rulership.[61] Equally fundamental was the return to a vision of Islamic society rooted in the ideals and practices of Muhammad's community. But as expounded by religious leaders like Morteza Motahhari and Mahmud Taleqani, these ideas took on new meanings. The differentiation between religion and politics was rejected, and opposition to unjust government became a religious duty. And in contrast to the atomized and individualistic society produced by the shah's tyranny and sponsorship of modernization, they put forth a vision of trust, interdependence, and mutual responsibility. God, asserted Taleqani, was the absolute owner of all property, which was given to man in trusteeship for the sake of the community. Marxism was wrong, he said, in seeking to abolish private property entirely, but capitalism was equally misguided in making property rights inviolable.[62] Some followers of this line of interpretation went further, claiming that "now personal wealth could and should cease. Science has given us the means to construct a society in which the trusteeship actually is collective."[63] Taleqani himself advocated enough redistribution to ensure freedom for all short of collectivism.[64]

These ideas were subsumed under the traditional injunction to struggle against evil and enjoin the good. The struggle against evil was seen to entail the fight against autocracy; the duty to promote the good necessitated efforts to create a just society. Islam in this respect was claimed to be superior to Christianity, which has "no substance." "Islam came to reform society and to form a nation. Its mandate is the reform of the whole world. . . . While Christianity does not cross the frontiers of advice, Islam is the religion which covers all the activities of human life."[65]

In this view, the just Islamic society would free the oppressed from many of their economic and social bonds. But the question of democracy is more

[60] Fouad Ajami, *The Vanished Imam* (Ithaca, N.Y.: Cornell University Press, 1986), 215.

[61] Enayat, *Modern Islamic Political Thought*, 5.

[62] Yann Richard, "Contemporary Shiʿi Thought," in Keddie, *Roots of Revolution*, 210–11; also see Mottahedeh, *Mantle of the Prophet*, 279–80.

[63] As presented in Mottahedeh, *Mantle of the Prophet*, 280.

[64] See Ayatullah Mahmud Taleqani, Ayatullah Murtada Mutahhari, and Dr. Ali Shariati, *Jihad and Shahadat: Struggle and Martyrdom in Islam*, ed. Mehdi Abedi and Gary Legenhausen (Houston: The Institute for Research in Islamic Studies, 1986), 50.

[65] Ayatullah Mutahhari in ibid., 89.

equivocal. In his opposition to the Constitutional Revolution Nuri had argued that the will of the majority cannot be a foundation of political authority in Shiʿite law.[66] He had then concluded that monarchy was the best provisional substitute until the return of the Imam. Although Islamic Shiʿite reformers rejected this conclusion, particularly in light of Muhammad Reza Shah's policies toward religion, suspicion of majority rule and democracy had deep resonance within the tradition.

Sharing Nuri's suspicion of majority rule, Khomeini could nevertheless not draw the same conclusion on the desirability and necessity of the monarchy. It was his special contribution to Shiʿite political thought to take the unprecedented step of advocating rule by the jurisconsult as a third alternative. Thus, to the Sunni elements of Khomeini's standpoint alluded to earlier—the reassertion of political activism, the modification of the doctrine of taqiyyah—he added the more traditional Shiʿite elitism and emphasis on superior knowledge. Only those with religious knowledge and experience—Khomeini himself had undergone profound training in erfan, a form of Islamic mysticism[67]—had the wisdom and courage to lead the society during the occultation of the Imam. The logic, but not the content, of the resulting synthesis is reminiscent of Leninism: a curious combination of extreme elitism and a call for militant mass participation. Like Lenin, Khomeini sought to resolve the possible tensions between these elements through restrictions on political parties and an exaggerated power of the executive. Some reformers, such as Taleqani, objected to these controls, advocating a more open and pluralistic system.

There was no final authority, no pope, to pronounce upon the acceptability of these different variations on the shared themes of the need to fight against the autocracy and restore Islamic values to the society. The diversity of interpretations was further amplified by the contributions of lay thinkers like Mehdi Bazargan, Abol-Hassan Bani-Sadr, and especially Ali Shariati. Detailed discussion and comparison of their ideas would take us too far afield, but a few remarks on the significance of Shariati are indispensable because of the enormous influence of his ideas.[68] Born in 1933 into a well-known religious family, in his youth Shariati was imprisoned for his participation in the National Front. After his release he went to

[66] V. A. Martin, "The Anti-Constitutionalist Arguments of Shaikh Fazlallah Nuri," *Middle Eastern Studies* 22, no. 2 (April 1986): 190.

[67] Mottahedeh, *Mantle of the Prophet*, 183–85.

[68] Many of his works have been translated into English. Numerous commentaries and discussions also exist. See, for example, Yann Richard, "Contemporary Shiʿi Thought," in Keddie, *Roots of Revolution*, 215–25; Enayat, *Modern Islamic Political Thought*, 155–59; Akhavi, *Religion and Politics*, 144–58; and N. Yavari-D'Hellencourt, "Le radicalisme shiʿite de Ali Shariʿati," in *Radicalismes Islamiques*, ed. Olivier Carre and Paul Dumont (Paris: Editions L'Harmattan, 1985), 1:83–119.

France to study, imbibing from Marxism, existentialism, anticolonialist theories (Fanon), and Louis Massignon's researches into mystical Islam. These diverse and indeed contradictory intellectual influences are indicative of the later eclecticism of his thought. Whatever the degree of intellectual consistency, however, the mixture seems only to have broadened his appeal as an engaged Islamic sociologist.

The concept of *towhid* (God's unity) is fundamental to Shariati's thought. Unity was not just a theological doctrine, but implied reconciliation and justice in human society. The present age is dominated by greed and strife, but through dialectical struggle, represented by the figures of Cain and Abel, history could reach its fulfillment. One could say that Shariati gives a moralistic interpretation to the Marxist dialectic; or alternatively, a Marxist interpretation to the Shiʿite eschatological vision. Ultimate victory will depend on the intellectual revival of Shiʿism and the willingness of its partisans to sacrifice themselves against tyranny, class exploitation, and Western imperialism. Third Worldist influences from Fanon and the Algerian struggle against the French, as well as from the nationalist opposition to the British and Americans in Iran, are thus incorporated into this framework. But nationalism and Marxism he judges to be inadequate because of their materialism and atheism; so, too, both Western democracy and Eastern communism stunt "the free growth of the essential nature of man."[69] Only Islam can ensure material well-being, social justice, and the unfolding of man's divine nature.

Shariati attacked the Iranian ulama for what he called their Safavid Shiʿism—their passivity and subservience to the state. Many clergy, in turn, were suspicious of his secular education and lack of credentials to speak on religious matters and, needless to say, resented his attacks on them. But he also established contact with some leading figures, including Motahhari, with whom he established the famous Husayniyah Irshad, an independent religious school founded in 1965 with the help of a philanthropist.[70] From there he courageously lectured on his views on the need to forge Islam as a weapon in the struggle against tyranny. His teaching and writings, circulated clandestinely, aroused enormous enthusiasm among young people seeking a response to despotism and Westernization, as well as among many members of the middle class and intelligentsia less open to more traditional religious messages.

Armed with these ideas, many clergy and religiously inspired laymen went beyond the traditional base of the ulama in the bazaar and sought to propagate their ideas among new groups—shantytown dwellers, workers,

[69] Ali Shariati, *Marxism and Other Western Fallacies* (Berkeley, Calif.: Mizan Press, 1980), 16.

[70] Motahhari later became extremely critical of Shariati and his ideas, and helped close down the Husayniyah Irshad.

even students and middle-class intellectuals whose world views had heretofore been permeated with Western values. Their activism among these new groups, made possible by the fact that Shiʿism was not a prohibited ideology or an underground sect, provides another important clue to one of the puzzles of the Iranian revolution: how traditional religious leaders were able to gain a hearing in the cities of a significantly modernized country. Their timing was propitious, as the shah's modernization schemes and political repression augmented social and cultural dislocation and aroused much popular opposition among broad sectors of the society. Entering the slums and the universities, religious activists cast the shah in the image of Yazid, one of the great villains of the Shiʿite belief. He was responsible for all ills, his regime the main barrier to towhid. Concrete grievances were reinterpreted in terms of religious imagery, giving rise to a political culture of polarization. The dualistic elements of traditional Shiʿism were given modern garb and given specific political content. Religious consciousness maintained ties with the past, but its activation required that it take on ideological dimensions.

Militant Shiʿism, rooted in traditional Iranian culture, could thus forge connections among ideas and movements in a way impossible for Russian Marxism. Whatever their differences, both the conservative and the reformist clergy had been educated in the same traditions and participated in a common institutional framework. Despite his sympathies for radical ideas, Ayatollah Taleqani was still one of them, part of that cultural world made increasingly cohesive by the policies of the regime. Both sectors of the clergy were able to extend their influence into the middle class. For example, the engineers and physicians who participated in the Islamic revival were not interested in reformist ideas so much as traditional culture.[71] Yet the example and ideas of men like Taleqani and Motahhari could reach strata inaccessible to the conservative clergy. In addition, the importance of lay reformers like Shariati in promoting Islamic values among the educated young can hardly be overestimated. Extending the chain, young religious students inspired by clerical and lay reformist perspectives also diffused these ideas among the masses, to which their work gave them a natural outlet. Less ideologically sophisticated men of religion also preached antiregime ideas among the masses using emotional language and vivid images of injustice and martyrdom from the Shiʿite tradition.[72] Added together, these diverse connections brought much of the new urban Iran under the influence of one form or another of subversive religious

[71] Said Amir Arjomand, "Traditionalism in Twentieth Century Iran," in Arjomand, *From Nationalism to Revolutionary Islam*, 218.

[72] For a lengthy example, see Thaiss, "Religious Symbolism and Social Change," 322–35. This is the transcript of the sermon of a *rowzeh-khan*, popular preachers and tellers of religious stories, often of limited education.

ideas. The traditional base of the clergy in the bazaar and old urban quarters remained intact.

The relative weakness of corporate organization and fixed hierarchy, expressed, for example, in the absence of formal membership in a local "church" and the ill-defined relations of authority among the leading Shiʿite figures, contributed to the extension of the mass base. People at the grass roots could choose their local mosque according to their sympathies, just as more committed believers could choose among a variety of different Islamic ideals. In these circumstances, the local clergy could not be aloof from the needs and concerns of the people and tended to shape their actions and statements according to what was expected of them. Thus, "religious and popular aspirations came together in a dialectical relation."[73] Like the Russian Marxist intelligentsia, the ranking Shiʿite clergy could influence and give shape to the movement, but they could not impose doctrines or strategies on the local level. In a very different context, then, Luxemburg's ideal of the relations between leaders and led was largely realized. In Russia, the weakness of the "organizational weapon" and the strength of local initiative stemmed from autocratic repression; in Iran it was connected with fundamental traits of the contractually, not corporately, organized society (see chapter one).

Receptivity to Shiʿite ideas was thus multiplied by the organizational and ideological diffuseness of the movement. But Shiʿism, like Marxism, could never have penetrated so deeply into so many layers of society if it had not successfully identified the major grievances of a great many people. In Russia, a class diagnosis made sense because of the interpenetration of the state and independent social elites. In Iran, class ideologies made very little headway except among the students, hardly at all among workers. For the Iranian state was so much more independent, voluntaristic, and arbitrary that the key conflict clearly loomed as the modernizing state versus Iranian society and culture as a whole. Even the regime's beneficiaries did not really believe in its model of rule. Shiʿism, as an alternative to Western capitalism and Eastern communism, promised to restore a sense of distinctive identity to individual Iranians and the nation as a whole, giving the society towhid. In its various manifestations, it could be all things to all people: traditional and modern, populist and elitist, religious and—to the extent that it was the major basis of national identity—secular. Finally, its ability to join people together, to create ties among engineers and shantytown dwellers, to give a sense of belonging to a larger community: all this was intoxicating to a people accustomed to mistrust and social atomization.

Special strengths and advantages inevitably exact their price. In becom-

[73] Behrang, *Le maillon faible*, 328.

ing more akin to an ideology—defining its goals more precisely, identifying friends and enemies, specifying doctrines—militant Shiʿism opened itself to the vulnerabilities of ideology. Ali Shariati exalted what he called Islam-as-ideology over Islam-as-culture for the purpose of movement and mobilization. Such systematization, however, threatens Islam both as a personal posture and as settled loyalty to a particular historical community. As policies become defined according to their Islamic nature, believers have to ask unaccustomed questions. Is this my Islam? And, if it is not, is this still my community? Religion as a cultural underpinning of social life may thus become sacrificed to a religion that makes no distinction between the religious and political realms.[74] Thus, this radical reversal of the traditional Shiʿite model of the relations between religion and politics will also force believers to ask political questions of religious government.

The second vulnerability of militant Shiʿism leaves many questions unanswered. Whatever its flaws, Russian Marxism had some preliminary responses to the question of modernization and the nature of modern society. However, the traditional elements of Iranian Shiʿism, so effective for creating temporary unity and a sense of cultural identity, may well be incompatible with the requirements of modern social life. This first attempt to combine revolution—heretofore a phenomenon of modernization and modernity—with tradition and religion may well also, if it fails to provide guidelines for modern social and economic institutions, be the last.

[74] See the critique of Hamid Dabashi, in Nasr, Dabashi, and Nasr, *Expectation of the Millennium*, 373–87.

Conclusion

Structural Crisis and Revolutionary Dynamics

The Making of the Revolutions

SOCIAL and political unrest with potentially revolutionary implications was not new to Russia in February 1917 or Iran in 1978. The regimes of both Nicholas II and Muhammad Reza Shah had already been repeatedly challenged by opposition of different kinds, which sometimes reached peaks of intensity that called into question the survival of the regimes. Russia in 1905–1906 and early 1914, and Iran in 1960–1963 had already been stirred by broad-based movements that gave a foretaste of events to come. In addition, even in periods of relative quiescence, when the mass of the population appeared subdued, there were always groups and parties of committed adversaries of the regimes to suggest to the rulers and elites that beneath the calm surface there still lay multiple sources of discontent. This recurring and persistent nature of opposition in both countries demonstrates the limitations of any thesis of the accidental character of both revolutions. Like all other revolutions, they were not inevitable; but clearly Russian and Iranian society in the decades before the revolution provided fertile soil for discontent and radical challenges to the regimes.

Keeping in mind the long-term nature of the regimes' predicaments, one must still insist upon the importance of situational factors specific to the periods of acute revolutionary crisis. In Russia, of course, the sufferings brought about by the war and the regime's handling of it provoked widespread dissatisfaction among both the elites and the masses of the population. Rumors about the court's German connections (the tsarina, we recall, was of German origin) and dismay over the corruption and ineptitude connected with Rasputin undermined the public's sense of the competence and integrity of the rulers. The economic dislocations imposed unimaginable sacrifices on the army and the civilian population alike, whose remarkable patience was not limitless. And while demanding self-abnegation and renewed commitment from the population, the regime was unwilling to make any political concessions parallel to those made by the German political leaders. The old political myths, symbolized by the tsar's fateful decision to assume direct command of the army, were seized upon in a senseless attempt to apply outworn ideas to a modern war requiring new connections between state and society.

February 1917 was the culmination of these mounting tensions. The previous year had seen a dramatic rebirth of the strike movement as well as renewed attacks on the regime by the liberal opposition. On these grounds alone it would be idle to attribute the Russian revolution to hungry women clamoring for bread. But the continuity between the events of February 1917 and earlier patterns of opposition rooted in the nature of the regime becomes even clearer when one goes beyond the usual stereotypes.[1] The hungry women who inadvertently initiated the revolution were largely textile workers who had previously participated in wartime strikes. The "food riots" erupted in the Vyborg district of Petrograd, the district long known as the center of proletarian militancy in the capital. The factories in which many of the demonstrating women worked were located next to two metal factories with militant traditions. Socialist activists from the area got involved in the demonstrations very rapidly and succeeded in giving a degree of coordination and direction to events. Although it is true that the leadership of the socialist parties had extremely limited involvement in the early stages of unrest, many of these grass-roots worker activists had had prolonged contact with the parties and were committed to socialist ideas.

Despite considerable government repression in the following days—the bloodless character of the February revolution, according to which the army and the regime just collapsed, is a myth—the movement gathered strength in the capital. At first the Petrograd garrison was willing to shoot down crowds of marching workers, but the choice imposed upon the soldiers—whether to continue the bloodshed in defense of a regime whose flaws were only too evident to many of them—soon led to the disaffection of first one, then other units of the garrison. In a matter of days the military foundation of the regime had collapsed and a new "Provisional Government" had been proclaimed by liberal groups that had not been the spearhead of the revolution. Unlike the Iranian Revolution, in which the period of mobilization against the regime lasted for many months, the defeat of the centuries-old Romanov dynasty was accomplished with amazing speed. It did not leave time for the mobilization of the whole country against the regime or for the regime to attempt to gather together its supporters. The government was routed in the capital in large part by the industrial proletariat. The significance of their action for Russian society and politics would only become clear in the following months, as various elites sought to organize and make use of different social groups for the sake of their own programs.

Uniquely among modern revolutions, the Iranian Revolution was un-

[1] The best account of the February revolution can be found in Tsuyoshi Hasegawa, *The February Revolution: Petrograd 1917* (Seattle: University of Washington Press, 1981). Hasegawa effectively disposes of the thesis of the "spontaneity" of the revolution, pointing out the accumulation of experience that lay behind the revolution and the role of seasoned activists.

connected to foreign or civil war and did not depend upon the prior decay of the army. There were, instead, a whole series of events that weakened the shah and embittered and emboldened an ever-widening opposition. The high-inflation and bottlenecks brought on by the oil boom fueled economic discontent and undermined confidence in the shah and the technocrats. Particularly irritating was the elite's continuing display of tasteless consumption in the face of real material need. The regime's attempts to counteract the economic discontent through the use of the Rastakhiz party in the campaign against profiteering clearly backfired. In fact, the entire bizarre effort to establish a one-party system in an autocratic regime was counterproductive, engendering not loyalty but anger. After his downfall even the shah recognized that it had been a costly mistake.[2]

With the inauguration of Jimmy Carter in January 1977 the shah suffered another blow, not so much because the new American government actually exerted much pressure in favor of liberalization, but more because many domestic opponents assumed that it would, and that they would have the tacit support of the American government. The shah, too, undoubtedly felt the prospect of more pressure for reform than he had experienced under the previous two Republican governments, which basically gave him carte blanche with respect to domestic repression. In response to what they assumed would be a new atmosphere, members of the moderate opposition, including leading professionals and intellectuals, addressed open letters to the shah, in which they complained of his intolerable human rights record and pointed to the failure of his reforms. Possibly also because of the shah's cancer, these protests met with a tolerance that would have been unthinkable a few years before.

These middle-class protests, somewhat reminiscent of similar campaigns among Russian liberals in 1904, clearly helped prepare the atmosphere for the outbreak of mass protest. But no more than the activities of the various leftist guerrilla groups, who had never suspended their bold feats of opposition, could such forms of protest play the decisive role in revolutionary mobilization. The critical event was the vicious attack on Khomeini in a government-related newspaper in January 1978, accusing him of harboring secret ties to the British. The following day religious students in Qom demonstrated against the government, which reacted violently, killing at least seventy people in the following two days.[3] From this time forward the religious forces never relinquished their leadership in the movement, which over the next year came to involve virtually all social groups in the country in protests of increasing intensity that astonished the world.

It would be impossible to do justice to the course of the 1978 events in

[2] Mohammed Reza Pahlavi, *The Shah's Story*, 154–55.

[3] Keddie, *Roots of Revolution*, 243.

the short space available to us here, and in any case they have been described in detail in numerous works on the revolution. Nonetheless, several striking characteristics of the revolutionary year should be highlighted. Most important, although there is some debate about the relative weight of the various social groups participating in the revolution, there is no doubt that the clergy provided the leadership and organizational framework of the revolution. The nationwide network of mosques, with their ties to the bazaars and the urban lower classes, already gave them an overwhelming initial advantage as compared with the positions of the liberals, guerrillas, or the Communists. In addition, the clergy and theology students actively formed revolutionary committees in the large urban centers, particularly the capital, both on the local level to coordinate grass-roots struggles and on a citywide basis.[4] It was largely these organizations, with their multiple ties to other groups, that gave coherence to the year's multifaceted protests, from mass popular demonstrations of hundreds of thousands of people, to industrial strikes and guerrilla operations. It was they, for example, who determined the slogans of the huge street manifestations and provided the surprisingly high degree of discipline evident in them.[5] Of special significance was the role of the Ayatollah Taleqani, closely in touch with Khomeini in Paris, whose office in the capital has been described as the coordinating center for the revolution. It helped direct not only the activities of the religious activists, but also organized workers' strikes. Taleqani can almost be seen as a symbol of the revolution before the arrival of Khomeini, for he advocated unity in the struggle against despotism. Ideologies would only divide the people. "Let us have one voice on the basis of what we have in common among us all—[to fight for] freedom."[6]

Leading the all-national movement against the shah, the clergy thus came to seem to represent the Iranian people as a whole. And indeed, it would be hard to locate a social group that did not make its contribution to the escalating revolutionary crisis. Almost universally, observers agree that the revolution came to embrace virtually all of urban Iran[7] and that even the peasantry became involved, though on a reduced scale and in re-

[4] See Ramy Nima, *Wrath of Allah* (London: Pluto Press, 1983), 77–80.

[5] Behrang, *Le maillon faible*, 53; Shaul Bakhash, "Sermons, Revolutionary Pamphleteering and Mobilisation: Iran, 1978," in Arjomand, *From Nationalism to Revolutionary Islam*, 177–94, esp. 180–81. Bakhash makes clear that a number of other groups, such as students and members of the National Front, became involved in these activities, but they nonetheless used religious imagery and language.

[6] Quoted in Irfani, *Revolutionary Islam in Iran*, 161.

[7] Abrahamian attempts to dissect the various roles of the different groups. The traditional middle class, he asserts, provided the opposition's nationwide organization; the modern middle class initiated and fueled the revolution, and also struck the final blows; and the working class was the revolution's "chief battering ram." See *Iran between Two Revolutions*, 533–36.

sponse to the larger events in the cities. (It was reported, for example, that during the summer of 1978 large numbers of villagers, including women, came to the cities to join in the marches. The impressive participation of women in the revolution has also frequently been noted.)[8] The analytical problem, therefore, is not to determine the social base of the revolution, which was universal, but to understand its leadership and how the different social groups were interrelated. If a comprehension of the Russian Revolution requires an analysis of how groups defined themselves in opposition to each other, especially on a class basis, the Iranian Revolution demands an opposite approach: how previously isolated and mutually suspicious groups came together to participate in an all-national movement. The previous chapter sought to clarify this fundamental contrast between the two revolutions through a consideration of differences between their respective experiences of autocratic modernization: the Russian regime's more complex relationship with social elites fed class conflict between the elites and masses, whereas the more statist pattern of development in Iran weakened class definitions; and the Iranian regime's more provocative assault on traditional groups and institutions encouraged a more unified nationalist counterreaction.

The prolonged character of the Iranian Revolution as compared with the shorter duration of the Russian Revolution also had important consequences. First, because the army remained intact virtually until the end and was intermittently used against the insurgents, the death toll was much higher in Iran than in Russia before the downfall of the regime. (Whereas the February revolution in Petrograd claimed roughly 400 dead and over 1,200 wounded, the comparable figures for Iran have been estimated at 3,000 dead and 12,000 wounded.)[9] In addition, whereas the tsarist regime fell before any set of leaders could establish effective control over the revolution, by the time of the departure of the shah, Khomeini and his associates had clearly established their predominance—although the fact and meaning of their victory was not entirely clear to the numerous other groups who had also participated in the revolution.

In Russia the overthrow of the tsar set in motion revolutionary processes that eventually culminated in the victory of the Bolsheviks in October 1917. The details of the political interlude between the tsarist regime and the Bolshevik assumption of power are enormously complicated—the intraparty splits, the strategies and alliances, the fruitless changes of government made in order to keep pace with shifting moods and aspirations. But

[8] Mottahedeh, *Mantle of the Prophet*, 375; on the role of women, see the comments in Behrang, *Le maillon faible*, 54.

[9] For Russia, see Hasegawa, *February Revolution*, 303; for Iran, see A. Ashraf and A. Banuazizi, "The State, Classes, and Modes of Mobilization in the Iranian Revolution," *State, Culture and Society* 1, no. 3 (Spring 1985): 22.

beneath all this instability and turbulence was an underlying social logic that gives coherence to the events. Throughout 1917, confronted with deteriorating economic conditions and the continuation of the war, the urban working class increasingly came to regard class conflict as irreconcilable. The workers therefore rejected compromise with their class enemy and opposed any government that sought to mediate between the classes as inimical to their interests.[10] By October, in their overwhelming majority they were willing to support that party, the Bolsheviks, that advocated a class government to rule in their interests. The peasantry did not play such an important part in the critical events of 1917, but they did act upon their interpretation of their rights and interests as these had developed under the tsarist regime. Although they did not spearhead the revolution, their militancy nonetheless undermined the Provisional Government and helped prepare the ground for the victory of the radicals.

The authority of the Provisional Government, composed largely of members of the former liberal opposition, was tenuous from the beginning. In the springtime of the revolution, workers and peasants were willing to suspend judgment, particularly because the closest approximation they had to political leadership, the various socialist parties, advocated temporary compromise in the class struggle. Yet this temporary truce was always conditional and was to prove remarkably evanescent. The various coalitions of the Provisional Government interpreted their role as the above-class mediation of conflict in the interest of the formation of a liberal political system, but they had no significant social base and their fundamental outlook on the revolution was inconsistent with that of the workers and peasants, who had their own perspectives and aspirations based on their experiences under the tsarist regime. In particular, as we have seen, neither peasants nor workers accepted the legitimacy or property rights of the upper classes, and they quickly lost patience with these liberal governments bent on compromise. More than any other party, the Bolsheviks, for their own reasons, were willing to accommodate their policies to the impatience of the masses, born of both long-term grievances and circumstantial deprivations. By October Lenin's party could act with the confidence that it had gained the overwhelming support of the workers and that its land program would be enthusiastically received by the peasantry.

Stated so laconically, the interpretation seems too simple to be true. And, of course, it does neglect the nuances and details necessary for an adequate comprehension of the concrete historical processes involved. Yet it does, I believe, explain the basic social and political conflicts during 1917, and it does so by linking these events to the larger pattern of autocratic modernization in prerevolutionary Russia, which, as we have seen,

[10] See McDaniel, *Autocracy, Capitalism, and Revolution in Russia*, 297–394.

gave rise to class conflict more intense and persistent than in Western countries, where the contradictions of modernization were not so deep or unresolvable.

By the time of the shah's forced departure from the country, it was already clear that the Ayatollah Khomeini enjoyed preeminent authority as the embodiment of the revolution. In addition, the clergy had been able to guide the course of the struggle both at the grass roots and in national political life. There was widespread acceptance of the idea that the revolution had been made for the sake of a return to an authentic national identity, which would allow the country to free itself from the bonds of dependency. But the implications of these initial conditions were not yet clear, for national independence and cultural renewal meant many things to different people and the all-national struggle against the shah had allowed people of conflicting perspectives to cooperate temporarily.[11] Just as important, each group—student guerrillas, workers, government employees, the bazaaris—could lay claim to the legacy of the revolution on the basis of their own participation and sacrifices. (In Russia only the workers could plausibly do this, although the industrialists made feeble attempts to associate themselves with the overthrow of Nicholas.)

The shah left the country in mid-January 1979. Within a month the cabinet of Prime Minister Bakhtiar, whom the shah had chosen to attempt to appease the opposition and restore order, had been swept away. Even before its demise, Khomeini had already asked Mehdi Bazargan, a devout Moslem and also an engineer who had participated for many years in the National Front, to head a new government. Bazargan's goals were in some ways parallel to those of the Russian Provisional Government and departed somewhat from Khomeini's own. He saw his mission as to prepare the way for an Islamic government in the future; in the meantime he was committed to economic reconstruction, the restoration of order, and democratic procedures based on free elections.

The challenges to Bazargan came from many different sides. The revolution had given birth to a multitude of political groups and movements, from moderate nationalists to leftists of various persuasions and to the various religious groupings. Few of these were committed to the kind of moderate democratic procedures espoused by Bazargan, and they often took matters into their own hands without regard to the wishes of the government. Leftists, secular and Islamic, sought to mobilize workers and peasants for the sake of workers' control or the expropriation of land. The cler-

[11] For example, many intellectuals and writers believed that the religious leadership was largely symbolic, embodying the concept of the unity of the nation, and would be temporary until a stable secular government emerged. See Gheissari, "Ideological Formation," 335.

ical committees that mushroomed during the revolution were equally committed to the immediate establishment of an Islamic republic.

It had always been clear to those who chose to listen where Khomeini himself stood. In the summer of 1978, well before the victory of the revolution was assured, he contested Bazargan's pleas for moderation, at the same time asserting his belief that "Iran's recent, sacred movement . . . is one hundred percent Islamic." A referendum of the public had already been taken in the form of mass demonstrations under the banner of Islam, he claimed, and "the whole nation, throughout Iran, cries out: 'We want an Islamic Republic.' "[12]

Although the degree of commitment to an Islamic government and the meaning that this concept had for different sectors of the Iranian public cannot be precisely gauged, it is certain that those groups who supported this program started out with immense initial advantages. The middle-class nationalists, student activists, guerrilla groups, and the Communist party all lacked significant mass bases. None of them had a leader to compete with the spiritual and political authority of Khomeini. Rather, many of them, including the Communist party leadership, had been quite compromised by their actions during the shah's regime. Finally, none of them had at their disposal anything parallel to the organizational network of the mosques or the extensive ties of the clergy with diverse social groups. Thus, the following years witnessed the inexorable consolidation of clerical power and the systematic defeat, one by one, of all opposition groups, in some cases with great bloodshed. Particularly dramatic and violent was the struggle between the powerful Islamic Republican party and the leftist Islamic Mojahedin, which culminated in the summer of 1981 in the Mojahedin's unsuccessful attempt to overthrow the government through terror and assassination. Although many leading figures of the Islamic regime were assassinated and the government appeared to be shaken, it fought back with equal ferocity and greater resources, initiating the bloodiest period of terror in the revolution.[13]

The defeat of the moderates and the left did not resolve all the uncertainties of the revolution. Important cleavages on socioeconomic issues and the precise interpretation of Islamic government within the ruling party and the government remained. The outcome of many of these disagreements is still in doubt, as "moderate" and "radical" Islamic leaders continue to espouse different positions on issues such as the government's role in the economy, land reform, and relations to the outside world. Yet these disagreements rage *within* the clerical party, who, in accord with their paramount role in the movement to overthrow the shah, continue to domi-

[12] Both quotations from Bakhash, *Reign of the Ayatollahs*, 48.

[13] Ibid., 221.

nate Iranian politics—the first time in modern history that a revolution has been headed by religious leaders acting in the name of traditional beliefs and values. But it was only through the incorporation of numerous modern elements into their practices and institutions—the reshaping of beliefs into ideologies, the adoption of more sophisticated forms of communication, the attempt to reach and mobilize new sectors of society—that this "traditional" elite was able to lead a modern revolution.

Autocratic Modernization and Revolution

Revolutions arouse great passions. Partisans will always be able to point to the long-term tendencies that made them inevitable and thus legitimate. Only now may it become possible for Soviet scholars to deny the thesis of the deep historical inevitability and rationality of the October revolution. No doubt many Iranian clerics are inclined to see in the Islamic revolution the fulfillment of the will of God until such time as the Imam returns. Victims and adversaries of the revolutions are equally committed to the view that they were "accidental" and could have been avoided if certain strategic errors had not been committed or certain events not occurred. Thus, opponents of the Russian Revolution have often blamed World War I, Rasputin, the tsarina, or the treachery of the liberals for the downfall of the tsarist regime. In the case of the Iranian Revolution, Jimmy Carter has been held culpable; others have pointed to the debilitating effects of the shah's cancer upon his will power.

An examination of the position of one version of the revolution-as-accident argument as applied to Iran will help clarify the implications of the very different perspective developed in this book. According to Hamid Enayat, "Western sociological concepts, whether Marxist or non-Marxist, have been freely used to explain both the background, and the rapid collapse of the imperial order." Most of these, the author claims, "fall wide of the mark," for they cannot answer what for him is the cardinal question: how did the regime's apparatus of social control break down to the extent that it was unable to handle the mounting opposition? The regime, claims Enayat, was *not* experiencing a crisis in any way comparable to those of prerevolutionary France or Russia. Perhaps the explanation should be sought, he suggests, in changed relations with the United States or the "mental wanderings" of the shah.[14]

Enayat is right, I think, to point out the limitations of more sociological analyses of revolutions. If Richard Nixon had been president of the United States in 1978 or the shah had been perfectly healthy, the revolution might

[14] Enayat, "Revolution in Iran 1979," 195.

well never have occurred. Yet an exclusive focus on the events and circumstances that precipitate revolutions may distract attention from what, contra Enayat, strikes me as the really fundamental question: how do we explain the differential vulnerability of societies to revolutions whether or not they actually occur. I admit that to pose the question this way invites the danger of retrospective teleological reasoning. Yet inexact fields of study like the social sciences cannot avoid such risks. On the basis of our knowledge and our theories we should be able to give approximate estimates of a society's degree of vulnerability. Surely, for example, no one could have doubted that Iran of the 1970s was more likely to give birth to a revolution than the United States in the same period. There were also good historical and theoretical reasons to think that it was potentially more unstable than many other industrializing countries.

Throughout this book I have argued that an autocratic regime's attempts to give birth to urban industrial society involve it and the society in a web of intractable contradictions. These contradictions, in turn, foster the emergence of revolutionary situations that, depending on the correlation of events, may culminate in revolutions. This global approach permits us to address a set of larger questions about revolutionary Russia and Iran that go beyond particular, accidental events. Why were Nicholas II and the shah so unwilling or unable to introduce and follow through on reforms? What compelled their governments to make repeated promises that they could not keep? What explains the striking inconsistencies evident in both regimes? How did the political characteristics of the regimes affect the interrelations among social groups, and these latter, in turn, condition the prospects for reform? In my view only a more inclusive model of the pattern of social change in society as a whole can illuminate such issues and relate them to each other.

In this book I have sought to illustrate this claim as well as to argue it more abstractly. I have developed a model of what I take to be the key dilemma in both societies, the tensions inherent in the attempt of a political autocracy to modernize society at a relatively advanced stage of development. I have traced the consequences of this project for the state, the society, and the interrelations between them. The model will be convincing to the extent that it has helped comprehend the processes of social change in Russia and Iran. Let me conclude then by summarizing the ways in which the model of autocratic modernization explains the vulnerability of the two societies to revolutionary challenges.

First, as was discussed in general terms in chapter four and illustrated in the substantive chapters, the process of autocratic modernization saps the effectiveness and legitimacy of the state. No coherent administrative apparatus can develop, and the conflicting ideas inherent in this pattern of development inevitably deepen political cleavages and administrative conflicts within the bureaucracy. Different agencies are left free to pursue conflicting goals with no means available to reconcile the inconsistencies. The Russian state's incoherent labor policy, with its tensions between the Ministries of Finance and Interior, and the Iranian regime's changing and inconsistent programs for rural change illustrate the consequences eloquently. As a result, both regimes displayed a striking inability to resolve the fundamental social and political issues confronting their rapidly changing countries.

The lack of coherent policies and the commingling of contradictory principles also undermined the state's legitimacy in the eyes of virtually all social groups. The regimes proclaimed their above-class character, but inevitably acted to protect the interests of the elites, though often ineffectively. They sponsored modernization, but sought to keep much of the traditional social structure and system of political authority intact. They promised to incorporate new social groups into the changing society, but failed to make good their promises. In traditionalist terms they promised to protect all social groups, and they also advocated greater freedom of action in accord with the logic of modern society, but those who took either commitment seriously suffered grave disappointments.

By the time of the revolutions, then, neither regime had a significant social base, despite ineffectual efforts to win over both traditional and modern groups, both upper and lower classes. Even more, a large number of groups in both societies came to regard the regimes as fundamentally unjust, unable to honor their own commitments or operate on the basis of explicit or implicit standards of political morality. The word of the rulers meant little; there was little predictability or consistency in government policy. The states remained foreign to the societies, operating upon them from outside in arbitrary ways.

Just as much as the states, the societies subject to the process of autocratic modernization also suffered from fundamental weaknesses that made them ripe for revolutionary challenges. As we have seen, the regimes' policies and actions weakened all social elites, both in their ability to play a dynamic role in social change and in their capacity to claim the allegiance of other social classes. Thus, when the rulers were overthrown in both countries, no group of social elites—either traditional or modern, rural or urban—could assume the mantle of leadership. The Russian industrialists made the most ambitious claims, declaring themselves to be vital for the country's progress both in the past and in the future, but their assertions had a pleading and desperate tone. The Iranian industrial and rural elites were all but invisible throughout the whole course of the revolution. Probably all those who could simply fled with their property, knowing that they had no basis on which to fight for leadership in the new society. The weakness of social elites determined that the revolutions would go far beyond the overthrow of the regimes, that they would inevitably reach deeply into social life and institutions.

Both societies also lacked the dense undergrowth of corporate organizations necessary for the effective functioning and stability of an industrial society. The consequences of the lack of authoritative modern organizations were significant in a number of respects. The weakness of corporate organizations inhibited collective private initiative, and so diminished overall economic dynamism. The sociological impact was at least as significant. The new social groups and classes that emerged with continuing industrialization could not be integrated into industrial society in the absence of trade unions, professional associations, interest organizations, and the like. No leadership with a stake in the society involving multiple ties, both horizontal and vertical, arose to direct and control social groups and movements. Public social life became impoverished, and a split developed between people's inner worlds and true beliefs and their public statements and actions. People were not connected as participants to the broad range of economic, social, and political institutions that give a sense of concrete reality to modern society, that would have substituted for the primary ties characteristic of less complex social forms. This lack of solidity, this insubstantiality, was augmented by the weakness of law in both societies, which further diminished people's sense of trust and predictability. Prerevolutionary Russia and Iran were both, in the words of a scholar of Stalinist Russia, "quicksand societies."[15] Fortunately, no Stalinist party-state was there to make use of this social fragmentation in order to create a fully totalitarian society.

In such societies people have less capacity to gauge events on the basis of their own experience. They lack the tacit knowledge that gives stability to political judgments in more predictable environments. They are more likely to be willing to believe that society can be totally recast according to visions of a better world. Socialism and Islamic republics loom not as disembodied abstractions, but as proximate goals with at least as much reality as the puzzling and unpredictable societies in which people lived. And by what may appear to be a coincidence but is really an expression of the way in which general social patterns shape and pervade the culture of groups throughout the society, this pattern of development also gives rise to elite cultures able to make partial contact with mass movements and mobilize them for very ambitious goals of social reconstruction. Among the competing groups seeking to organize opposition and develop a mass base, autocratic regimes unwittingly give all the advantages to those tendencies most dangerous for their own survival. The traits of Russian Marxism and Iranian Shi'ism discussed in chapter seven allowed the movements to sur-

[15] Moshe Lewin, *The Making of the Soviet System* (New York: Pantheon, 1985), 44.

vive in the face of oppression and gain support among significant social groups for uncompromising visions of total change.

Autocratic modernization does not thereby inevitably culminate in revolution because of the vulnerabilities of state and society, but it does give rise to persistent challenges. In addition, when situational crises do occur, unrest can only be put down by repression. If repression is initially effective, surface tranquillity can be restored; but once a certain threshold has been passed, force loses its potency. A new psychological climate emerges which encourages heroic and solidary action; and when enough people become willing to take risks, the threat of violence on a vast scale becomes altogether unrealistic. Weber may have been right that all states ultimately rest on the threat of force; but when they are so cut off from society and when society itself so lacks means of conflict resolution, the threat of repression in times of crisis is all that remains. And if the crisis is serious enough, even this seems hollow.

By themselves sociological models may be able to do no more than explain the relative vulnerabilities of modernizing societies to revolution—which would be no small accomplishment. In order to explain various other dimensions of the revolutions, however, historical particularities of the different societies must be taken into account. Thus, considered apart from the specific traits of Russian and Iranian institutions, the model of autocratic modernization would not be able to explain the very great differences in the social bases and outcomes of the revolutions. As we have seen, in both countries revolutionary events were centered in the cities, but in Russia the focus of attention must be on class conflict in the modern sector. In Iran the revolutionary movement was much more broad-based, but traditional urban groups and institutions, the ulama and the bazaar, clearly led the revolution and defined its goals.

On the most fundamental level, I have traced these very different outcomes to the historically very different roles of the states in social change and their relationship to social elites. For centuries the Russian state had sought to modernize Russian society from above. Its limited success had taught the rulers that they must make use of social groups, rule through and by means of them, in order to anchor state policies in society. This strategy had its own dilemmas, as the state weakened and controlled the very elites whose initiative it wanted to encourage. Nonetheless, by the late nineteenth century the Russian autocracy had multiple ties of interdependence with social elites—politically, primarily with the nobility and economically, increasingly with the modern elites. Therefore, despite its proclamation of tutelary goals through which it sought to integrate the lower classes into society, the Russian state was largely forced to ally itself with both agrarian and industrial elites. Yet this arrangement only further undermined the legitimacy of both the regime and the elites in the eyes of the masses, who never regarded their masters as anything more than usurpers. State favoritism toward them only enhanced the appeal of a class interpretation of social relations, which was then, with the help of the socialists, turned upon the state itself.

The Pahlavi shahs in Iran inherited no such tradition of state-led modernization. Nor had there developed a complex interweaving of state and social elites along the Russian pattern. Rather the shahs had endeavored to stay in power through subtle strategies of divide and rule and other forms of manipulation. With the Pahlavi modernization beginning with Reza Shah, the rulers built up armies and administrations largely free of the noble dominance characteristic of Russia until the last years of tsarist rule. Local government also did not depend heavily upon the dominance of the gentry. Thus, with American support and the immense influx of oil wealth, the Iranian state could embark on a much more aggressive policy of modernization with little regard for the position of the landed gentry and without much immediate need to encourage the development of an efficient and independent class of entrepreneurs. The resources at its disposal and its apparent autonomy from social forces engendered voluntaristic policies that undermined the people's sense of cultural identity and plunged them into a whirlwind of unpredictable changes. Cultural identity, national independence, and despotism, not class conflict, loomed as the most significant issues for the vast majority of Iranians. In this context, it was only natural that the traditional guardians of the nation's cultural heritage, the ulama, who had been attacked and in some respects weakened, but far from defeated, by the shah's regime should emerge to lead a revolution not in the name of a single class, but for the sake of the Iranian people as a whole. With their ancient ties to traditional urban groups, who had never been brought fully under the control of the state or effectively displaced, and with their new ideological appeals to the modern middle classes, the ulama were perfectly situated to combine the contradictory tendencies that made up the revolutionary movement.

The hollowness of the ulama's claim to represent all Iranians, which became clear after the consolidation of the new regime, suggests a final irony of social change in modernizing autocratic regimes. Through processes previously described, the autocracies had inadvertently forged links between ideological elites and mass movements based on a limited convergence of beliefs and goals. At the same time, by curtailing public life the regimes had made it impossible for the different sectors of society to be able to take the measure of each other without prejudices and illusions. Thus, in a flash the workers could change their image of the Bolsheviks. No longer privileged and untrustworthy outsiders, during 1917 they became for the vast majority of politically aware workers the truest defenders of their class interests. Likewise, in a short space of time the clergy were able to shed their reactionary reputation among many modern social groups in favor of their revolutionary image as guardians of the nation's identity. Even the Tudeh party came to accept that, in the words of a leading party theoretician, "the principles of the socialist program for social transformation have similarities to those of Islam with respect to justice, equality and a combative spirit." "The situation would be different," wrote the secretary-general of the party, "if the matter concerned the creation of a theocratic state. But as far as we know, the Iranian religious leaders have not called at all for anything of the sort."[16]

Mutual group perceptions in both societies were thus just as unstable and groundless as were other social phenomena. Critical knowledge vital to rational decision making on the part of individuals and social groups was masked in both societies. Workers had no real sense of what support for the Bolshevik party implied. The middle classes were equally ignorant of the implications of an Islamic republic for men like Khomeini. Among their many other vices, this legacy of ignorance was one of the most tragic consequences of autocratic rule, for it ensured that the new regimes would recapitulate many of the worst features of the rulers they had successfully displaced.

[16] Both quotations are from documents to be found in *MERIP Reports* 75–76 (March–April 1979): 29–30. For a retrospective critique of the strategy of the left see Val Moghadam, "Socialism or Anti-Imperialism? The Left and Revolution in Iran," *New Left Review* 166 (November–December 1987): 5–28. According to Moghadam, the left should have advocated a "social liberation model" grouping together the modern strata of the society, not an all-national coalition.

Select Bibliography

Abrahamian, Ervand. *Iran between Two Revolutions*. Princeton: Princeton University Press, 1982.

———. *The Iranian Mojahedin*. New Haven: Yale University Press, 1989.

Akhavi, Shahrough. *Religion and Politics in Contemporary Iran*. Albany: State University of New York Press, 1980.

Al-i Ahmad, Jalal. *Occidentosis: A Plague from the West*. Translated by Robert Campbell. Berkeley, Calif.: Mizan Press, 1984.

Arjomand, Said Amir. *The Shadow of God and the Hidden Imam*. Chicago: University of Chicago Press, 1984.

———. *The Turban for the Crown*. New York: Oxford University Press, 1988.

Arjomand, Said Amir, ed. *From Nationalism to Revolutionary Islam*. Albany: State University of New York Press, 1984.

Ascher, Abraham. *The Revolution of 1905*. Stanford, Calif.: Stanford University Press, 1988.

Bakhash, Shaul. *The Reign of the Ayatollahs*. New York: Basic Books, 1984.

Balta, Paul, and Claudine Rulleau. *L'Iran insurgé*. Paris: Sinbad, 1979.

Banani, Amin. *The Modernization of Iran: 1921–1941*. Stanford, Calif.: Stanford University Press, 1961.

Bater, James. *St. Petersburg*. Montreal: McGill–Queen's University Press, 1976.

Behrang. *Iran: Le maillon faible*. Paris: François Maspéro, 1979.

Bendix, Reinhard. *Nation-Building and Citizenship*. Berkeley: University of California Press, 1977.

Berman, Harold. *Law and Revolution: The Formation of the Western Legal Tradition*. Cambridge: Harvard University Press, 1983.

Binder, Leonard. *Iran: Political Development in a Changing Society*. Berkeley: University of California Press, 1962.

Black, Cyril, ed. *The Transformation of Russian Society*. Cambridge: Harvard University Press, 1960.

Bonnell, Victoria. *Roots of Rebellion*. Berkeley: University of California Press, 1984.

Cherniavsky, Michael. *Tsar and People: Studies in Russian Myths*. New York: Random House, 1969.

Cottam, Richard. *Nationalism in Iran*. Pittsburgh: University of Pittsburgh Press, 1979.

———. *Iran and the United States*. Pittsburgh: University of Pittsburgh Press, 1988.

Enayat, Hamid. *Modern Islamic Political Thought*. Austin: University of Texas Press, 1982.

Gerschenkron, Alexander. *Economic Backwardness in Historical Perspective*. New York: Praeger, 1965.

Gilsenan, Michael. *Recognizing Islam*. New York: Pantheon, 1982.

Goldstone, Jack, ed. *Revolutions*. San Diego: Harcourt Brace Jovanovitch, 1986.

Goodell, Grace. *The Elementary Structures of Political Life: Rural Development in Pahlevi Iran*. New York: Oxford University Press, 1986.

Graham, Robert. *Iran: The Illusion of Power*. New York: St. Martins Press, 1980.

Haimson, Leopold, ed. *The Politics of Rural Russia 1905–1914*. Bloomington: Indiana University Press, 1979.

Halliday, Fred. *Iran: Dictatorship and Development*. Harmondsworth: Penguin, 1979.

Hodgson, Marshall. *The Venture of Islam*. 3 vols. Chicago: University of Chicago Press, 1974.

Hooglund, Eric. *Land and Revolution in Iran 1960–1980*. Austin: University of Texas Press, 1982.

Huntington, Samuel. *Political Order in Changing Societies*. New Haven: Yale University Press, 1968.

Huntington, Samuel, and Joan Nelson. *No Easy Choice: Political Participation in Developing Countries*. Cambridge: Harvard University Press, 1976.

Kapuscinski, Ryszard. *The Emperor.* San Diego: Harcourt Brace Jovanovitch, 1983.

Katouzian, Homa. *The Political Economy of Modern Iran 1926–1979*. London: Macmillan, 1981.

Keddie, Nikkie. *Roots of Revolution*. New Haven: Yale University Press, 1981.

Krieger, Leonard. *An Essay on the Theory of Enlightened Despotism*. Chicago: University of Chicago Press, 1975.

Lambton, Ann. *Landlord and Peasant in Persia*. London: Oxford University Press, 1953.

———. *The Persian Land Reform 1962–1966*. Oxford: Clarendon Press, 1969.

Lapidus, Ira. *Muslim Cities in the Later Middle Ages*. Cambridge: Cambridge University Press, 1984.

———. *A History of Islamic Societies*. Cambridge: Cambridge University Press, 1988.

McDaniel, Tim. *Autocracy, Capitalism, and Revolution in Russia*. Berkeley: University of California Press, 1988.

Manning, Roberta Thompson. *The Crisis of the Old Order in Russia*. Princeton: Princeton University Press, 1982.

Montesquieu. *The Spirit of Laws*. Berkeley: University of California Press, 1977.

Moore, Barrington. *Social Origins of Dictatorship and Democracy.* Boston: Beacon, 1966.

Mottahedeh, Roy. *The Mantle of the Prophet*. New York: Pantheon, 1985.

Nasr, Seyyed Hossein, Hamid Dabashi, and Seyyed Vali Reza Nasr, eds. *Expectation of the Millennium*. Albany: State University of New York Press, 1989.

Raeff, Marc. *The Wall-Ordered Police State*. New Haven: Yale University Press, 1983.

———. *Understanding Imperial Russia*. New York: Columbia University Press, 1984.

Raeff, Marc, ed. *Russian Intellectual History: An Anthology*. New Jersey: Humanities Press, 1978.

Riasanovsky, Nicholas. *Nicholas I and Official Nationality in Russia 1825–1855*. Berkeley: University of California Press, 1955.

———. *A History of Russia*. 4th ed. New York: Oxford University Press, 1984.

Rogger, Hans. *Russia in the Age of Modernisation and Revolution 1881–1917*. London: Longman, 1983.

Shanin, Teodor. *Russia as a "Developing Society."* London: Macmillian, 1985.

Skocpol, Theda. *States and Social Revolutions*. Cambridge: Cambridge University Press, 1979.

Smith, Steven. *Red Petrograd*. Cambridge: Cambridge University Press, 1983.

Starr, S. Frederick. *Decentralization and Self-Government in Russia, 1830–1870*. Princeton: Princeton University Press, 1972.

Tilly, Charles. *From Mobilization to Revolution*. Reading, Mass.: Addison-Wesley, 1978.

Von Laue, Theodore. *Sergei Witte and the Industrialization of Russia*. New York: Atheneum, 1963.

Wildman, Allan. *The Making of a Workers' Revolution: Russian Social Democracy 1891–1903*. Chicago: University of Chicago Press, 1967.

Index